Rag Rug Making

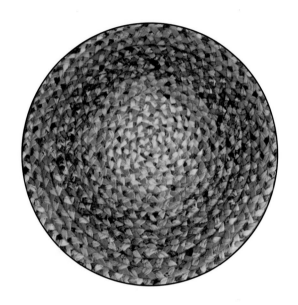

ACKNOWLEDGEMENTS

I would like to thank:

Mollie Midgley and all the people who have told me their rag rug memories;
Rhiannon Bydawell for giving me the initial impetus to make rugs;
Doris Tunley for her generous sharing of techniques;
Gail and Christopher Lawther for their hard work and encouragement;
all the rug makers who have contributed their work,
and Debbie Davies and Janet Bradley for letting me photograph their vintage rugs.

First published in 2003 by
Traplet Publications Limited
Traplet House, Pendragon Close, Malvern,
Worcestershire WR14 1GA

Reprinted 2007

Publisher: Tony Stephenson

Text © Jenni Stuart-Anderson
The Birches, Middleton on the Hill, Leominster,
Herefordshire HR6 0HN

Photographs © Jenni Stuart-Anderson, or as credited
The following photographs were taken by Lynsey Piff,
© Traplet Publications: front cover, pages 3 (bottom),
4, 8, 17, 18, 26, 30, 32, 38 (top), 46-47, 51, 53, 75, 89, 92
(bottom), 94, 103, 107, 108-109 (edges).
Photographs on the gallery pages supplied by the artists.

Illustrations by Gail Lawther and Danny McBride,
© Traplet Publications

Studio scans and pre-press work by Neil Blowers

The designs, projects, illustrations and other material
in this book may not be used for workshops without
the prior permission (in writing) from the author.

ISBN 978 1 900371 53 7
British Library Cataloguing in Publication Data
A catalogue record for this book is available from
the British Library

Designed and edited by Teamwork,
Christopher and Gail Lawther, 44 Rectory Walk,
Sompting, Lancing, West Sussex BN15 0DU

Set in Gill Sans and Breughel

Printed by
Printed by Wa Fai Graphic Arts Printing Co., Hong Kong

Rag Rug Making

Contemporary projects, techniques and inspirations for a traditional craft

Jenni Stuart-Anderson

Craftworld Series

Introduction

JENNI STUART-ANDERSON

I used to work as a freelance architectural/interior designer and lecture part-time at a London art college. In 1977 I spent a winter in France, learning simple rug weaving and dyeing, and the following year moved from London to the country-side, converting my cottage in Herefordshire myself.

I saw some rugs made by a local resident on the floor of a friend's house, and traced the maker when I decided to try the craft myself. She was delighted to show me some traditional techniques, and we remain good friends, although she doesn't make rugs any more. She's very proud of me!

I'm into sustainable lifestyle, waste minimisation, sourcing materials locally if possible, and other eco issues. I believe in treading lightly on the planet and taking only what we need.

My aim in this book is to inspire you to try your hand at rag rug making and to explore your creativity by experimenting with fabrics. I want to share with you the pleasure of making things and the satisfaction I get from breathing new life into recycled textiles. By combining different colours and textures you can discover wonderful creative possibilities.

I hope too that you'll share my respect for the generations of working people who recycled their threadbare clothing into rugs to create a meagre bit of comfort in their homes. I think of rag rugs as the unsung art of ordinary people. When I demonstrate at shows, my work always stimulates reminiscences from other people who have practised or observed rug making. Throughout the book you'll discover quotations, stories and anecdotes from many different individuals; they are people who have seen me working and shared their own memories with me.

You can make the projects in the book without spending much money, by recycling old clothes and furnishings. The huge selection of textiles available today - both new and recycled - provides a richer palette than our grandmothers ever had. If you can't find a particular colour, improvise: be bold. Whichever fabric comes to hand may look better anyway!

I started making rag rugs in 1985, at home with my baby, in rural isolation. I had to give up my work and needed a creative activity which I could fit around childcare. So I asked Mrs Tunley, a local resident who had hooked and progged rugs for over 50 years, to teach me. There are many other ways of making rag rugs; in the techniques section I explain various different methods, and the projects feature the ones I use most.

By the way - this craft can be addictive!

> "When my mum died, a lady in the village taught
> my father how to make mats out of baler twine.
> He used to sit doing it and reckons it saved
> his sanity."

Contents

A Tradition in the Making

19th century Vermont rug made by Alan Last's grandmother; a precious piece of carpet is preserved in the centre of the rug.

Early coverings for floors of stone, earth or boards were made from straw or rushes, and kitchens typically had sand on the floor which could be swept up when dirty. Did rug hooking originate in Britain, Canada or America? It's a matter of conjecture among textile historians. The technique of hooking woollen loops through a base fabric was used by the Vikings, whose families probably brought it to Scotland. We can only guess whether settlers from Britain took the technique of rug hooking to the New World, or whether it developed from needlework skills there and came to Britain with mail-order commercially-printed rug hessian in the 1890s. Certainly during the 19th century in Canada and America, pictorial rug hooking reached great heights as a medium for artistic expression.

French settlers in Nova Scotia and Quebec made rugs using a sewn yarn technique before 1800. Until about 1820, 'ruggs' of yarn loops sewn on homespun wool or linen were made as bed covers. Worked with a large needle and a running stitch, up to six strands of crewel wool formed loops on the top, which were sometimes cut. Handworked textiles, including woven or knotted carpets – too precious to put on the floor – were displayed on tables and chests.

As the production of machine-made carpeting increased, floor coverings became generally fashionable. Worn-out clothing and linen were made into braided rugs and patchwork quilts, and sewn, poked, or hooked into a linen base to make rugs. Rag hearth rugs were used to protect the carpets of those who could afford them. By the late 1850s jute hessian (burlap) from India was widely obtainable in Europe and America, and rug makers used it enthusiastically as a base. In Canada and America hooked rugs developed into a rich folk art, depicting scenes from daily life including flowers, animals and landscapes.

Alan Last's 19th century braided seat pads from Vermont

Proddy by Jane-Ann and Frances Frost, 1938
(Collection of Debbie Davies)

In Newfoundland in the 1890s, the English doctor Wilfred Grenfell founded a mission which built schools and hospitals serving the British immigrants in villages along the coast. He remarked that rug hooking was a thriving tradition in the fishing community – a skill which must have been brought by their ancestors from Devonshire, Cornwall and Scotland. With artistic input, the Grenfell Mission developed this local rug making into a thriving industry. The beautiful and desirable Grenfell rugs were sold locally, and many also crossed the border to be sold in America and even in England.

Rag rug making in Britain can be traced back to the beginning of the 19th century, but few early examples remain since rugs graduated through the house, ending up as a dog bed or on the compost heap.

My mother – she died in 1950 – used to put a new rug on the bed, then on the bedroom floor and it would move through the house. It was cold in Yorkshire in the winter; the wind was cutting.

Drawing of typical early American floral design for a hooked rug

Rug making was a winter evening occupation involving the whole family – the children cutting the pieces for the adults to put into the rug. It was considered restful after the extra-long working days of summer, especially in agricultural communities.

Revived again in the 1960s, the craft has been developed into a thriving art form which typifies the current enthusiasm for sustainability. Rag rug making can be a wonderful way of filling the need lots of us have for creative self-expression; a therapeutic antidote to a stressful lifestyle.

Prodded rag mat, c 1890, made by Hannah Jones of Montgomery, Wales.
(© National Museums & Galleries of Wales)

Memories of times past

These memories were shared with me by people who grew up in Britain, during times when it was harder to get the basic necessities, and rag rug making was common in town and country.

> *The more rag rugs you had, the richer you were –*
> *(it meant) you could afford to have new clothes. We'd sit*
> *around the fire with the rugs on our laps, which kept us*
> *warm. They were old potato, flour and sugar sacks.*

Rug making and dominoes at Derwentside, England, during the miners' strike of 1892.
(Beamish North of England Open Air Museum)

> "We made them because we couldn't afford a carpet. They did smell when a cinder fell out of the fire onto them and they smouldered. We had one to step out onto by the bed because we had lino in the bedroom."

Mollie Midgley remembers:

> "My great grandmother came to Yeadon (in Yorkshire) from Birmingham via Rotherham, where her husband came from. He worked in the mines until his leg was shot off in World War 1. My granny was in service: in a mining village there wasn't much else for them to do. She was the oldest of 13 - few survived. Her mother got up at 5am to pump the bellows and get the fire going in the forge at the end of the garden. She would make either a pound of nails or a yard of chain, then she would sell it to buy something for grandad's breakfast. They all had forges at the end of the garden and were called 'out workers'. All the chain would get joined together later."

Lively hooked and braided rug featuring a bird design – from New England, 1910-20

(Reproduced by permission of the American Museum in Britain, Bath ©)

> *Granny had a day for washing, a day for finishing (starching, ironing, mending), a day for baking, a day for cleaning, and on Saturday she would do the shopping.* Mollie would get sixpence pocket money from her granny *for scrubbing the two great big flagstone steps and putting white on the edges, so you could see them.*

Mollie's granny and her neighbours would get together in each others' houses on Friday nights to make a rug, working for an hour then sharing supper and, during World War 2, putting 1/6d (the equivalent of about 7½p, or around 10c, today) in a pot for the Red Cross, for soldiers. When they went to other houses the kids slept over, three to a bed.

> *All the men disappeared on Friday night. We lived at number 3 and when we walked across the yard to number 8 we would just have supper there - it was a one up, one down, not big enough for a rug frame. Numbers 1, 2, 3 and 4 had the outside toilets, then the mill. 5, 6, 7 and 8 faced the coal houses.*

For two shillings they bought a bundle of fabrics from the mill – nearly enough for a rug. Or they bought from jumble sales held by the women's section of the British Legion.

> *There was a Geordie [someone from the Newcastle area] who came who used to cut the tabs on the diagonal and prodded them with a sharpened broken dolly peg [clothespin]. There was an influx of glassblowers from Tyneside who came to make light bulbs when Crompton Parkinson opened their factory. A whole housing estate was built for the workers.*

An example of an early 20th
century hooked rug
(Collection of Janet Bradley)

> *Everything that happened in my youth is gone: the school,*
> *the house where I lived 'till I got married, the Methodist*
> *church I got married in. There's a main road through the*
> *churchyard now. It's all built on.*

Rag rugs were made all over the country, particularly in the
industrial North. One man recalled:

> *It was a huge thing in the mining community. In Blythe,*
> *the industrial town where I lived, it was a big part of their*
> *social life going to people's houses to help make a mat.*
> *Most, but not all houses had a frame.*

I've also been told of a shared rug frame in a village which
would move from house to house in turn, with everyone coming
in to work for a while on the mat and have a cup of tea.

> *My mother was from near Durham and I was born there,*
> *then we moved to West Hartlepool where I live now. I'm 83.*
> *They used to chew toffees when they were making rag rugs*
> *to keep the fluff from going on their lungs. It's like the*
> *miners - my father used to chew tobacco down the mine and*
> *spit it out. It kept the dust from their lungs. The men*
> *couldn't afford it but if they were given it they'd work an*
> *extra shift.*

> *I'm 80. I come from Otley in the West Riding [a part of*
> *Yorkshire], and we used to make these in the evenings when*
> *I was a child. We had no TV. I can remember getting our*
> *first radio and the neighbours used to come in to listen to it.*
> *Especially Monday nights - there was a programme called*
> Monday Night at Eight. *Oh it was a real treat! Nowadays*
> *they live a completely different kind of life. I can't come to*
> *terms with it.*

A 1943 photograph of proggy mat-making, taken by a child using a box camera
(Beamish North of England Open Air Museum)

"*We used to make them in the war in Coventry. Things were a lot harder then, we didn't throw anything away - not like today. That's when Jelly Babies were called War Babies; and after the war they called them Jelly Babies again. We had powdered milk - you couldn't get fresh - and coupons for food.*"

Developments in loom widths and machine efficiencies brought carpets within the reach of the mass market, and rag rug making declined. It has, however, reappeared at times of economic hardship.

Another example of an early 20th century hooked rug
(Collection of Janet Bradley)

> *My dad had a clothing factory in Leeds. The textile trade was really thriving in those days and he would bring home fabric ends. We would sit on the back doorstep, we three children and mum and dad, pegging a rug. We used them on the floor. My dad would say which colours went where but I don't remember him drawing a design. They were stripes, or going round the edge in various shades of gent's suiting.*

One woman told me:

> *Seeing you doing that has taken me right back to my childhood. I've had strokes and don't remember things, but seeing you has taken me right back to happy days in Birmingham. My dad taught me to make rag rugs and he was blind. He used to feel the wrinkles on my mother's face as she was getting older. He felt my face the day I got married, with tears streaming down his face because he couldn't see his daughter on her wedding day.*

And a man shared his experiences:

> *I was evacuated to Lincolnshire and put to work making rugs from my uncle's shirts. I think of it as a penance. I enjoyed finishing one! My sister was in the land army - she married a farmer. They used to put rag rugs on the bed and on the floor.*

> *We used to make proddies: the whole family in the evenings. My dad probably did the design - he was more into that sort of thing. He was from London, and I used to visit relatives a lot but didn't see much rag rug making there. But when I was grown up and used to visit my Auntie Eva in the war, they were still making them in Salford.*

> *Does this bring back memories! When you went in anyone's house they only had these rugs and a big coal range. Then later me and me dad started doing Readicut rugs.*

Designing Rugs

Inspiration

For me, the impetus to begin rag rug making wasn't the need for something warm to put my feet on, but a need to do something creative which I could pick up and put down at a moment's notice. It also had to be a cheap hobby – and the recycling involved in rag rug making fits perfectly with my belief in a sustainable lifestyle.

My inspiration comes from many sources, and it's my first step in designing a rug. I rip pictures out of magazines, collect cards and postcards, and sometimes make little sketches of things which inspire me. I take photographs, and collect fabrics if I like the colour or texture: these can be old clothes, furnishings or remnants. Sometimes a piece of fabric is the starting point for a rug: this is especially true for plaited rugs, which show off the surface of the fabric. Scattered through this section of the book, you'll find collections of rugs which have been inspired by different aspects of the world around us.

Nature is my greatest source of inspiration, either observed directly or from other people's creative response to it; this response can be in the form of fine art, individual artefacts, even buildings. If you'd like to make rugs, collect things which inspire you. Even if you don't use something now, you might use it later to inform a piece of work.

Looking – **really** looking – at nature, people, animals, exhibitions, your environment, helps to build a visual vocabulary which you can draw on for your creative work. The more you work with colours and textures, the more you sharpen your awareness and enjoyment of them. As you'll see from the inspiration pages, I've used history, geometric patterns, mythology, children's drawings, abstract textures, artefacts, and particular items such as leaves, flowers, animals and birds to give me ideas for my rugs.

INSPIRATION: **Abstract**

Rug making is the perfect medium for revelling in textures and tones, as you can see from the progged rugs featured here. The fabrics available today, and the contrasts they can create, can be enough on their own, without needing a formal pattern. The Easy Peasy Proddy rug on page 51 is a quick and easy way to create a wonderful abstract rug.

These are all progged rugs by JSA.
A *'Squiggle' rug: woollens on hessian*
B *Hearth rug; wool/mohair on hessian*
C *Rug made from progged rug kit by JSA*
D *Detail of washable rug; cottons on rug canvas*
E Rose Garden *oval rug; cottons on hessian*
F *Fine Indian cottons on hessian*

A

D

B

C

E

F

INSPIRATION: **Nature**

These photographs of moss and tree bark show the kind of thing that could act as a starting point for a rug; the inspiration could be the form, the colours, the texture, or an idea they stimulate. Take a look at water, sunsets, landscapes, wood, plant forms of all kinds.

A *Butterfly; hooked woollens on hessian by JSA*
B *Hooked and progged sampler with added pearl buttons; mixed fabrics, by JSA*

Design Considerations

Photograph by Keith Morris

Where will your work go: on the floor, a seat, or the wall? Does it need to fit into an existing colour-scheme, be hard-wearing, be washable? How will it be viewed – from one position or from different angles? These considerations all affect the size, materials, technique and design of a piece. In some cases it will be a question of what you can do with the tools or materials you can get – or what you can fit into the time you have available. If you've done a design but you're not sure what colours or fabrics would work best with it, make a small sample to try out your chosen technique in several fabrics. If you do sketch a design and you are not sure about which colours to use, make some photocopies of the basic design and colour them in different combinations to find which looks best.

If you don't yet have a design in mind, or panic at the thought of designing your own rug, try one of the projects in the rest of the book. Working with different fabrics and yarns will help to give you some ideas for future rugs of your own design. Enjoying the process of making is the most important bit, I think; and even if you use a pattern created by someone else, the choices you make of colours and fabrics will still make it your own unique piece.

Colour

Fairly early on in your designing, you'll need to think about the colours that you're going to use. You may decide, in the time-honoured rag rug tradition, simply to use whichever colours are available. As one woman remembered: *'They had a dark 5in or 6in border, with a red line inside it and a red diamond in the middle. The size of the line and diamond would depend on how much red fabric they could get.'*

An intuitive, spontaneous approach to choosing colours can produce original results, and this may be the direction you'd like to explore to develop your personal creativity. However, if you want to manage colour combinations to produce particular effects (as artists do), it's useful to understand the basic principles of colour. Using a system like the colour wheel shown here makes it relatively easy to devise effective colour schemes.

White light is composed of the colours seen in a rainbow, when it passes through raindrops and breaks into the visible spectrum. Black and white aren't really considered colours: an object appears black if it absorbs or transmits all the white light, and white if it reflects all the light.

Colours are defined by various different qualities: hue, value, intensity and temperature.

• **Hue** is the basic quality by which we define colour: red, yellow etc. The *primary* colours (red, yellow and blue) are the ones from which all other colours are derived. The *secondary* colours result from mixing two primaries; they are orange (red + yellow), green (blue + yellow) and purple (blue + red). *Tertiary* colours are the mixtures of primaries and secondaries; they can be described as yellow-orange, red-orange, purple-blue etc

Opposite colours on the wheel are called *complementaries*: red/green, orange/blue and yellow/purple. Complementary pairs intensify and electrify each other, but can also be used to balance each other in different values and intensities.

Colours next to each other in the colour wheel are called analogous (eg red and orange, blue and green).

- The **value** of a colour depends on the amount of black or white in it, determining its lightness or darkness. Light values are called tints; dark values are known as shades.

- The **intensity** (or **saturation**) is the purity of a colour – how bright or dull it appears.

- **Temperature** refers to how warm or cool a colour appears. Warm colours (generally those in the red/yellow range) seem to advance towards the viewer and make an area appear larger, whereas cool colours (generally in the blue/green range) seem to recede and appear smaller. This concept also applies to value, with darker colours receding visually and lighter colours advancing.

The fabric texture and the rug technique you use will both affect how a particular fabric reflects or absorbs the light, and therefore how the colour appears. A colour seen in isolation will look different next to other colours, so by juxtaposing different combinations of colours you can achieve very different effects. When I've decided on a range of colours, I assemble fabrics of different textures and try moving them around each other. Another factor to consider is the way a fabric's appearance is altered by the rug technique. Progging softens the look of patterned fabric; ripping cotton fabrics instead of cutting them does the same.

Some people like to make a detailed coloured drawing of their design, then find the rags to fit. I usually start with an outline of a design, and fill it out as I choose and work the fabrics. Often I decide that a touch of a totally different colour will enhance a rug when I'm making it. This organic way of working is one of the things I like about rag rug making; I do apply the ideas outlined in this section, but I also welcome the unexpected.

A great way to train your eye is by keeping a scrap book in which you can sketch, write and stick things; the book could also be used as a visual record of how different colours and textures interact. Experiment with different materials and textures - sweet wrappers, plastic bags, net - and include photographs, scribbles and doodles. It's fun to compile a scrap book, and it means that you have a very useful resource to turn to when you're designing a rug

INSPIRATION: **Animals**

Animals were a traditional theme for rag rugs; the irregular texture of the rug could imitate fur, fins or feathers. Here's a selection of wild and domestic animals; see too the ginger cat rug (page 80), Doris' sheep rug (page 60) and the copy of an old cat rug (page 44). All these examples are hooked woollens on hessian.

INSPIRATION: **Animals**

A *A rug I made for a man in New York*
B *Siberian Tiger by Lorenzo Gavarini*
C *Another tiger by JSA*
D *Cat 'n teapot by JSA*
E *Mel by JSA (this was featured in a magazine, and was seen by the man who then commissioned A on the opposite page)*
F *Two cats in a summer garden (commission)*
G *Cat on a cushion by JSA*
H *Taurus by Lorenzo Gavarini*
I *Fizz by Lorenzo Gavarini*
J *Dark Chanting Goshawk with twisted raw fleece trim*

Materials

Base/ground fabrics

I started making rugs on jute sacks, in the traditional way, but mostly I use 10oz common jute hessian now as a base for both hooking and progging. The exception is when I need a rug to be machine washable, in which case I use open-meshed rug canvas. This comes in different widths and gauges from craft or needlecraft suppliers, and is usually stiff with starch, so it can be used without a frame for hooking. I prefer double thread with 7mm (¼in) squares; it softens with use and washing, but it is much more expensive than hessian. Hessian can be obtained from upholsterers and comes in different widths. I have occasionally used coloured hessian with a tighter weave when the backing might be seen, but I find it harder to poke the tools into. Hessian smells when it's damp so it wouldn't be suitable for a bath mat, but it can be hand washed.

I've been told that in the early days sacks were used double, as they came, or opened out. *'For a hearth or "best" rug the maker would join two sugar sacks. The new rug would be placed at the hearth and the previous one would move to the back of the room, then to the kitchen.'* Some animal feed and wholefoods come in hessian sacks if you want to try using them. I have also used linen scrim, doubled, which is softer, more flexible and more expensive than hessian.

If you need to join two pieces of hessian, overlap the edges by at least 15cm (6in), stitch two lines of stitching with the thread parallel with the two edges, then hook or prog through the two layers together.

INSPIRATION: Leaves

Leaves come in an endless variety of shapes, colours and textures – enough to inspire a lifetime's rugs. On holiday in Italy, I picked up a leaf, made a sketch of it and used it as a design for my first hooked leaf rug when I came home – the one shown in B. Have a look at the hooked leaf rug on page 85 if you fancy creating your own version.

All by JSA.
A *Hooked rug; woollens on hessian*
B *Pesaro leaf; woollens on hessian*
C *Hooked rug; woollens on hessian*
D *Hooked rug; woollens on hessian*
E *Hooked and progged fantasy leaf; mixed fibres*

A *Woollens, suitable for hooking. Only felted sweaters will survive progging.*

B *Sumptuous, mixed-fibre woven textiles. Best for plaiting and hooking; check if they fray too much for progging.*

Collecting rags

Once you start making rag rugs, you look at all textiles as potential material for your next rug. These textiles can include your own wardrobe, and the clothes of your friends and family! Jumble sales are a great source of fabrics, and there are often bags left over at the end which the organisers will be happy for you to take away for a contribution. If you ask, charity shops may sell you items which are too worn for them to display, and once your friends know about your new obsession (oops, I mean hobby), they may give you their shrunken sweaters and other cast-offs. Curtains, blankets and tablecloths provide larger amounts of a single fabric. Fabric shops often sell off ends of rolls at reduced prices, and of course there are always sewing remnants.

Try working small samples of different textiles to find ones you like for the different techniques. If you need to calculate how much fabric you'll need for a specific area, measure a square of fabric, cut it up and see what size it covers when you hook or prog it into a piece of hessian. Then you can multiply it by the number of times that the small area fits into the area you want to fill.

Types of rags

Almost any fabric can be used for progged rugs, but I tend to use all cottons or all woollens for a piece. I use mainly woven fabrics such as dress cottons, woollen skirts, curtains, blankets. Any pattern in the weave or on the surface of the fabric will look blurred and impressionistic when it's been progged in. Tweeds, checks, stripes, all look very different when they're cut up and progged and provide visual interest, and strong prints become muted by the process.

C *More shiny woven textiles which I use for hooking and plaiting and – less often – for progging.*

D *Woven cottons which I use for progging and plaiting, and occasionally for hooking.*

For hooking I like using sweaters; these have a spring and resilience which makes them puff out and cover a greater area when hooked than other fabrics. Medium and lightweight machine knits hold together better than loose hand-knits when they're cut into strips. If the strip doesn't hold together when you pull it gently, it probably can't be hooked.

I use tweeds if the colour and texture fits my design, and velvet or needlecord adds richness to any type of rug. Fair Isle or patterned jumpers produce interesting effects; sweatshirts, T-shirts and children's clothes are brightly coloured, easy to get hold of, and hook well. Plain or printed cottons work too. I sometimes add silk, net, synthetics or glitter fabrics if the effect works well on a particular piece. For plaited rugs I collect textiles with an attractive surface colour and/or texture, and I have used dress fabric, leaving the lace sewn on it, for textural variety.

So, look around and collect any textiles you like the appearance of. Even if you don't make a particular fabric into a rug, yet, you might copy a motif or colour combination which works well. Unusual fabrics from faraway places offer inspiration. Coloured tights, old swimsuits, chiffon scarves, could all enliven a piece of work. Don't stop at garments – knitting wool hooks well, and a bit of lace or trimming could be just what you need when you make an experimental wall-hanging.

D

Storing rags

I store sweaters in transparent plastic sacks, separated by colour, and have shelves piled with folded fabrics. I store the ones I'm using currently in a large basket which I move around to where I am working. I store blankets in a trunk and plastic sacks, with lavender to repel moths.

It's visually stimulating to have beautiful fabrics around, if you have space and your family doesn't complain. (Quite a few women have told me their husbands wouldn't let them take up another craft requiring storage space ...)

Preparation

Woollen fabrics cut into strips for hooking, plus two of my hooks

If you're using hessian sacks, it's a good idea to wash or steam iron them first, in case they contain any moth eggs. When you're ready to make a rug, draw the outline of it on the hessian with a marker pen, leaving a seam allowance of 10cm (4in) around the outside. Use a ruler: don't follow the weave, which is often not square on 10oz common hessian.

I wash rags before I store them but I don't try to shrink sweaters: often they are already felted, but new wool has been treated so it doesn't felt in the wash. My teacher used to cut up her fabrics before storing, but I cut them as I need them. (The sizes I use for different techniques are covered under those sections; see page 34 for cutting techniques.) Always cut one or two pieces and hook or prog them first to see if the width is right for that particular fabric (before you cut lots of pieces the wrong size). If the fabrics are very creased, iron them before cutting them up – it makes it much easier.

INSPIRATION: **Spirals**

Spirals occur throughout nature and have been used symbolically by many cultures since early times. You can see them in ammonites, shells, flowers and many amazing spiral galaxies. For a simple progged project to get you started, try the spiral seat pad on page 56 – or, if you're feeling more ambitious, try the mixed technique rug on page 98. All these rugs are based on spirals, and are by JSA.

A *Hooked and progged; mixed fibres*
B *Hooked and progged woollens*
C *Hooked woollens*
D *Hooked, progged and plaited mixed fabrics*
E *Hooked, progged and plaited mixed fabrics*

Tools and Equipment

Vintage rug-making tools on an old Welsh woollen patchwork quilt

Rug tools

One of the great things about rug making is that you can do it with a minimum amount of equipment, but there are some specialised tools which make the work quicker and easier. I've listed below everything that I use to do all the techniques in this book, but some of this equipment is optional. It's always easier to use the correct tool for a job, and at the beginning of each Technique section you'll find a picture of the appropriate rug tool along with instructions on how to use it. You'll find the sections explaining the individual techniques, and the relevant tools, on the following pages:

prodding; page 47

progging; page 53

hand hooking; page 76

hooking with a speed shuttle; page 78

plaiting/braiding; page 89.

Rug making tools:
A *Cutting gauge*
B *Two rug hooks; yew and brass, and tulip wood and steel*
C *Speed shuttle*
D *Bodger rug tool*

Useful items

I find all the following tools and bits of equipment useful for doing specific jobs when I'm making rugs.

- metre rule, yardstick or straight edge to draw the edges of your design
- tracing paper, for transferring designs
- large sheets of paper for the drawings of finished designs
- sticky tape for joining paper or photocopies
- marker pens for drawing designs on paper and hessian
- transfer pencil
- dressmaking pins
- needles and threads, including a bodkin for lacing plaited rugs, and a large needle and strong thread for finishing rugs and stitching hessian to a frame
- sharp dressmaking scissors
- scissors for cutting paper
- string for frame (see page 38)
- staple gun if you use a stretcher or picture frame (see page 38)
- carpet tape for finishing
- latex carpet adhesive (see page 106)
- an iron will be useful, occasionally
- sewing machine; not essential, but quicker for some techniques than hand stitching

Cutting tools

I cut fabrics along the warp threads and down the length of knitted sweaters. I also rip woven fabrics (children really enjoy doing this).

Scissors

First you need some good dressmaking scissors to cut fabric: sharp scissors are a pleasure to use and make a satisfying snip, snip sound. It's a whole different experience using blunt ones. I also use a small pair of embroidery or nail scissors to trim ends while I'm hooking, but they aren't essential.

Cutting gauges

These gauges were originally used for cutting Turkey wool to make mats with a latchet hook. They work for long strips of rag, too; you wind them round the gauge, then run scissors along a groove in the side of the gauge, snipping as you go (see left). This produces a number of pieces ready for prodding or progging. Remember to wind the strip along the length of the gauge no more than two layers thick; if you wind it round and round in one part of the gauge only, the fabric will be too thick to cut.

Rotary cutters

Self-healing cutting boards, used with rotary cutters and non-slip rulers (see photo opposite), make faster work of cutting strips for hooking and pieces for progging. For progging pieces, I cut several layers of fabric simultaneously, so it's much faster. The mat and ruler have centimetres and inches marked on them, so I just line these markings up with the fabric. The rotary cutters are *extremely* sharp, and even though they have a safety lock they shouldn't be left around where children can get hold of them.

Cloth stripping machines

There are various different American-made machines on the market which cut fabric into strips. They're worth the investment if you intend to make a lot of hooked rugs. I cut strips for hooking on a Rigby Cloth Stripping Machine. The cutter wheels come in different widths: I use mainly the ⅜in and sometimes the ¼in cutter. (These have to go back to the maker for regrinding when they're worn, but they last a long time.) I cut sweaters into manageable-sized panels and feed them into the cutter against the guide, turning the handle so that two strips come out the other side.

Cutting tools:
A *Cutting gauge*
B *Large scissors*
C *Rotary cutter*
D *Rule for use with rotary cutter*
E *Mat for use with rotary cutter*
F *Rigby strip cutter*

Before I bought my cutter I became quite fast at cutting strips of fabric side by side on a table, using scissors. It makes a change when you're hooking to stop and cut a pile of strips. Iron any creases out of cottons or synthetics, to make cutting easier and more accurate.

I'm not recommending the following method of cutting garments for rugs, which Molly Midgley's granny used, but it makes interesting reading!

> *She would work out which was the warp and cut along it. The warp's the strongest thread, you can tear the weft more easily. Clothes were made with the warp going down for strength, particularly skirts and coats. Granny would hammer one of grandad's safety razors between the pine table planks, with the sharp side facing up and inwards, and she would pull the fabric across it, for speed.*
>
> *She would fringe the end for us kids to tear into strips. We would sit under the rug frame - that was our tent - with one of grandad's hankies around our faces, holding the fabric to rip between us in the semi darkness. We had the oil lamps. She made everything fun. She'd have to scrub the table before she made bread.*

INSPIRATION: **People**

I occasionally include human figures in my work; as with all the other inspiration sources, they can be treated realistically or stylised. Simplification and strong lines are keys to translating complex forms with the chunky medium of rag strips. All these rugs are hooked woollens on hessian; A, B and E are part of a series of the 12 zodiac signs made for an exhibition in Hereford called *Sky Hooks*.

A Aquarius, *based on a Kenyan Masai tribesman; wall-hanging by JSA*

B Virgo; *wall-hanging by Lorenzo Gavarini*

C Pearl Diver *by Lorenzo Gavarini*

D *Detail of* Masks *by Lorenzo Gavarini*

E *Detail of* Libra *by JSA*

INSPIRATION: Geometric

19th century rag rugs often copied the geometric designs used on patchwork quilts. Simple geometric rug designs are easy to draw with minimum equipment and look very effective. Architectural features like the mosaic flooring in the photograph below can provide ideas for rug designs, and Islamic art is also a rich source of inspiration for geometric designs. All by JSA.

B

A

A *Hooked woollens hanging, inspired by traditional Belouch rug motifs and colours*
B *Hooked cottons rug; the person who commissioned this asked for a geometric design on a pentagon-shaped rug, in particular colours to match her decor*
C *Hooked cottons rug*
D *Progged woollens hearth rug*

C

D

Frames

If the backing material is held taut by a frame it's easier to push in a rug hook, and both hands are then free for hooking. For hand hooking you could staple the hessian to a simple frame such as an artist's stretcher, which just needs to be fitted together, or you could use a picture frame and secure the hessian with staples or drawing pins (thumb tacks). If the frame is smaller than the finished piece, you'll need to move the hessian from time to time, with the working area on the frame. For hooking relatively small items a rectangular needlepoint/embroidery frame works well, and you can roll the hessian around the rotating ends. I hand hook with my frame horizontal on the table (I put something heavy on it to hold it steady), with the bit I am working on projecting over my lap. A frame for hand hooking needs to be narrow enough for you to reach the middle with one hand above and one below (see the instructions on page 76).

If you're hooking with a speed shuttle it's essential to stretch the hessian on a large frame (see below). I sit or stand at it, turning it upside down if it makes access to a particular part of the design easier. When I'm working, I like to see the whole of the rug, so I use a frame which adjusts to different sizes. I had extra-long frame uprights made for a rug which exceeded the size of my square frame. Large rugs are very heavy, but people have told me about hooked stair carpets and rugs which covered the sitting room.

Putting the hessian on a frame

To use a speed shuttle you need to stretch the hessian on a frame; this frame then stands on the floor and leans against a wall while you work. These instructions are for a frame which has webbing attached to two of the pieces; my frame is 1.5m (roughly 5ft) square. I thread my frame before putting the design on the hessian. Note that because a speed shuttle pokes the loops into the hessian from the back you work with a mirror image of your design. For designs like the leaf on page 85, it doesn't matter which way round you hook it, but with a portrait or writing you need to reverse the image. To do this, trace the full size drawing, flip the tracing paper over and transfer the reversed image onto the hessian.

These instructions for threading the frame are for right-handers; if you're left-handed, reverse the directions when appropriate.

a

b

B

A

c

table

B

left hand holds
hessian here
*

A

B

d

webbing
folded
under frame
during
marking

A

e

1 Lay the frame flat on a table, with the bolts or pegs of the frame holding it in a rectangle which allows for the design plus at least 15cm (6in) all around the design (**a**).

2 Cut a piece of hessian as wide as the rectangle made by the frame, and 10cm (4in) longer (top to bottom) than the rectangle. Fold over about 3cm (1½in) of the two sides of the hessian which will be vertical, and tack (baste) them with strong thread (**b**).

3 Slide the frame towards you so that the bottom piece (A) projects beyond the table about 15cm (6in), and fold one horizontal edge of the hessian over 1cm (½in). Holding the right-hand edge of the fold on the frame's webbing (**c**), stitch the folded hessian edge to the webbing, keeping the fold against the frame as you stitch. Work from right to left, using back stitch in a strong cotton or linen thread.

4 Before you can sew the hessian to the frame at B it has to be cut to a size that will ensure that it's stretched between sides A and B. Push the loose end of the hessian under the frame at side B and, using the inside of B as a ruler, draw a line on the hessian with a marker pen (**d**). Cut along this line and fold the cut edge over 1cm (½in).

5 Slide the frame so that side B projects beyond the table (I move round to the other side of the table!). In order to sew the hessian to the webbing as you did at side A, you'll need to undo the bolts/pegs through side B and carefully slide B towards A, just enough to enable you to to sew all along the webbing as before (**e**). Check the measurement between sides A and B as you go, to make sure they remain parallel while you sew; the stretching won't work properly if they aren't.

6 Now you can put the bolt/peg back on one side of piece B. You'll find that you need to pull hard to get the other side of B over the second bolt/peg.

INSPIRATION: **Flowers**

The lily in this photograph would make a superb rug just on its own. Flowers can be interpreted artistically in many different ways: realistic, stylised, abstracted – or they can be used as part of a rug border design. Early rug makers frequently used flowers on hooked rugs, which were often based on earlier needlework motifs. (See the traditional 19th century vase of flowers design on page 11.) All hooked woollens on hessian by JSA.

A Poppies, *inspired by a painting by Sir Robin Philipson RA PPRSA (1916-1992). I love poppies.*
B *Vase of flowers with contour-hooked background*
C Rose-shaped rug
D *as A*

INSPIRATION: Children's Art

Children's drawings are a wonderful source of inspiration, and making rugs out of them will preserve them for posterity. These rugs also make marvellous gifts for the artist's parents or grandparents. All of these rugs were made by me from drawings by my daughter Rhiannon. They are all hooked; A has a progged border as well.

A Hooked hanging with progged border from an Easter card

B Teddy and robot – two drawings combined

C Rhiannon drew these figures when she was only four years old, and she was so proud when I used them on this hooked rug which we displayed on the wall

D Horsey

A

C

B

D

Transferring an Image

Enlarging using a grid system

If you're confident, you can use this method to enlarge an image straight onto the hessian, working in one colour of marker pen for the grid, another colour for the drawing (try red) and a third (maybe black) for final drawing including any corrections. Or, if you need to reverse the image, enlarge it onto tracing paper first and turn it over before you draw round the image – in which case you won't need to draw the grid onto the hessian.

a

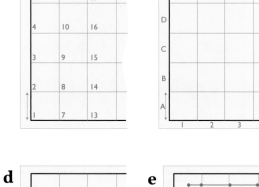

TIP *Greaseproof kitchen paper makes quite good tracing paper.*

To work one of the rug designs from this book, you can enlarge it using a grid; we'll use the sheep design on pages 64-65 as an example (**a**). Look carefully at the template, and check how many squares there are in the grid, both vertically and horizontally; you need to reproduce this grid full size, so check that you have a piece of paper large enough. For this design you need six 10cm (4in) squares vertically, and ten squares horizontally. Now draw the grid on your paper, making every square the specified size. Number the squares to identify them, on both the template and your new grid; either give each square a number (**b**), or use numbers across the bottom, letters up the side (**c**).

Look at the first square – we'll begin at the bottom left-hand square of the design, but you can begin anywhere that seems sensible – and note where the corner is; make a dot. Now notice where the line crosses the grid: is the line of the border half way up the grid square? Less? More?

b **c**

d **e**

f

g

Make another dot on your new grid at the place where the drawn line crosses the grid (**d**). Then, where does the line cross the next box? Mark it and follow it, marking where the line crosses each line of the grid (**e**). Then you just join the dots to create your line. On a straight line like this border, it's easy, and you follow exactly the same process with the curved lines as well, as shown in **f** and **g**.

a

b

c

You may want to use this system to enlarge an image you've chosen from another source (**a**). In this case, decide on the finished overall size of your rug, and how big the image needs to be to fit comfortably inside it. Divide the width of the image into round increments: for instance, if the rug will be roughly 1m (say, a round 40in) wide, that divides neatly into ten 10cm (4in) widths.

d

If you want to preserve the original image (a photograph, for instance), take a photocopy. Measure the height and width of the image and divide by 10: this will give you the size of the boxes for the grid, which you can draw over the image in pencil. Start by finding the middle of the image (measure the width, divide by two); draw a vertical line through the centre. Measure the height, divide by two, and draw a horizontal line through the centre (**b**). Working out from those two centre lines (which form a cross), draw a grid with all the boxes the same size (**c**). Now follow the instructions in the preceding section to enlarge and transfer the image (**d**).

TIP *If you enlarge something complex (eg an animal or person) from a picture, trace the outline first so you're then enlarging a simplified line drawing. Draw lines round areas of shadow etc.*

Enlarging using a photocopier

Trace the image first so that you have a simplified line drawing. Decide on the finished size of the rug (measurement A). Measure the image (measurement B) and divide A by B to get the enlargement ratio. For instance, if a rug is to be 1m (100cm) wide, and the image measures 20cm: 20 goes into 100 five times, so the image needs to be enlarged to five times its size, or by 500%. (Or, if you don't fancy doing the maths, just keep enlarging until you're happy with the size.)

INSPIRATION: **Places & History**

'Travel broadens the mind' they say, and it can certainly provide us with a wealth of ideas for rugs. Artists have always taken inspiration from the art of previous generations, and we can do it too for our rugs. Two of the rugs shown here (C and E) are ones I based on early American hooked rugs; the geometric one was probably inspired by patchwork.

A Hooked and progged country scene with plaited border by JSA; woollens on hessian

B Hooked woollens rug by JSA; design taken from an ancient South American mirror-back in semi-precious stones and mother-of-pearl.

C Hooked woollens rug

D Hooked mixed fabric hanging

E Hooked woollens made into a floor cushion

F Lion Mountain; hooked hanging made by Lorenzo Gavarini for his sister Albina. Their favourite spot in the Italian Alps to go camping.

INSPIRATION: **Mythology**

Many of my early rugs were inspired by mythology, ancient symbols and lore, and I've even been asked to interpret dreams and shamanic journeys as rugs and hangings which have made fascinating projects. All hooked woollens by JSA.

A Helice *made for Goddess exhibition, with crocheted web of silver thread*
B Wolf & Owl *hooked rug*
C *I Ching trigrams with yin/yang symbol*
D *Ancient labyrinth and Goddess symbols*
E *Scorpion rug for a Scorpio*

C

A

B

D

E

Techniques and Projects

Although there are many ways to make rag rugs, I'm going to describe prodding, progging, hooking and plaiting/braiding. In this section of the book I'll explain the techniques as I do them; there are other ways of doing the same basic techniques though, and you may adapt them depending on your tools, materials and circumstances. I've also included some projects you might like to try.

I'm still learning all the time too. Sitting beside a woman with a learning disability I took the very varied bits of fabric she was cutting up (with difficulty) and wondered how to work them into a small progging sample. Some were big and some were really small and, as I progged them in, I wondered why I always cut my pieces exactly the same size – hers made a much more interesting texture!

Prodding

Prodding

"Happy days! I used to make rugs with my mother and sister in the evenings. That was near Newcastle. We used a sharpened peg. It was great – they kept your knees warm; we didn't have any heating except one coal fire. You had your corner to do. Happy days!"

Prodding, as its name implies, involves literally prodding or poking a piece of fabric through a base. Rugs made by this technique have different names around the British Isles: 'pegged' in Hull, 'pricked' in Dewsbury, 'clippies', 'proddies', 'stobbies,' and (in Scotland) 'clootie mats'.

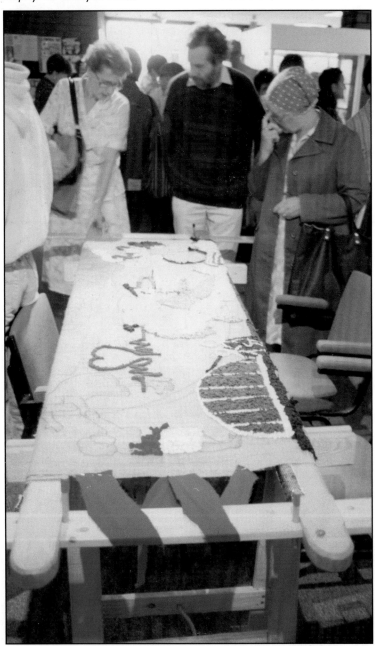

A traditional frame set up for visitors to have a go at prodding. I took the picture at the Ragtime exhibition at Shipley Art Gallery in 1988.

"I did this with my mother. She cut the strips and I cut them to bits. Four of us used to hold a corner and shake it. Mother said 'Don't shake it too hard or the pricks will fall out.'"

Thick woollen fabric (often coats) was cut into strips, and then into pieces which were sometimes called 'tabs' or 'lists'. A base fabric, usually a hessian sack, was stretched on a frame and the pieces were poked (poke mats) or prodded (proddies) one end at a time from the top. The ends were pulled through by one hand held beneath the hessian. With this method the finished effect is a shaggy, cut pile on the right side. I've been told that they used to have these rugs upside down during the week and best side up on Sundays!

"Granny used to get sacks from the mill – they were called 'sheets' – all held together with wooden skewers. They were full of wool which would go into the machine. They were reused and sent back where they came from, but if one was damaged, we could get it."

How to do it

1 Mark the design on the hessian and stretch it on a frame.

2 Cut the fabric, along the weave, into same-sized pieces about 10 x 2.5cm (4 x 1in). You can cut the pieces with a rotary cutter or scissors, or you can use a combination of scissors and an old-fashioned cutting gauge (see page 34).

3 With your writing hand, push a gap between the hessian threads where you want the first piece of fabric to go (**a**). Now use the prodder to poke the end of a fabric piece through the hessian (**b**), receiving it beneath the hessian with your other hand.

c

d

e

single   double

4 Make a second hole about a centimetre, or half an inch, away from the first (**c**), and prod the other end of the strip through it. With the underneath hand, pull the ends of the strip even (**d**).

5 There are two ways you can proceed now: **single prodding**, which spaces the pieces of fabric out more and results in a lighter-weight rug; or **double prodding**, which is more densely packed and results in a thicker rug (some people would say more hard-wearing).

For single prodding: leave four or five threads of hessian beyond the hole where the first fabric piece emerges, then repeat steps 3 and 4.

For double prodding: prod the first end of the next fabric piece into the same hole that the previous piece emerges from (**e**). (This means that every hole has two pieces of fabric emerging from it.) Follow step 3 to finish prodding the second fabric piece, then continue in the same way.

When Mollie Midgley's grandma made a proddy, which she called a tab rug, she used a frame and made big separate holes for each fabric 'tab.' The tab ends were cut on the diagonal so they went through easily, poked from the top and pulled through from beneath. If it was to be a small door mat she didn't use a frame and put each tab in the same hole as the last one. '*You couldn't do that for a large one – it would be too heavy to lift. She used a wooden skewer with a rag wrapped round the end, so she didn't get a blister. The frame used to sit between the table and the back of the settee, and you could get four people working on it, or one at each end.*'

Painful memory. I'll tell my sister my past came back to haunt me. My mother and father, one at each end prodding, and I had to cut up with big scissors which hurt my hands. We had flagstone floors in the country and nothing else to cover them. (Dorset)

TIPS ON PRODDING

* You may need to vary the width of the strips depending on the thickness of the fabric. Cut a few pieces first and poke them through the hessian. If they are hard to push through, cut them a bit narrower – or wider if they seem as though they might fall out.

* If you cut the ends of the fabric (the 'tabs') diagonally, as Molly Midgley's granny did, this makes it easier to prod them through the hessian.

Easy Peasy Proddy

Sometimes the people who come to my workshops tell me that they're 'no good at art,' or 'can't draw.' The good news is that you don't need to be good at art to make a wonderful proddy rug like the one shown below and on page 47. You only need to draw a simple shape — a square or a rectangle. For the prodding you can use old T-shirts or whatever other materials you have (except jumpers, which don't work so well with this technique).

It's much easier to prod the fabric pieces through the hessian if it's stretched taut on a frame. This doesn't need to be a complicated specialist frame; something like an old picture frame will do (see page 38). Working from the wrong side, you simply use whichever colour you fancy and make the rug as small or as large as you like. By the time you're half way through, you'll be planning your next one!

TIP *40 x 60cm (16 x 24in) or smaller is a reasonable size for a first rug which you can then finish quite quickly; your sense of achievement will spur you on to other things.*

You will need

➤ hessian base the size of your rug plus extra 10cm (4in) all round

➤ assorted fabrics — eg old clothes, furnishings, sewing remnants

➤ rug prodder (pointed stick, half a wooden peg or similar)

➤ simple frame

➤ to fix hessian to frame: staples, drawing pins (thumb tacks), or large needle and thick thread

➤ straight edge (long ruler) to draw outline

➤ sharp scissors

➤ marker pen

➤ dressmaking pins

➤ needle and strong thread

INSTRUCTIONS

a

1 Decide on the size and shape of your rug. (If this is your first rug, stick to a square or rectangle as these are the easiest shapes when it comes to sewing the edges under after the prodding.) Use the marker pen and straight edge to draw the outline onto the hessian base; make sure that there is an extra 10cm (4in) of hessian all around the line, to turn under later.

2 Use staples, drawing pins (thumb tacks) or thread to attach the hessian to the frame. Stretch the hessian by pinning one side, then the opposite side.

3 If you're recycling materials, cut out all seams, zips etc. Cut the fabrics along the width into pieces measuring about 7.5 x 2.5cm (3 x 1in), as shown in **a**. (You may need to vary the width depending on the thickness of the fabric – see page 50.)

TIP *A traditional way of making a random rug is to mix all the cut pieces in a bag and use whichever colour comes out when you put your hand in the bag.*

b

4 Following the general instructions for prodding on page 49, begin to prod the pieces through the stretched area of hessian (**b**). (You'll be working from the back of the hessian; the diagrams show how the prodding will look on the right side.) You can use single or double prodding; if you use double prodding, the rug will be thicker and harder wearing. I tend to prefer it. Rugmakers used to make doormats this way because the mats got a lot of use.

5 Working in parallel lines about 1cm (½in) apart, fill in the stretched area of hessian, then if necessary move onto the adjacent area by rolling the rug if your frame allows this. (If you're using a picture frame or similar, move the frame under the next area to be worked, re-stretch the hessian and secure with staples, drawing pins or thread.)

c

6 When you've filled the whole of your marked area with prodded pieces (**c**), remove the rug from the frame. Follow the instructions on page 104 for finishing off your rug (**d**); add a separate backing if you wish.

Variations

d

- If you prefer to prog rather than prod, use a bodger rug tool and work from the right side without a frame.

- If the mood takes you, you could work the rug in simple stripes.

Progging

Progging

My parents used to make progged rugs. Once my father used my mother's red coat – she hadn't thought it was worn out yet! They moved from Yorkshire to Surrey in the Depression and sent money back home – everyone did. The family didn't know how hard up we really were. They would never have let him marry her if they had known. My dad used to go to the coal yard and get coal dust and mix it with dirt, to make sort of brickettes for the fire. My mother never told the family back in Yorkshire she had to walk two miles to work to send them money. In fact she realised much later they were better off than her. She was sending them money to go to the pub!

Progged rugs look the same as prodded rugs but are usually worked from the top, right side up. The fabric pieces are pulled through a hessian base with a 'bodger,' a spring-clip tool with small jaws. I frequently use a bodger, with all kinds of different fabrics. For this technique, the hessian doesn't need to be on a frame. Progging is good for flowing, blended designs, so isn't the best one for pictures. If you do want to prog pictorial detail, use bold, simple shapes and make use of contrasting colours to make them stand out as Doris has done (see pages 108-109).

Traditionally, progged rugs had a dark border and random infill of whatever colours the maker had, sometimes with a shape in the middle in one colour. Mollie Midgley remembers asking her grandmother, *'Why do we always have to have black borders?'* The answer was, *'Because of all the black fabric generated by funerals. People would rush to find black for funerals, even dyeing coats. When Queen Victoria was in mourning for Prince Albert everyone wore black. Plain for everyday, and sateen finish with embroidery for Sundays.'*

How to do it

1 Begin the progging along an outline on your design. Holding the bodger in your writing hand, poke the point into the hessian and out again about 1cm (½in) further along the marked line (**a**).

2 Depress the lever to open the jaws of the bodger and catch the first piece of fabric by one corner (**b**).

3 Pull the bodger back out of the hessian, leaving the piece sticking up like a bow (**c**).

4 Push the bodger back into the last hole it made (where half of the 'bow' sticks up), and out again a further 1cm (½in) along the marked line. Repeat this process (**d**) until you've progged one line all around the border (**e**). Working in parallel lines about 1cm (½in) apart, fill in the shape.

I was born in 1920 and my mother taught me to make rugs at a young age. Between 1930 and 1940 we were making them – perhaps I was even younger. No self-respecting household would be without a bodger.

TIPS ON PROGGING

• If the progging seems too densely packed, just leave a wider gap between the lines from time to time as necessary. The aim is not to have the base fabric visible from the right side.

• You may need to vary the width of the strips depending on the thickness of the fabric. Cut a few pieces first and pull them through the hessian. If they are difficult to pull through (this may well be the case with woollen fabrics) cut them a bit narrower; if they seem as if they might fall out, (which might happen with fine cotton fabrics), cut them wider.

Spiral Seat Pad

I worked this swirling spiral seat pad in dress-weight cottons; it's designed to be used like a chair cushion. You could make a set in toning colours for dining chairs – and one or two would make a lovely present. Once you've made this project you'll be able to use the same technique to work up your own designs.

FINISHED SIZE:
roughly 39cm (15½in) diameter
(the approximate sizes of the projects in inches follow the metric dimensions)

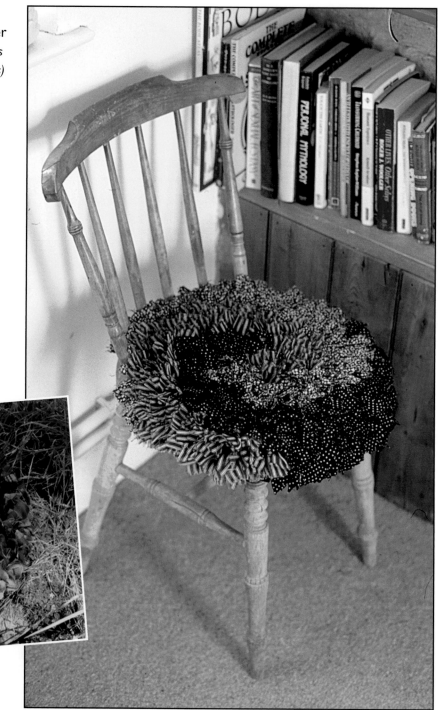

You will need

➤ hessian base (ground) fabric at least 50cm (20in) square

➤ fabrics for progging, plain or patterned, in three colourways

➤ backing (lining) fabric

➤ a bodger rug tool

➤ sharp scissors

➤ marker pens in three different colours

➤ ruler

➤ needle and thread

➤ pins

➤ wadding (optional)

INSTRUCTIONS

1 Select woven fabrics of similar weight, eg cotton dresses or woollen skirts (if you're recycling fabrics). Remove any seams, waistbands etc.

2 There are two different ways in which you can enlarge the template on page 59 to the correct size (see page 42). Either: scale up the drawing onto a large piece of paper, enlarging the grid so that each square measures 5cm (2in). Or: using a photocopier, enlarge the design to measure 39cm (15½in) diameter. Transfer the enlarged design (not the grid) onto the hessian base with marker pens (**a**); you can do this by cutting round the circle and drawing round it, then cutting out the curved shapes one at a time and drawing in the shape. Draw an extra 4cm (1½in) around the edge (**b**), to act as a seam allowance, but don't cut it yet.

TIP *If you're making a set of seat pads, but need to cut up the paper shapes to draw around them, make a paper copy of the full design first to keep for reference, and use tracing paper templates to cut up each time.*

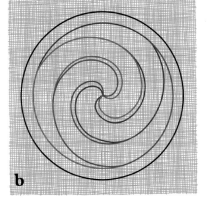

3 Cut the fabrics into pieces along the weave to create strips 10 x 3cm (4 x 1¼in), as shown in **c**, keeping the three batches of colours separate.

4 Follow the instructions for progging (see page 54) to outline one section with fabric pieces in the appropriate colour (**d**). Fill in that section, working in parallel lines about 1cm (½in) apart (**e**).

Outline and fill the two other sections in the same way with the remaining colours (**f**).

5 Cut round the outer circular line (**g**); place this circle on the backing fabric and use it as a template to cut an identical circle from the fabric (**h**). On both circles, fold the seam allowance to the wrong side; pin and tack in place.

6 Place the two circles **wrong** sides together and pin. Slipstitch the folded edges together neatly (**i**).

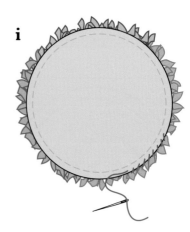

Variations

- Thick fabrics, such as woollens, will create a thicker, warmer seat pad.

- For a more cushion-like effect, lay a circle of wadding (39 cm/15½in diameter) on the underside of the progged area and secure it with stitching before adding the backing fabric.

- If you prefer, this project could be made on a frame with a prodder instead of a bodger.

- Enlarge the whole design to make a rug.

5cm (2in)

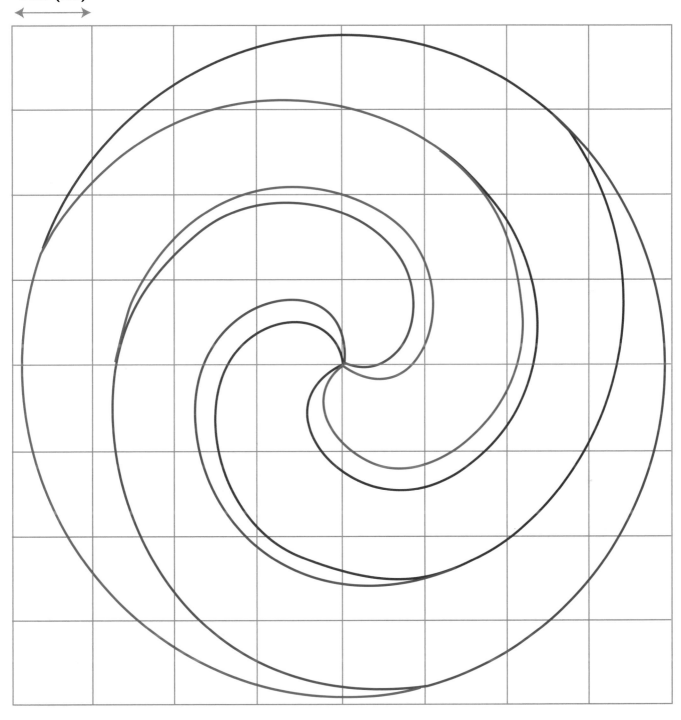

Doris' Sheep Rug

Mrs Doris Tunley is the blacksmith's daughter who taught me hooking and progging (see page 108). She made rag rugs for more than 50 years until her husband Stan died. When she told me she was giving up, I asked her to make one of her lovely traditional rugs for me; now you can do your own version of this typical Herefordshire design featuring a dark-faced Clun sheep. Study the picture and collect old woollen clothes in those colours: coats are ideal. Woven fabric is hard-wearing. The flowers and parts of the sky were made from matted sweaters.

FINISHED SIZE: roughly 102 x 59cm (40 x 23in)

You will need

➤ hessian base at least 122 x 79cm (48 x 31in), which includes an extra 10cm (4in) all round the design for turning

➤ a selection of woollen fabrics

➤ sharp scissors

➤ marker pen

➤ ruler

➤ long straight-edge to draw the outline

➤ paper and pen (if you enlarge the design by squaring up)

➤ bodger rug tool (see page 33)

➤ dressmaking pins

➤ needle and strong thread

TIP *Doris always worked the dark border first and then hemmed it, so that the hessian didn't fray while she progged the rest. You could follow her example, or leave it until you have finished progging as I've described below.*

INSTRUCTIONS

1 Select woollen fabrics similar in weight (for instance, cream blanket for the sheep). Remove any seams, zips etc.

2 Enlarge the drawing on page 64-65 to the correct size (see page 42). To do this, either scale up the grid on paper so that each square measures 10cm (4in), then draw in the lines of the design. Or, using a photocopier, enlarge the design to measure 102 x 59cm (40 x 23in); enlarge it in sections and tape the photocopies together. Transfer the enlarged design (not the grid) onto the hessian base and draw in the lines with marker pen (**a**). Make sure that you have a minimum of 10cm (4in) of hessian outside the border shown on the drawing, for turning to the back of the work later.

a

b

*Reverse side of Doris' mat showing
her neat lines of progging*

3 Cut the fabrics along the weave into pieces 7.5 x 2.5cm (3 x 1in) as shown in **b** on page 61, keeping the colours separate. (You may need to vary the width of the strips depending on the thickness of the fabric – see page 55.)

4 The rug is worked right side up. Using a dark colour, with the hessian resting on a table, work around the outer line of the border first, from right to left, turning the piece of hessian as you go so that the area you're progging is near you. Continue until you've progged a single line all round the border (**c**) then, working in parallel lines about 1cm (½in) apart, fill the border with the same colour (**d**).

5 Prog two yellow pieces for each eye. Now work round the outlines of the sheep (**e**), and then fill in the shapes with parallel lines of progging (**f**); the detail *above* shows how these lines look on the back of the rug. Next prog the flowers (**g**) and fill in grass and sky (**h**), which can be a mixture of strips of woollen cloth and woollen jumpers.

c

d

e

f

g

h

i

6 On the back of the rug, turn the raw edges of the hessian under 5cm (2in), then turn them under again in a double hem, so that they are folded out of sight beneath the progged area (**i**). Secure with pins, and stitch in place using a needle and strong thread; make sure that the hemmed edge is stitched to the hessian, not just to the progged pieces.

Variations

- The colour of the border, the flowers or even the sheep can be varied.

- For a smaller rug, try working the design without a border.

- This design can be made on a frame, using a prodder instead of a bodger, if you prefer.

10cm (4in)

Christmas Wreath

*This quick-to-make seasonal decoration looks great on the
front door or indoors, and makes an unusual present which
can be used year after year. For my wreath I used old woolly
clothes and sparkly dress fabrics.*

FINISHED SIZE: 27.5cm (10½in) diameter

You will need

➤ hessian base at least 34cm (13in) square

➤ green, red, and silver or gold fabrics

➤ a bodger rug tool

➤ scissors

➤ marker pens

➤ tracing paper

➤ cardboard

➤ fabric glue

➤ red ribbon to decorate (optional)

➤ string or fine ribbon to make a hanging loop

➤ large, fat needle or sharp skewer

TIP *A recycled cereal box can be used for the cardboard pieces.*

INSTRUCTIONS

1 Lay the tracing paper over the diagram on page 70 and trace one quarter of the wreath. Do this four times, rotating the design until you've traced the whole circular wreath (**a**). Don't worry if the circles aren't perfect – they are just a guide. Cut out the shape around the circumference and inner circle (**b**).

2 Lay this doughnut shape onto the cardboard and trace round it twice; cut out two card doughnuts (**c**).

TIP *Keep one pair of scissors just for cutting paper and card, as these blunt your fabric scissors.*

3 To transfer the design, place the paper doughnut shape in the centre of your hessian base fabric and draw round it with marker pen. Make sure that there is at least 3cm (1¼in) of hessian left all around the outer circle to turn under later, but don't cut the hessian yet. Mark the positions of the smaller circles around the wreath (**d**).

a

b

c

d

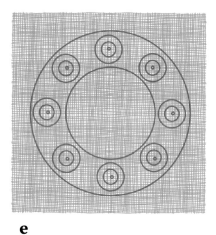

e

4 Cut one of the smaller doughnut shapes out of the paper and align it with one of the marks on the hessian. Using the paper shape as a template, draw round the edges; repeat the process, moving the template round the dots marked on the wreath until you've drawn eight double circles (**e**).

5 Cut the fabrics into pieces:
from the red, cut 32 pieces measuring 3 x 7.5cm
   (1¼ x 3in), cut with straight ends (**f**)
from the silver, cut 96 pieces measuring 3 x 8.5cm
   (1¼ x 3½in), cut with straight ends (**g**)
from the green, cut 72 pieces measuring 3 x 10cm
   (1¼ x 4in), cut with angled ends (**h**).

You may need to vary the width of the fabric strips depending on the thickness of the fabric (see page 55).

6 Start by working round the green circles, just inside the marked lines. Follow the instructions for progging on page 54, until you have filled one green circle using nine pieces of fabric. Repeat round the other seven green circles (**i**). If your fabric is thin, poke the bodger into the hessian for a distance of slightly less than a centimetre. Fill in the red circles using four pieces per circle (**j**).

7 Fill in each area between the circles with twelve pieces of silver fabric (**k**). The diagram of the back of the work (**l**) shows how the strips are distributed.

8 Cut out the wreath leaving a seam allowance of 3cm (1¼in) around the outer and inner circles (**m**). Clip these borders, as shown (**n**), so that they can fold flat behind the

f   **g**   **h**

i   **j**

k

green
red
silver

l

m

n

1cm (½in)

o

p

q

progged area later; don't cut closer than 1cm (½in) to the progging.

9 Position one cardboard circle on the back of the progged area (**o**); fold over the seam allowances of the hessian and stick them to the cardboard (**p**), working on small sections opposite each other and holding the hessian against the card until it sticks.

10 Glue the second cardboard doughnut over the back of the wreath to finish it off neatly.

11 For the hanging loop, use the needle or skewer to make a hole through both thicknesses of card 1.5cm (¾in) in from the outer edge. Thread the string or fine ribbon through and tie it to form a loop.

12 If you wish, make a large bow with red satin ribbon and attach it to the bottom of the wreath (**q**).

Happy Christmas!

Variations

- You could use different colours and fabrics to make a decorative wreath or one to celebrate a special occasion such as a wedding, engagement or anniversary.

- In Italy they hang flowers and a bow on the front door to announce a baby's birth - pink for a girl, blue for a boy. You could make a wreath like this as a welcome present for a new baby.

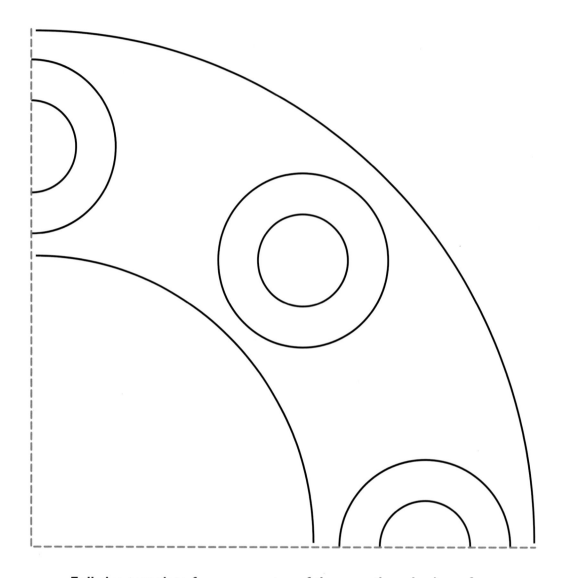

Full-size template for one quarter of the wreath and mirror frame

Mirror Frame

I used the same pattern for this fun frame as I used to make the Christmas wreath on page 66. You can create this design in any colours or fabrics; I made this one for my teenage daughter using her favourite colours. The pink fabric I used was silk, so to prevent it from fraying badly I cut it at an angle using pinking shears (see step 4); the silver-blue fabric was dress-weight cotton, and was slightly stiffer. If your fabrics are significantly thicker or finer, you might need to alter the widths of the strips (see page 55).

FINISHED SIZE: 27.5cm (10½in) diameter

You will need

➤ hessian base at least 34cm (13in) square

➤ three different lightweight fabrics (I used silks and cottons)

➤ a bodger rug tool

➤ scissors

➤ optional pinking shears (to stop the silk from fraying)

➤ marker pens

➤ tracing paper

➤ cardboard

➤ fabric glue

➤ double-sided adhesive tape

➤ circular mirror approximately 17cm (6¾in) diameter

➤ thin ribbon to make a loop for hanging

➤ large, fat needle or skewer

INSTRUCTIONS

a

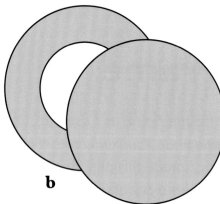

b

1 Follow the instructions for step 1 on page 67 to create a doughnut-shaped template in paper (**a**). Trace round the complete template onto the cardboard once, and then trace just the outer line; cut out one doughnut shape and one complete circle 27.5cm (10½in) in diameter (**b**).

2 Place the paper template in the centre of the hessian and draw round it with marker pen. Make sure there is at least 3cm (1¼in) of hessian all around the outer circle to turn under later, but don't cut the hessian yet. Mark where the smaller double circles come around the wreath (**c**).

3 Cut one of the smaller double circles out of the paper and use it as a template to mark the small doughnut shapes onto the hessian. Align it with the marks on your hessian and move it round the wreath until you have drawn eight double circles (**d**).

c

d

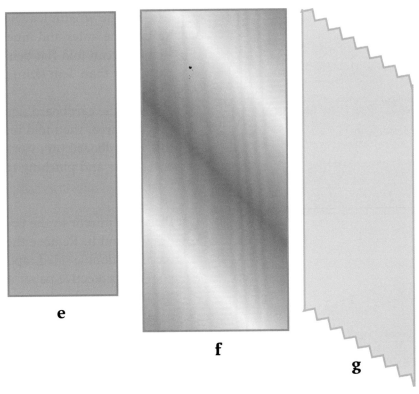

e

f

g

4 Cut the fabric into pieces:
from the deep pink cut 48 pieces measuring 3 x 7.5cm (1¼ x 3in), cut with straight ends (**e**)
from the silver-blue cut 96 pieces measuring 4 x 8.5cm (1½ x 3½in), cut with straight ends (**f**)
from the pink cut 80 pieces measuring 4 x 10cm (1½ x 4in), cut with angled ends using pinking shears (**g**).

5 Start the progging by working round the pink circles. Working just inside the marked lines, use ten pieces of fabric to make one circle; repeat round the other seven pink circles (**h**). Fill in the darker pink centres using six pieces per circle (**i**). Fill in each area between the circles with twelve pieces of silver fabric (**j**); the close-up diagram of the back of the work (**k**) shows how the different areas are filled with progged pieces.

h

i

j

k

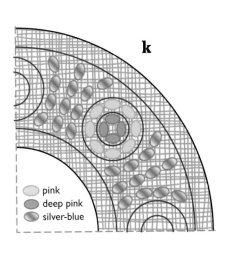

○ pink
● deep pink
◍ silver-blue

l

1cm (½in)

6 Cut out the wreath leaving a seam allowance of 3cm (1¼in) around the outer and inner circles. Clip these borders so that they can fold flat behind the progged area later; don't cut closer than 1cm (½in) to the progging (**l**).

7 Position the cardboard doughnut shape on the back of the progged area, then fold under and stick the hessian borders to the cardboard (**m**), working on small sections opposite each other and pinching the hessian against the card until it sticks.

m

8 Place the mirror in the centre of the circle of card and draw round it. Remove the mirror and stick overlapping pieces of double-sided tape around the drawn circle (**n**); peel the protective paper off the pieces of tape, and stick the mirror in place (**o**).

9 Spread glue on the area of card surrounding the mirror (**p**) and press the back of the progged wreath firmly onto the card backing (**q**), pinching the card edges together until they are stuck.

10 Use the large needle or skewer to make a hole through both thicknesses of card, 1.5cm (¾in) in from the outer edge. Thread the ribbon through and tie it to form a loop and a bow (**r**).

n

o

Variations

• You can use the same design to frame a special picture or photograph instead of a mirror.

• Try other fabrics; opulent ones such as velvets or strips of ribbon look very good.

p

q

r

Hooking

Hooking

" My mother wouldn't have hookies, only proggies. She said if you pulled a piece out of a hooky, too much came out. If you pulled a piece out of a proggie, it was only one piece. There were seven of us kids, you see. "

Hooking is the technique to use if you want to make pictorial rugs or hangings. Strips of fabric are pulled up through hessian (stretched on a frame) to make a series of loops on the right side, where the design has been drawn. You can do this technique with either a hand hook or a speed shuttle (shuttle hook). For hand hooking I work with my frame horizontal on a table, projecting over my lap so that I can hold the strip under it and the hook above it. Quilting frames work well, or even a picture frame or artist's stretcher (see page 38).

Hooking with a hand hook

This is easiest to do using a proper rug hook, which fits snugly in your hand and has a shaft which is wider towards the handle. The shaft makes a big hole in the base fabric, making it easier to draw the strip to the front as a loop. It's possible to use other, improvised tools, but in my experience they aren't as good as one designed for the job. Before Mrs Tunley showed me how to do it properly, I made a hooked rug with a crochet hook, which hurt my fingers and took two years! (I gave up for some years after that.)

Rug hooks come in different sizes – many Americans use a small hook for really fine detail. My rugs are made with a coarse or medium hook and are quite chunky and thick. You can also hook wool (yarn), several strands together (see the cat rug project on page 80), or mix rag and yarn in the same rug. In fact, you can make it up as you go along – if you think something will look good in your rug: hook it, prog it or even stitch it!

How to do it

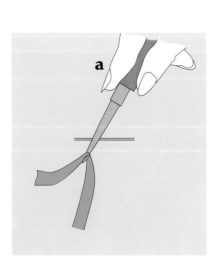

1 Mark the design onto the hessian and stretch it on a frame; lay the frame so that part of the design protrudes over the edge of a table. Begin hooking along an outline of your design; work with the hook in your writing hand above the hessian, and hold the fabric strip in the other hand underneath the hessian. Plunge the hook into the hessian on the marked line, pushing it in right up to the handle so that the wider part pushes a hole between the threads of the fabric.

2 With your lower hand, loop one end of the strip around the hook (**a**), then pull the end of the strip through to the front of the fabric (**b**).

3 Two or three threads further along the marked line, push the hook through the hessian again; loop the fabric strip round it (**c**), and pull it through to the surface to make a loop (**d**). Continue along the marked line, creating loops of an even height, until you reach the end of the strip; pull the end through to the surface, then trim both ends of the strip level with your loops (**e**).

4 Carry on in the same way with another strip; continue working round all the outlines, then fill in the gaps with lines of hooking.

TIPS FOR HAND HOOKING

• Try varying the lengths of the loops you're working, to emphasise different parts of your design.

The rugs were hooked mostly with rags cut into 1in strips and folded in half. The hooks were ground down from an old screwdriver, or made from broken or rusty spindles out of the shuttles from the mill. There were 11 mills in Yeadon. All gone now.

Hooking with a speed shuttle (shuttle hook)

I use a speed shuttle because it's much quicker than working with a hand hook. The shuttle pushes a series of same-sized loops to the front of the hessian – which must be stretched taut on a large frame (see page 39). The aim is to form a dense loop pile so that you can't see the hessian on the right side.

How to do it

These instructions are for a right handed person; however, left-handed people usually find it easy to do it the same way.

1   Stretch the hessian on a frame, then draw the design onto the back of the hessian. Cut your fabric into strips about 1cm (½-⅜in) wide, along the weave. With the frame leaning against a wall, work from the back (wrong side) of the hessian. Thread a strip through the small metal ring and up through the eye of the shuttle, leaving about 2cm (1in) dangling through the eye (**a**); let the strip hang down.

2   Hold one side of the shuttle firmly in each hand. With the needle side in your right hand push it through the hessian where you want to begin the first line of loops (**b**). I work the outlines of shapes first, then fill in. Now push the left-hand side of the shuttle in and pull back the right-hand side (**c**); there should be a click each time you push and pull. Carry on pushing it in, up to the wood. Don't walk the shuttle along – it moves along of its own accord; all you do is push and pull with the needle side facing the way you want to go. I find it easiest to work from left to right and bottom to top.

3   When you've used up your strip, poke its two ends through to the front with something pointed like a bodger. Thread another strip and continue where you left off. Work in lines next to each other to cover the other side of the hessian with loops. Keep poking the strip ends to the front, and from time to time turn the frame round and trim them level with the loops.

TIPS ON HOOKING WITH A SPEED SHUTTLE

- If you can see bits of the hessian on the right side between the loops, it probably means that you've 'walked' the shuttle rather than letting it move at its own place. You can pull out the faulty strip and work it again, going more slowly, and just pushing and pulling the shuttle hook carefully so that the loops are closer together.

- If, when you turn the frame round, you find that a detail (for instance, an eye) isn't clear, you could unpick it and hand hook it from the front later.

- If the shuttle is hard to work, your strips could be too thick – it should move smoothly and rhythmically, without difficulty. Try cutting your strips a little narrower.

Hooking backgrounds

There are various different ways of hooking backgrounds. You can see one in my copy of the 1880 American rug made into a floor cushion (the cat and rat design on page 44) where I followed the maker's meandering lines. I hooked a similar background for the cat on a cushion (see page 25); compare it with the background on the rug from my daughter's drawing (*Rhiannon '88*, see page 41), where I worked the figures first, then hooked round and round them in various shades of cream jumpers. If you don't know how far your materials will go, this technique – known as contour hooking – is a way of blending slightly different shades together (as your jumpers run out). It also emphasises the figures. The background for *Mel* (see page 25) is different again, giving a sense of perspective.

Blending colours

If you want to make a blended transition from one fabric to another, you can blend them by hooking two thin strips together, one of each colour. Or introduce a row of the second fabric, then work a few more rows of fabric 1, then another of fabric 2; gradually space out the rows of fabric 1 until you're working almost exclusively in fabric 2, with increasingly widely-spaced rows of the original fabric. This technique is useful if you don't have enough of one fabric to hook a large area, or if you want to break up a dense block of a single texture or shade.

Ginger Cat Rug

This rug featuring a contented-looking ginger cat was made by Lorenzo Gavarini, who hand-hooked carpet wool (yarn), four strands at a time, through a hessian base. You could make it using any wool or yarn (for instance knitting wool), or strips of rag. Although there are several shades of orange in Lorenzo's cat, one only would look good too, and would be simpler to make. Any variations in the thickness of your wool and the loop size will add to the one-off, hand-made look.

FINISHED SIZE: 56cm (22in) diameter

You will need ➤ Hessian base/ground, big enough for a 76cm (30in) diameter circle (this includes an extra 10cm/4in all round the design – but don't cut the circle out until you've finished hooking)

➤ plenty of wool (the exact quantity depends on the thickness) in the following colours:

one or two shades of orange

brown

black

white

a little blue or green for the eye

➤ rug hook

➤ sharp scissors

➤ marker pens in two colours

➤ ruler and paper (if you enlarge the design by squaring it up)

➤ dressmaking pins

➤ needle and strong thread

➤ frame

INSTRUCTIONS

1 Enlarge the design on page 84 (see page 42). You can do this either by enlarging the grid onto paper so that each square measures 10cm (4in), and then drawing in the lines of the design, or by enlarging the whole on a photocopier until the diameter of the cat is 56cm (22in). To transfer the full-size design (not the grid) onto the hessian base (**a**), use the enlarged circular design as a template and draw round it on the hessian, making sure that you have at least 10cm (4in) extra all around the cat to turn under when you finish (**b**).

2 Attach the hessian base to a frame with thin string, drawing pins or staples depending on the type of frame. If the frame is big enough, the cat should be in the middle. If the frame is small, work on a section of the cat at a time, moving or rolling the hessian on the frame when you need to start a new section. If the hessian is attached top and bottom, stretch the hessian sideways with some string, which can be tightened when the hessian sags.

a

b

3 Place the frame on a table with one side projecting over your lap. Start by working the black outlines. Follow the basic instructions for hooking on page 76, holding four strands of wool in one hand beneath the hessian. (You might need to use more or fewer strands of wool depending on the thickness you use. The aim is for the loops to form a pile on the right side of the work which covers the hessian completely.) Work from right to left along the drawn outline, skipping two hessian threads between each loop and leaving the loops about 1cm (½in) high.

4 Continue hooking until you've worked two lines of loops around the outside edge (**c**), then fill all the other black areas (**d**).

5 Fill in the other colours in the same way, working in order through the eye (**e**), the white areas (**f**), and the brown stripes (**g**), then fill in with the orange. All ends should be pulled to the top and trimmed level with the loops as you go – I use nail scissors for this.

c

d

e

f

g

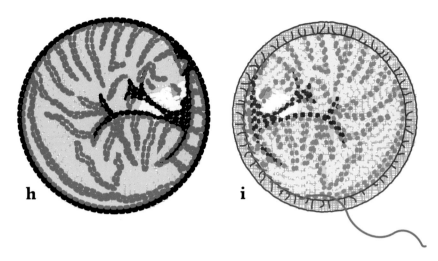

h   **i**

6 Take the rug off the frame. Cut round the border 10cm (4in) outside the cat; turn the raw edges under 5cm (2in), then under again beneath the hooked area (**h**). Secure the turned edge with pins, and stitch in place with needle and thread (**i**).

Variations

- Cats come in all shapes and colours; try using different colours to produce a tabby, a tortoiseshell or a Siamese - or create a portrait of your own cat.

- The background too can be varied to complement your own decor.

- A strip of rag can be used instead of the strands of wool (see the hooked rag project on page 85 for details).

- Enlarge the grid for a bigger rug, or make it smaller for a seat pad.

- If you prefer, add a fabric backing (see the finishing instructions for the progged seat pad on page 58), either stitching it on or glueing (see page 106).

- This project can also be hooked using a speed shuttle and frame (see page 78).

10cm (4in)

Leaf Rug

Make a leaf rug in natural colours or use your imagination — nature's palette is infinite. You could hook this rug with a speed shuttle (shuttle hook) or a hand hook. My leaf has a mixture of woollen fabric strips and wool (yarn). When you're choosing the sweaters which will be recycled, machine knits are best; nothing too loosely knitted. If you can't find enough sweaters, use any wool fabrics.

FINISHED SIZE: 81 x 57cm (32 x 22½in)

You will need

➤ 10oz common hessian, at least 110 x 97cm (43 x 38in)

➤ a selection of woollen sweaters

➤ speed shuttle

➤ large frame with webbing attached to two sides (see page 39)

➤ scissors

➤ rotary cutter, rule and board (optional)

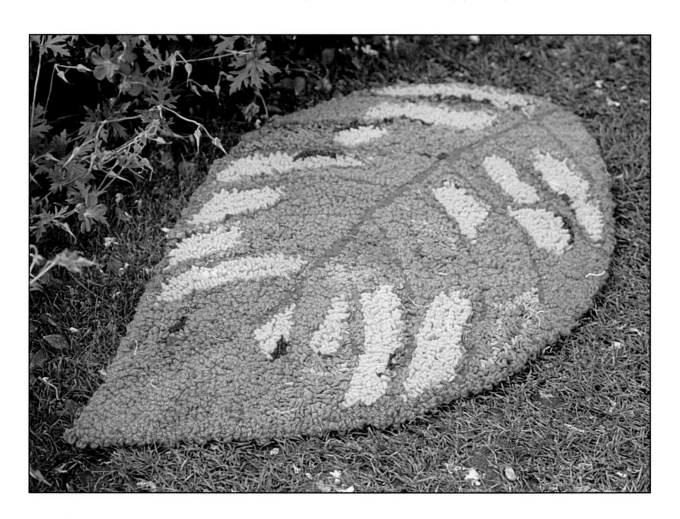

➤ large needle

➤ strong thread

➤ string

➤ paper and pencil (if you're enlarging the design by squaring up)

➤ marker pens in three colours

INSTRUCTIONS

1 Follow the instructions on page 39 to attach the hessian to the frame. Remember that for this method you're working from the back of the hessian.

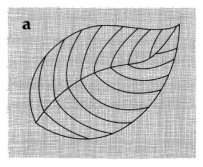

If you're confident, draw a freehand leaf shape onto the back of your hessian base, making it no larger than 60 x 80cm (24 x 32in). If you prefer to use my leaf design, enlarge the diagram on page 88 to full size, either by re-drawing the grid onto paper so that each square measures 10cm (4in), then drawing in the lines of the leaf, or with a photocopier. Transfer the enlarged design onto the back of the hessian (**a**).

TIP *Even though you're working from the back, it doesn't matter which side of the hessian you draw on as long as you can see the line when you're using the shuttle.*

2 Choose a colour for the spine and veins of the leaf, and cut the relevant sweater into strips about 9mm (⅜in) wide. Pull a strip gently and, if it pulls apart, increase the width a tiny bit.

3 Lean the frame against the wall with the drawing facing you. Thread the shuttle with a strip of sweater fabric and, following the instructions for working with a speed shuttle on page 78, work two rows for the spine of the leaf first, then one row for each of the veins (**b**).

f

g

My leaf also has an outline – a single row in the same colour (**c**). Fill between the veins with other shades and colours (**d** and **e**), following the shape of the veins.

TIP *If you need to, turn the frame upside down to work the bottom part of the design.*

4 Take the hessian off the frame and cut around the leaf shape (**f**), leaving a border which will vary in width, depending on how you decide to finish the rug (see page 106). Finish the edges in your chosen method (**g**).

Variations

- If you don't have a speed shuttle, work from the right side using a hand hook and suitable frame (see page 38).

- Vary the colours to reflect a particular season of the year (**h**).

- Try working the design in only fabric strips or only yarn.

- Create your own leaf shape – a realistic one from nature, or a stylised one from your imagination. See page 27 for more ideas on leaf rugs.

h

10cm (4in)

Plaiting/Braiding

Plaiting/Braiding

Plaited rugs don't seem to go as far back in Britain as they do in America. Many people have told me about the rugs they plaited from silk or lisle stockings in the 1930s and 40s, but the only old plaited rugs I've seen myself were Canadian ones. I came across these when I stayed with a friend in England; his Canadian grandmother's rug with a braided border, and her braided seat pads (see pages 9 and 10), were in my room.

In plaited rugs I combine fabrics which are similar, such as all cottons, so that they will wash and dry evenly. I gather fabrics which look good together and make a couple of test plaits, one with narrow strips and one with wider strips to see which looks and feels best. The width of the strips also relates to the thickness of your fabric. I don't sew the strips into tubes (the traditional American way), I just turn the raw edges to the back as I plait. These edges are then concealed by the fabric backing (which also consolidates the plaits). If you want a reversible rug you need to sew the fabric into tubes; some makers stuff these tubes with wadding or other materials.

How to do it

1   Cut or rip the fabrics into strips along the weave, and aim to start plaiting three strips about 1m (1yd) long. If your strips are short, join them with diagonal seams (**a**). If your strips are cut from something very long, such as curtains, roll up one end of each strip and secure it with a pin so that you're still working with metre/yard strips; longer strips will get tangled as you plait.

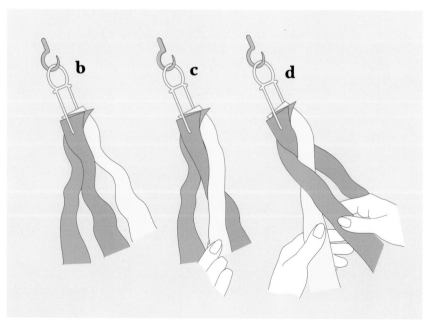

2   Choose three strips and fasten the top ends together with a safety pin; hook the safety pin over a cup hook screwed into something secure (**b**). Plait or braid the strips by picking up the right-hand strip and bringing it over the middle strip (**c**), then bring the left-hand strip over the new middle strip (**d**); continue in the same way (**e**), turning the raw edges of the strips to the back of the plait as you go. Keep the plait fairly soft and pliable. Leave about 20cm (8in) unplaited and secure the plait with a pin.

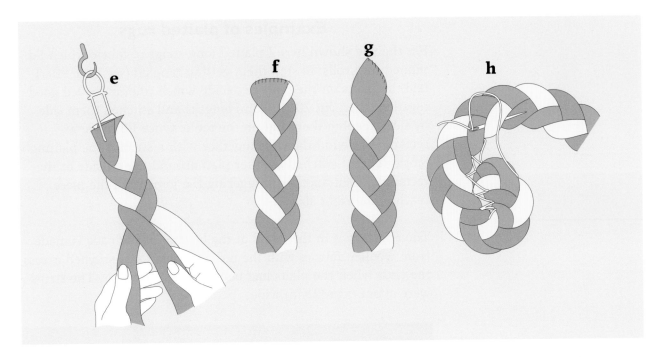

3 Remove the safety pin and neaten the starting ends. For an oval rug, such as the one on page 93, fold one of the strip ends over the other two to bind them neatly, sewing the strip in place (**f**). Similarly, for a circular rug, make the top ends of the plait into a pointed shape which forms the centre (**g**), then wind the plait round in a spiral. Lace the edges together with thick thread, taking the bodkin behind single loops of the plait on alternate sides so that the thread forms a 'ladder', then pulling the thread to bring the edges together and conceal the thread (**h**). Keep the stitching fairly loose so that it doesn't pull and deform the finished piece.

4 Once you've laced the plaited section, join more strips to your original ones, making sure that the joins on different strips aren't adjacent (to avoid making the plait lumpy).

5 When the rug is big enough, taper the strips to half their width over about 23cm (9in), and plait them. Lace and sew the tapered plait against the edge, tucking and stitching the end underneath.

TIPS FOR PLAITING/BRAIDING

- You can create rugs of various shapes with plaits; try squares and rectangles (see page 92) as well as circles and ovals.

- In addition to lacing, I like to sew the plaits together invisibly with a needle and thread, for a really smooth finish. You can decide if the lacing looks as though it's enough on its own.

Examples of plaited rugs

For the rug shown here I plaited long strips of fabric which I'd pinned into rolls, to stop them getting tangled (see page 90). I laid the plaits on the table to decide which colours looked good together, then cut 70cm (28in) lengths and stitched them side by side, keeping them flat on the table. Once I'd made a rectangle I bound the ends together with a strip of the plaiting fabric. Then I stitched another plait around the outside of the rectangle, then another, staggering the joins until the piece reached the right size.

The rug shown in the detail at the bottom of the page is made from woollen fabrics with the red felt woven and stitched across the ends when the plaits had been stitched together. The strips were about 6cm (2¼in) wide.

Oval Rug

Make a small rug for your first plaited project, and that will give you the confidence to work bigger. This one's made from recycled plain and printed cottons, and is enriched with pink and green velvet. It could be draped over a chair-back or put on the floor, maybe even in a bathroom.

FINISHED SIZE: 73 x 57cm (29 x 22½in)

You will need
- ➤ assorted cotton fabrics and optional velvets
- ➤ cotton backing fabric
- ➤ large safety pin
- ➤ tape measure
- ➤ scissors
- ➤ blunt needle (bodkin or lacing needle)

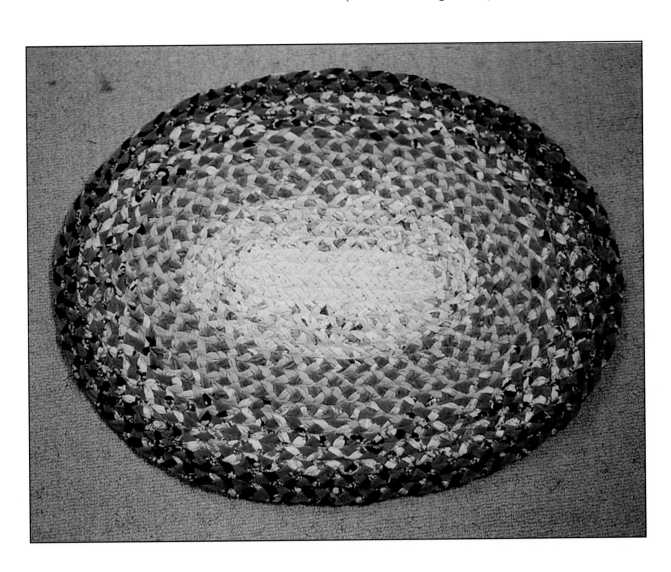

➤ thick thread for lacing (no 5 knit & crochet cotton or similar)

➤ sewing needle

➤ threads in colours to match the fabrics

➤ pins

➤ sewing machine (optional) for joining the strips

INSTRUCTIONS

1 Choose fabrics of a similar weight. The velvet I used was thicker than the dress fabrics, so I cut same-width strips of both and made a test plait, slowly reducing the width of the velvet strip until I achieved an even plait. It's worth making a short test plait anyway to see how wide the strips need to be for your particular fabrics. On my rug the strips of dress fabric were about 5cm (2in) wide.

TIP *Wider strips make bigger plaits which grow faster, but they need careful lacing/stitching so that their weight doesn't pull them apart.*

2 Cut or rip the fabrics into strips along the weave, and choose three strips about 1m (1yd) long to start off the plaiting. Follow the general instructions on page 90-91 to start and continue the plaiting, keeping the plait fairly soft and pliable. Leave about 20cm (8in) unplaited and secure the plait with a pin.

3 Remove the safety pin and stitch the top ends together neatly (**a**).

TIP *Subtract the width from the length of the finished rug to get the length of the centre starting plait for an oval rug.*

a

b

4 Double up the plait so that the centre strip is about 16cm (6in) long (**b**). Thread a large needle with the lacing thread and knot the end; bring the thread through the plait, concealing the knot. Change to the bodkin and follow the instructions on page 91 to lace the plaits together (**c**); the thread shouldn't show on the front of the rug. Once you've laced the centre strip, coil the plait around the strip and continue lacing (**d**). Work with the rug flat on a table, pulling the thread firmly but not so tight that the rug deforms. To produce the curved ends of the oval you'll need to miss out a loop on the plait being added as you're doing the lacing.

c

d

5 Follow the instructions on page 91 to add more strips to the end of your plait. Continue plaiting and lacing in the same way, working round and round the oval and adding

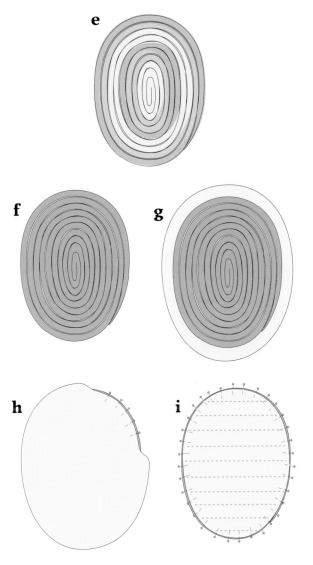

e

f   g

h   i

more strips as you go until the rug is as large as you want it. Decide, as the rug grows, whether you want wide bands of the same colours.

TIP *Changing the colour of one strip at a time creates a subtle colour transition. It emphasises the shape to make complete ovals before changing colour (e).*

6 When the rug is big enough, taper the strips to half their width over about 23cm (9in) and plait them; follow the instructions on page 91 to neaten and conceal them (**f**).

7 Place the rug on the backing fabric and cut round it leaving 2.5cm (1in) seam allowance (**g**). Turn the rug upside down and pin the backing to it, turning under the seam allowance as you go (**h**).

8 To hold the backing in place and to strengthen the rug, work backstitch across the plaits at right angles in parallel lines about 10cm (4in) apart (**i**). Sew neatly round the turned edges of the backing to secure it to the rug.

Variations

- If you want to make a larger rug, use wider strips.

- Smaller ovals, using finer strips, work well as place mats.

- Woollen fabrics would make a thicker, harder-wearing rug.

- If you enjoy using a sewing machine, try making fine plaits which can then be zigzagged together on the machine.

Mixed Techniques

Mixed Techniques

By mixing techniques in a piece of work you can create as many interesting textures and effects as you can dream up. I have progged borders on hooked rugs, like the ones on this heart wedding memento (top left), and I've sewn plaits as borders on hooked or progged rugs.

I love making mixed technique spirals and ammonites (such as the one centre left), which I start with a plait to define the shape and then fill in with other techniques – rather like doing a painting. Before starting, I pick a selection of fabrics which look good together, perhaps adding to them as I'm working and I get inspiration. With each row, other ideas for colours and variations come to me for the next bit. Each time I make such a piece, it gives me ideas for further variations on the theme.

I was commissioned by Hereford Museum and Art Gallery to make the piece at the bottom left for an exhibition called *Get in Touch,* which was mainly for the blind and partially-sighted people who are at college in that city. I chose the materials by feeling them with my eyes shut so that there was an interesting range of textures, including: smooth, shiny, slippery, soft, rough, hairy, fluffy, knobbly, warm, intricate and contrasting. I saw my work again recently in a *Recycling Through the Ages* exhibition on the Museum on the Move bus, and it had been touched by an enormous number of people!

If you're not sure which rug making technique to begin with, or if you've tried several techniques and want to branch out by mixing them, you could make a small sampler using various techniques and contrasting fabrics. Don't worry about the finished result, just enjoy playing around. I made the piece on page 20 at a workshop with teenagers; they didn't want me peering over their shoulders all day, so I hooked and progged some of the huge pile of fabrics we had, then sewed on some pearl buttons. The workshop was in a converted water-mill so I was inspired to give it a flowing feeling.

TIPS FOR WORKING IN MIXED TECHNIQUES

- Be flexible in your colour choice and change or add colours as you go along, if they complement the work. Think of it like painting a picture, and 'paint over' or change bits if it looks good. Be prepared to unpick sections if a new colour changes the dynamic, or if what you planned doesn't look as you expected.

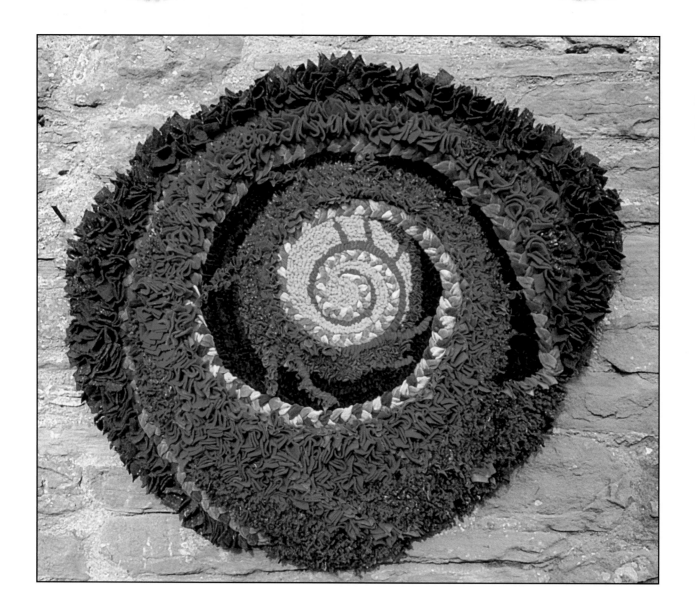

Ammonite

FINISHED SIZE:
80 x 75cm (32 x 29½in)

One way of achieving really striking effects in your rugs is by mixing techniques and fabrics. To give rich colours and textures on this spiral ammonite design I used golden curtain material, furnishing velvet, woollen and velvet skirts, glazed cotton, felt, wool/mohair fabric scraps and some carpet yarn. I began by stitching the plait onto the hessian in a spiral line, then filled the shape, first by progging, then hooking.

To make your own version of the spiral, choose colours that you like, with contrasting textures, and be prepared to enjoy improvising. I used two different shapes for my progged pieces, cutting some of them with straight ends and some of them with diagonal ends for extra visual interest.

You will need

➤ hessian background, 1m (39in) square

➤ bodger rug tool

➤ rug hook

➤ marker pens in two colours

➤ paper for enlarging the drawing

➤ scissors

➤ rotary cutter, ruler and board (optional)

➤ needle

➤ thread

➤ a selection of fabrics

INSTRUCTIONS

1 Enlarge the diagram on page 102 to full size, either on a photocopier or by using the grid method, so that each finished square measures 10cm (4in). Trace the enlarged drawing to make a template, and cut it out around the outline. Place the template in the centre of the hessian and draw round it (**a**). Cutting on the drawn lines, remove a section on the outside edge of the template, and draw the shape left behind (**b**). Continue cutting out adjacent sections of the template, drawing each line as you go until the whole ammonite design is drawn on your hessian (**c**).

2 Pick three strips of fabric 2.5cm (1in) wide for the first section of your plait (I used peach velvet and golden curtain fabric) and follow the instructions on page 90. To neaten the starting ends, taper them to a point and bind the point with one of the strip ends folded over the others, sewing it in place. After roughly 87cm (37in), add to the plait with strips 4.5cm (1¾in) wide (I changed one of the strips to a darker orange velvet) until the plait is the same length as the central spiral on your drawing. This increases the thickness of the plait as it spirals outwards.

a

tracing paper template

hessian

b

template with first section cut away

c

3 Make an additional plait to cover the outer arc of the design and sew both plaits onto the hessian, over the drawn lines (**d**), using thread that tones with the fabrics. Sew both sides of the plait to the hessian, concealing the stitches.

4 With a bodger, prog pieces alongside the outer edge of the spiral (**e**), starting about 46cm (18in) from the centre (see page 54 for general instructions on progging). Towards the centre of the design use pieces of fabric about 7.5 x 2.5cm (3 x 1in), gradually increasing the size to 9.5 x 4cm (3¾ x 1½in) and cutting the ends diagonally. I used tan-coloured glazed cotton for these pieces. Prog the same fabric on the lines radiating outwards. I finished progging the spiral in tan felt.

5 Have a good look at the photograph of my finished rug to get a feeling for improvising. Using another colour, prog a line or two next to the first ones. Prog more lines, working outwards, changing the shade/type of fabric. If you work a line at a time you can decide what to use next, depending on how it looks.

6 Using a rug hook (see page 76), hook a strip of tan fabric (about 1cm/½in wide) from where you started progging to the centre of the spiral, plus the lines radiating outwards (I added three extra hooked radiating lines, as shown in **f**).

7 Using either a strip of fabric or four strands of yarn, fill the central area with hooked loops (**g**). I used yellow rug wool. Hook strips of another colour round the spiral next to the plait – I worked with maroon velvet – then hook another texture/shade between the two. I chose a silky maroon fabric. Fill in the rest of the outer sections with progging. Grade the colours as you work outwards to emphasise the shape of the ammonite.

TIP *You might need to trim down some of the progging adjacent to the plait if the progged pieces flop over it. I trimmed some of the first progged pieces near the centre because they looked too long (this depends on the length of your hooked loops, the thickness of the fabrics and how they all interact).*

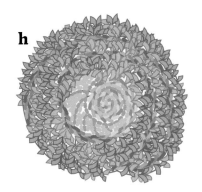

h

8 When you've filled in the whole shape, cut round the progged area, leaving a border of 4cm (1½in) outside the design. Choose one of the finishing techniques on page 104 onwards to complete your rug (**h**). You could hem the edge or sew on a backing (see the seat pad on page 58), or glue on a hessian backing and tape.

Variations

- Simplify the design by leaving off the outer plait and the radiating lines to give a straightforward spiral.

- If you prefer, you can cut all the progged pieces with straight ends.

10cm (4in)

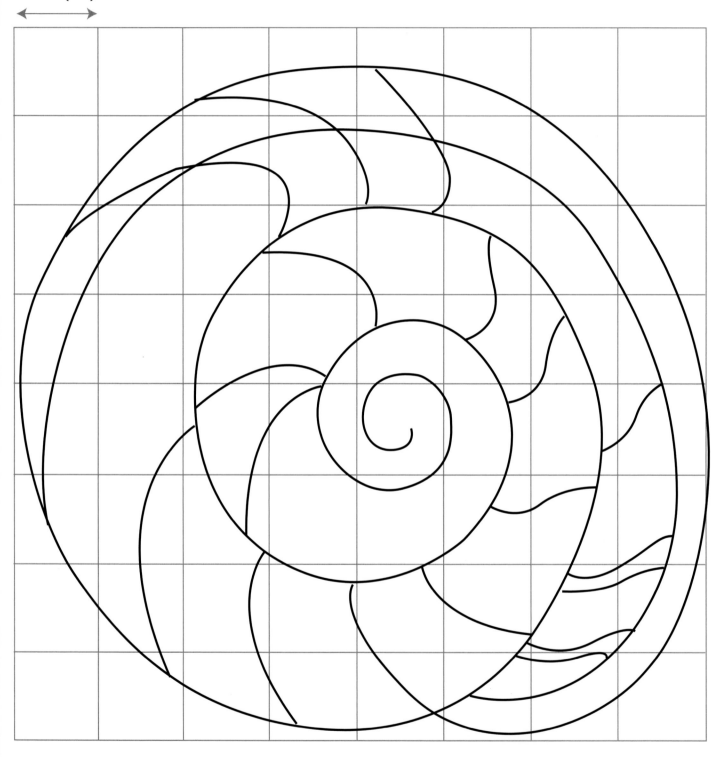

Finishing

Finishing

Traditionally prodded rag rugs were not backed (lined), so that the dirt would fall through them and not be trapped between the rug and the backing. An unbacked rug will be more flexible and drape, so if it's going on a wall, a backing will stiffen it. People often love the backs of rugs where you can see the design clearly. I usually back hooked, plaited and mixed technique rugs, but not progged ones.

Here are different ways of finishing off rugs:

Hemming

Simply fold back the unworked edges in a double fold and slipstitch them to the backing; make sure that you catch the actual fabric, not just any progged or prodded or hooked pieces. Fold in the corner of the hessian (**a** and **b**) and trim off the point, then fold the edges in twice, pin them and stitch (**c**). The sheep mat on page 60 uses this method of finishing.

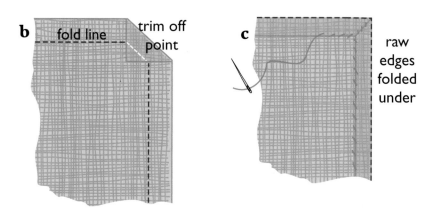

Cloth backing

After you've trimmed your rug to its finished size plus a border for turnings, cut a piece of backing cloth the same size (**a**). Fold the unworked edges of the rug to the back and pin or tack them, then pin the backing fabric in place, turning under the edges as you go (**b**). The seat pad on page 56 uses this method. For backing plaited rugs see page 95.

Binding

Cut away any surplus hessian, leaving a border of 3cm (1¼in) around the worked area (**a**). Pin cotton carpet tape (approximately 4cm/1½in wide) on the right side of the hessian and, using a heavy cotton thread, work a line of backstitch close to the worked area (**b**). Join the ends of the tape on a side of the rug, not a corner. Ease the tape around corners and points.

Turn the tape to the back, pin, and hemstitch the tape in place using strong thread (**c**); mitre any corners neatly. The final result is a neat line of binding all around your rug; it will show on the back, but not on the front (**d**).

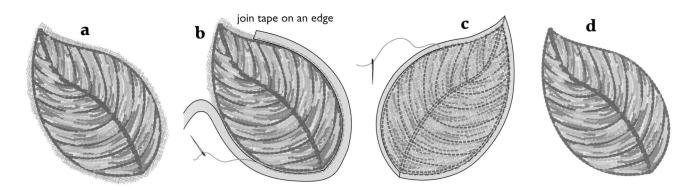

a   **b**   join tape on an edge   **c**   **d**

a

glue

worked area

b

second piece of hessian, trimmed to worked area

c

border folded back

d

carpet tape

Glued hessian backing

Cut away any surplus hessian, leaving a border of 3cm (1¼in) around the worked area. Cut the piece of hessian for the backing a bit bigger than the back of the worked area. Spread a thin layer of latex carpet adhesive on the back of the rug (**a**). Work in strips about 30cm (12in) wide; place the backing on the glued area and smooth it down with your hands. Repeat the process until the whole of the backing is glued down, then trim it back so that it covers the worked area only, leaving the hessian border (**b**).

Fold the border back, mitring any corners, and glue it lightly in place (**c**). Glue carpet tape over the raw edge of the border (**d**), using more adhesive to cover the tape.

TIP *Put some adhesive in a saucer and use a knife to spread it, but use just enough to stick it, not enough to soak the backing. Always use this adhesive in a well ventilated place, wear an apron, and follow the manufacturer's instructions.*

Ready-made hems

It's possible to hook or prog a rug onto a piece of hessian with ready-turned edges. Before you begin to work the design, trim the hessian so that there's a 5cm (2in) border around the outer edge of your rug design (**a**); then fold this excess over to the **right side**, mitre the corners, and tack/baste (**b**).

Now work your hooking or progging though the two layers of hesssian round the outer edge of the rug (**c**); the folded bit disappears under the ragwork. This technique gives a really neat finish, but it's harder and slower to work through two layers.

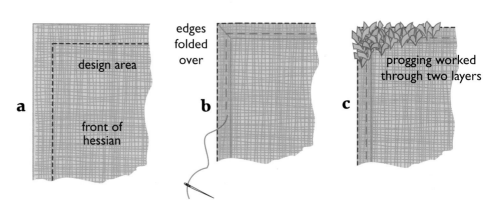

a

design area

front of hessian

edges folded over

b

c

progging worked through two layers

Working on a sack

If you're working your rug design on a sack, doubled, you could work right up to the edge; the edge of a sack is usually bound with string and therefore requires no further finishing.

Granny would work right up to the edge of the hessian then bind the edges with old shirts or anything she had. Posh rugs would have a separate lining made from sheets, blankets, curtains to protect the back.

Cleaning Rag Rugs

My mum said to my dad, you made the rugs, now you clean them. He put them on the line and beat them with a broom and ohh, how the dust came out in great clouds!

Before the days of vacuum cleaners, people used to shake rugs to get the dust out, or hang them over a washing line and beat them with a special cane carpet beater. In countries where snow is common in winter, people used to put their knotted rugs upside down on the powdery snow and walk on them, so that the snow acted as a dry cleaner.

I vacuum my rag rugs when I'm making them and when they are finished. When it's absolutely necessary, I hand-wash hooked and progged rugs in warm soapy water, in the bath, then rinse them and leave them to drain as they are so heavy when wet. Then I dry the rugs flat outside on a ladder or netting, to allow air to circulate around them. They take a while to dry so this is best done in the summer – but not in direct sunlight, which may fade the colours.

I have also used a commercial carpet-cleaning machine, generally used for large carpets, which spreads and then vacuums away proprietary carpet cleaner diluted with water.

I do machine-wash rugs made on open-weave rug canvas, but I pin them inside a pillow case before putting them in the machine. It's important that the edges have been sewn well so that the action of the machine doesn't fray them. This technique works for plaited cotton rugs too, which is why they make very good bath mats. Recently I had to retire one after 10 years because I was tired of looking at it!

A friend told me that her grandmother used to make the rag back doormat like a bag; then she would put newspaper between the rug and the backing, changing the damp paper every night.

Gallery

Many of these rugs are by non-professional rug-makers. As I mentioned earlier, Mrs Tunley taught me, and I taught most of the others rag rugging; Mona and Russell are self taught.

Doris Tunley

I was born Doris Colburn in Pontypool in 1924, and we moved to Herefordshire in 1926, in the big strike. When I was about seven I had an operation and callipers fitted, for foot trouble. My mother had to find ways to kill the boredom, so I got on to making mats on sacks from the farm - the mats had to be sack size. At that time we needed them for the floor to cover tiles or flags. We used to put the rags in using a stick cut to a point, but after a time we got nice peggers. Wool mats were made at our country school, along with pinafores, traycloths etc.

I left school life behind and did lots of different jobs. Then I had to come home and looked after my mother for four and a half years; I did a few mats at this time. In 1949 my Mum died, and I went back to work and kept home for me and my Dad.

BELOW: *Doris Tunley and the author, with Doris' sheep rug*
OPPOSITE: *Four small rugs made by Doris and her husband Stan*

In 1952 I met my husband (in the photo, right); we married and moved house, and Dad came with us. We needed floor covering, so Dad says 'Why don't you make some mats?' Dad cut up the rags for us; me and my husband Stan pegged

them. People around gave us rags – we used thick cloth army coats, flannel trousers and wool jumpers that had gone thick in the wash. We worked well together and enjoyed it. We put one in a show – 'something new out of something old' – and had first prize. We did lots of different ones after this.

Jenni Stuart-Anderson

For me rag rug making has been the start of a real fascination with textiles. After years at a drawing board working in millimetres, it was a liberation to use such a fluid medium with such scope for improvisation. I also believe in recycling and as I work a garment - a piece of someone's life - into a rug, I wonder about its history. I find I can tell a lot about a place from the contents of its charity shops (reading the rags?)

I made the progged rug below after looking at Mark Rothko's wonderful paintings. It's made from wool, cotton and mohair fabrics, plus woollen yarn put in with a latchet hook. Of course, it doesn't achieve the subtlety of Rothko's masterly composition and use of paint, but people who like his work see that I do too, and this includes Miriam, who sent me this poem after she saw my rug.

A Rag Rug

for Jenni Stuart-Anderson

A poem by Miriam Obrey

I want to make a rag rug like Rothko
might have done had he made one.
I'd lay my hessian-backed mat
across the kitchen floor, and say to all
who'd wipe their boots on it: *wait a bit
- look at it - it's all my own work;
see how the colours speak to each other;
see how they sing when the sun creeps in
to rest for a moment in the knap of them -
'velour, velour'; how the frayed edges kiss
where orange cotton meets blue polyester.*
Imagine, just for a moment, if you tried
to add a whisper of yellow, or to work in
purple, pink or green, how the world –
their world I call *kitchen* – would change.
Imagine how the tiles might talk back,
chipping in with their terracotta –
a sort of dark rhubarb mutter; and how
the gaps between might cough. Rothko,
you old rascal, no one can see my work
as they'd have done had you not come
before me with your dripping brooms
laying in swathes of mulberry and moss.

RIGHT: **Movin' On**, mixed technique wall-hanging made by Jenni Stuart-Anderson

BELOW: Miriam Obrey's hooked hanging **St Mark**, in his symbolic representation as the lion

Miriam Obrey

I like to feed the birds in my garden and believe in recycling so, when I'd accumulated a pile of peanut sacks, I thought of turning them into rag rugs. I enrolled on one of Jenni's courses and became hooked.

As a painter and poet, my work is influenced by medieval ideas: art, philosophy, colour, superstition and lore. With regard to my wish to recycle as much as possible, the fabrics I choose range from cotton velvets, sheer silks and glittering Indian rayons through to woollen blankets, knitted jumpers, T-shirts, brushed nylon sheets and stretch towelling, all of which I've found at jumble sales and charity shops.

ABOVE: **Dancers**, one of Lorenzo's hooked rugs
BELOW: **Masks**

Lorenzo Gavarini

My rugs begin with paper and pencils as I bring an idea to shape on the sketch pad. When a design pleases me, I am in for the compelling harvest – a swim through Jenni's overspilling bags of colourful old jumpers and skirts, all shaped with some body's memory.

Then the chosen clothing goes laughing in the soapy water and, when dried, becomes a meal for the gossipy scissors.

All this in preparation for the fervent flickering of the shuttle hook, a busy bird which picks up in its brass bill strip after strip of cut-up clothes and flies to the stretched hessian, into which the woolly picture gets prodded as a lasting nest for eyes or toes.

Rachel d'Albert

(Rachel was given one of Jenni's rugs – leaf D on page 27 – as a leaving present, which inspired her to come to a workshop.)

When I'm rug making I'm painting with fabric. I begin with a sketch and notes of how I hope the finished product may end up.

As I work I let the ideas flow and build up - constantly viewing my work from a distance to get a real feel for it. Also my rugs are very special to me - using my grandma's coat, mum's college scarf, and poncho fabric that I had as a youngster. Rag rug making is so exciting: I need a larger house to accommodate them all!

Two examples of Rachel's rugs, hooked using a speed shuttle.
ABOVE: **Leaves**
RIGHT: **Flower**

Esther Barrett

I studied embroidery, and have experimented with silk and cotton quilts and hangings, branching out into wool and recycled fabrics after a day school with Jenni. I make rag rugs, cushions and bags in my workshop at Brewery Arts, Cirencester.

I love working with material, exploring and playing with its textures, colours and patterns. I've demonstrated rag rug making at Cotswolds shows and at the Cotswold Heritage Centre; I particularly enjoy hearing people's reminiscences of rag rug making.

RIGHT: *Esther Barrett with Alec Martin and his football rug*
BELOW: *Leaf rug, hooked with speed shuttle*
BOTTOM: *One of Esther's progged rugs*

Janet Bradley

My aunt taught me to embroider as a child, encouraging my fascination for colour and textiles.

I was trained in fine art, and living in the south Shropshire hills inspired me to research and practise traditional country crafts, using natural materials and dyes including wool from my own sheep. Twelve years ago I started rag rug making after inheriting my family's tools and an unfinished rug. Using old coats, my mother made peg rugs on a sack (unpicked, washed and ironed), using a second sack for backing. The heavy mats were pushed against the back door to keep draughts out; they needed a good thump against the wall to get the dust out.

I demonstrate Victorian domestic rural skills and crafts, including rug making, at Acton Scot Historic Working Farm. I prefer to work traditionally, and I use recycled sacks, ragbag oddments and felted wool, prodded with an old, worn, adapted peg for have-a-go sessions with children and craft workshops.

ABOVE AND RIGHT:
Examples of Janet's prodded rugs

Russell Parkinson

I first saw rag rugs on a childhood visit to the museum in Scunthorpe, the steel town where I grew up.

Inspired to make my own by the vivid colours and bold designs of Kaffe Fassett, I started with a latch hook, which broke - so now I use a rug hook. My work is influenced by gypsy art and vibrant stained glass. As an astrologer I also think of my designs as symbols to be interpreted, as in my recent rugs of alchemical symbols.

My rug of a naked man spiralling through space (above right) was inspired by a Laurie Anderson song. It's full of wonderful images including 'kerjillions of stars' starting to shine and 'icy comets' whizzing by, and finishes by talking about 'the enormous night.'

Sometimes I think it looks like a man falling through a hole in the floor!

Heart

Red/white dragons

Lion eating sun, *in progress and* (right) *a detail*

Mona Callander
(of the rug business Thrum)

ABOVE AND BELOW: *Two examples of Mona's abstract hangings hooked using a speed shuttle.*

OPPOSITE: **Mother and Child**

I first became interested in rag rugging in the mid-nineties, after seeing traditional examples illustrated in a library book. The ready availability of materials and simplicity of technique encouraged my first attempts at small simple pieces.

The quality of colour unique to textiles, and the actual physical presence of a rug or hanging, as an object, quite different to that of a painting, seemed to make it the ideal medium through which I could develop my particular interest in abstraction.

I continue to refine my design ideas while increasing the scale of my work, and in the future I would like to focus on exploring the seemingly endless possibilities of the medium.

BIBLIOGRAPHY/FURTHER READING

American Hooked and Sewn Rugs by Joel and Kate Kopp, University of New Mexico Press, reprinted 1995

Handcrafted Rugs by Sandra Hardy, Guild of Master Craftsman Publications, 2001

Rag Rugs of England & America by Emma Tennant, The Decorative Arts Library, Walker Books, 1992 (now out of print)

Rag Rug Inspirations by Juliet Bawden, Cassell 1996

Rag Work by Lizzie Reakes, Lorenz Books, 1996

Rag Rugs by Ann Davies, New Holland, 1996 (now out of print)

Rag Rugs by Juju Vail, Quintet, Apple Press, 1997 (now out of print)

Rag Rugs, New Holland, 2002

Rugs from Rags by John Hinchcliffe and Angela Jeffs, Orbis Publishing, 1977 (now out of print)

Rugs from the American Museum in Britain by Sheila Betterson, The American Museum in Britain, 1981

Rare Hooked Rugs by William Withrop Kent, The Pond-Eckberg Company, 1941

The Hooked Rug by William Withrop Kent, The Pond-Eckberg Company, 1949

INTERESTING PLACES TO SEE RAG RUGS

The American Museum in Britain,
Claverton Manor, Bath BA2 7BD
tel 01225 460503
www.AMERICANMUSEUM.ORG

The North of England Open Air Museum,
Beamish, County Durham DH9 0RG
tel 0191 370 4000 www.beamish.org.uk

Museum of Welsh Life,
St Fagans, Cardiff CF5 6XB
tel 029 2057 3500

SUPPLIERS

Jenni Stuart-Anderson & Lorenzo Gavarini
The Birches,
Middleton-on-the-Hill,
Herefordshire HR6 0HN, England
tel 01568 750229
email: jennifay.sa@ukonline.co.uk
http://www.jenni.ragrugs.freeuk.com
Workshops, commissions, tools and equipment by mail order

Mona Callander
The Workshop, No 1 Cottage,
Lightfield, Gordon,
TD3 6LD, Scotland
tel 44 (0) 1573 410662
email: monacallander@btinternet.com
Commissions

Creative Grids (UK) Ltd
PO Box 207, Leicester LE3 6YP, England
tel 0845 450 77 22/fax 0116 254 11 66
email: sales@creativegrids.com
Rotary cutters, mats, non-slip rulers etc by mail order

Russell & Chapple Ltd
68 Drury Lane, London WC2B 5SP, England
tel 020 7836 7521/fax 020 7497 0554
email: info@brodies.net
Retail and mail order hessian

Brown & Cook Ltd
77 Allcock Street, Birmingham B9 4DY, England
tel 0121 766 7117/fax 0121 753 2155
email: sales@brownandcook.co.uk
www.brownandcook.co.uk
Suppliers of hessian, carpet tape etc by mail order

Rigby Cloth Stripping Machines
Route 302, PO Box 158
Bridgton, Maine 04009, USA
Fabric strip cutters

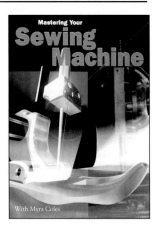

QUILTING WITH A DIFFERENCE
BY NIKKI TINKLER

Learn how to add visual interest to the surface of your work while you quilt with award-winning quilter, Nikki Tinkler.

Ref: QWAD

INDIAN INSPIRATIONS
BY GISELA THWAITES

Discover how to enhance your own patchwork and quilting in this Indian inspired resource for crazy patchwork enthusiasts of all skill levels.

Ref: IND

TWO BY TWO
BY LESLEY BRANKIN

Enjoy creating a truely timeless heirloom quilt that will be adored by children of all ages and loved by generation after generation. Tried and tested endearing design by needlecraft designer and prize winning quilter, Lesley Brankin. Full of helpful expert hints and tips, this complete pattern booklet contains comprehensive instructions and full size master templates.

Ref: TBT

LOG CABIN LANDSCAPES
BY DOROTHY STAPLETON

Discover easy ways to stitch your own fabric houses, countrysides and scenes from around the world in this fantastic book for quilting enthusiasts.

Ref: LCL

STAINED GLASS PATCHWORK FOR CHRISTMAS
BY GAIL LAWTHER

Create spectacular stained glass patchwork designs for the festive season with this fantastic book by award winning quilter, Gail Lawther.

Ref: SGP

p&p/s&h per book:
UK: £3.50
Europe: £4.50
W/Wide: Weighed and costed per order
USA & Canada: US$10.00
[Illinois residents add 7.5% sales tax]

All prices & details correct at the time of going to press and may be subject to change without further notification.

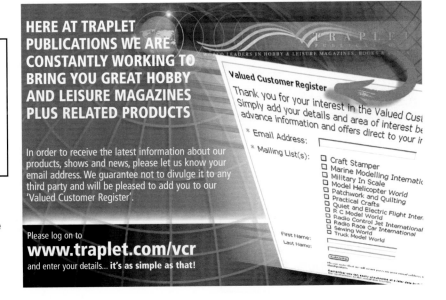

HERE AT TRAPLET PUBLICATIONS WE ARE CONSTANTLY WORKING TO BRING YOU GREAT HOBBY AND LEISURE MAGAZINES PLUS RELATED PRODUCTS

In order to receive the latest information about our products, shows and news, please let us know your email address. We guarantee not to divulge it to any third party and will be pleased to add you to our 'Valued Customer Register'.

Please log on to
www.traplet.com/vcr
and enter your details... **it's as simple as that!**

Valued Customer Register

Thank you for your interest in the Valued Customer Register. Simply add your details and area of interest below. Advance information and offers direct to your inbox.

* Email Address:
* Mailing List(s):
  - ☐ Craft Stamper
  - ☐ Marine Modelling International
  - ☐ Military In Scale
  - ☐ Model Helicopter World
  - ☐ Patchwork and Quilting
  - ☐ Practical Crafts
  - ☐ Quiet and Electric Flight International
  - ☐ R C Model World
  - ☐ Radio Control Jet International
  - ☐ Radio Race Car International
  - ☐ Sewing World
  - ☐ Truck Model World

First Name:
Last Name:

weddings

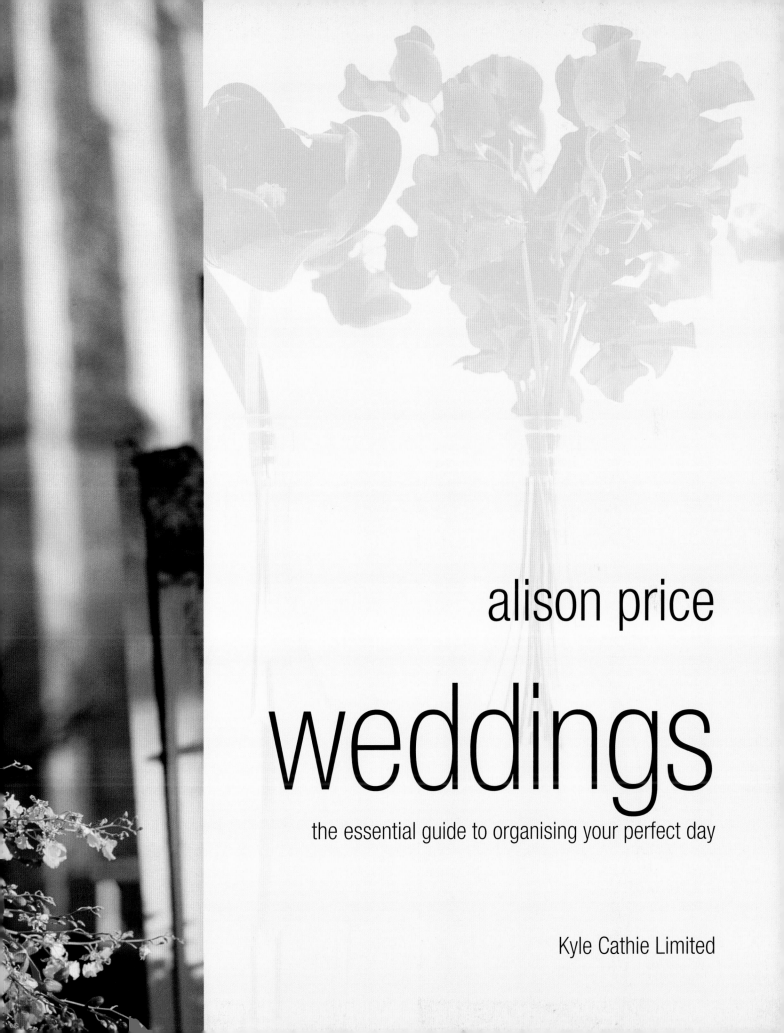

alison price

weddings

the essential guide to organising your perfect day

Kyle Cathie Limited

For Olivia and Lauren Alvarez, Elspeth White, Johanna Edwardsen

First published in Great Britain 2001 by
Kyle Cathie Limited
122 Arlington Road
London NW1 7HP
www.kylecathie.com
general.enquiries@kyle-cathie.com

ISBN 1 85626 387 8

Senior Editor: Helen Woodhall
Editorial Assistants: Andrie Morris and
Esme West
Copy editor: Gillian Haslam
Stylist: Pippin Britz
Designer: Paul Welti
Production: Lorraine Baird and
Sha Huxtable
Index: Helen Snaith

Colour separations by Colourscan

Printed by Tien Wah Press, Singapore

contents

introduction

Something old, something new, something borrowed, something blue – the centuries-old chant for a bride on her wedding day. The tradition of the wedding predates pagan times, when the bride wore a simple white dress as a sign of purity, perhaps with flowers in her hair, and exchanged wedding rings made from straw or crude bands of metal with her betrothed. Although the ritual and meaning of the wedding ceremony has its roots firmly in the past, marriage in the twenty-first century is still just as important as it was in ancient times.

We started our wedding planning business over twenty years ago and I have lost count of how many weddings we have organised. As a company, we have had the opportunity to travel far and wide and feel very lucky to be involved. Some brides allowed up to a year to plan their day, while others gave us as little as ten days! Each celebration is totally different, from the grand dinner and dance to a simple family lunch.

Yet whatever the scale of the celebration, one thing remains constant – above all, the occasion is very personal. To be able to create a day that is so special that it will remain in people's memories for the rest of their lives is certainly a great responsibility and honour. Watching as the bride appears for the first time is quite magical, as is observing the just-wed couple arriving from the ceremony so happy they rarely stop smiling. It is a privilege to hear wonderful speeches and to understand that we have played a major part in creating a very happy and memorable day.

And when it is over, I arrive home after all the months of planning, knowing every detail has been perfect. That we have helped to make a dream come true gives me a great sense of personal satisfaction. We have taken time to get to know the families and understand exactly how they would like the wedding to be. Not that it has necessarily been plain sailing all the way. There have been hours spent planning with the bride, making decisions on invitations, flowers, music, menus and drinks, the site, the style of dress and the number of attendants – the attention to detail all pays off on the day.

The advice I have given over the years is first of all to set a realistic budget and stick to it. Plan very carefully, taking into consideration the smallest detail, but do not become stressed over details you cannot change. This should be a happy time, so try not to become bogged down in the fact that you cannot have the car you wanted because it is already booked. The amount of decision making, attention to detail and sheer effort that is required can be quite daunting. Do make sure to discuss with your fiancé what you both want. It is very important not to make him and his family feel they are not included in the arrangements. There will be many times you may have to be the diplomat, so be ready to play that part.

No other celebration surpasses the importance of a wedding. Marriage is a rite of passage, and is celebrated in different ways throughout the world. Although it will probably be the most important day of your life, remember that your wedding is also a day to be enjoyed by all. Arriving at that point requires great planning. This is not too difficult to do, just pay lots of attention to detail. You have probably never had to arrange a wedding before, but by the time your wedding arrives you will be an expert planner. This book contains years of experience; it is full of valuable advice and ideas on styles, drinks and menus, flowers and entertainment. I hope it will give you the enthusiasm you need to plan your very special day, and to enjoy the whole experience.

Alison Price

first steps

So, the question has been popped, the champagne too, and now it's time to come back down to earth and

start organising. It may seem that there are a million and one things to do before the day, and the truth is,

there are. But by taking it step by step and keeping track along the way, you'll achieve your dream day.

the engagement

The traditional length of an engagement is six months, and during this period of time all the activities of planning the wedding will take place, but this is not to say you cannot be engaged for a shorter (or, indeed, longer) period of time.

ANNOUNCING YOUR ENGAGEMENT

Even in these modern days it is still appropriate for the man to 'pop the question'. However terrifying this must be, there comes a time in most relationships when this is the natural step. The tradition is for the man to ask the father of his fiancée for her hand in marriage, and I feel this custom is very charming and correct. Once this formality has taken place, he will then inform his parents. But in modern times, the couple will announce their intentions together.

Whatever you decide to do, there are some details and courtesies that are often followed. The groom's parents should write to the future in-laws expressing how delighted and thrilled they are. If the parents have not met, then an invitation from the groom's parents is usually extended for lunch or dinner. When families have been informed, start to tell other family members and friends. You may wish to announce your engagement in the forthcoming marriages section of your local or a national newspaper. The bride's family normally pays for this. Each family must be consulted, and parental divorce, remarriage and widowhood dictate the wording. Write a letter or send a fax confirming the details of the announcement. If you are unsure of the correct wording, your chosen publication will be able to guide you. Do take advice as it would be very embarrassing to make a mistake and unintentionally upset someone.

Here are some examples of typical engagement announcements.

> *Mr R.A. Graeme and Miss E.M. Garden*
>
> *The engagement is announced between*
> *Robin, elder son of Dr and Mrs Nicolas Graeme*
> *of Crosbies, Hampshire, and Emily, third daughter*
> *of Mr and Mrs John Garden*
> *of Georgetown, Suffolk.*

If the parents of the bride or groom (or both) have been widowed, the announcement may be along these lines:

> *Mr R.A. Graeme and Miss E.M. Garden*
>
> *The engagement is announced between Robin,*
> *the elder son of the late Dr and Mrs Nicolas Graeme*
> *of Crosbies, Hampshire, and Emily, third daughter*
> *of the late Mr and Mrs John Garden*
> *of Georgetown, Suffolk.*

Where parents are separated the announcement might read as follows:

> *Mr R.A. Graeme and Miss E.M. Garden*
>
> *The engagement is announced between*
> *Robin, elder son of Dr Nicolas Graeme of Kensington,*
> *London, and Mrs Julia Graeme of Crosbies,*
> *Hampshire, and Emily, third daughter*
> *of Mr John Garden of Georgetown,*
> *Suffolk, and Mrs Mary Garden of*
> *Knightsbridge, London.*

If the groom's parents are separated, and those of the bride remarried, the wording may be like this:

Mr R.A. Graeme and Miss E.M. Garden

*The engagement is announced between Robin,
elder son of Dr Nicolas Graeme of Kensington, London,
and Mrs Julia Graeme of Crosbies, Hampshire,
and Emily, third daughter of Mr John Garden
of Camp Street, Edinburgh, and
Mrs Mary Hunt of Seatons,
Devon.*

If both mothers have remarried after divorce, the announcement could read as below.

Mr R.A. Graeme and Miss E.M. Garden

*The engagement is announced between Robin,
elder son of Dr Nicolas Graeme of Kensington, London,
and Mrs Albert Hall of Hotpot, Lancashire, and Emily,
third daughter of Mr John Garden of Camp Street,
Edinburgh, and Mrs Mary Hunt of Seatons,
Devon.*

The bride may have been married and widowed, in which case she may be referred to by her married name:

Mr R.A. Graeme and Mrs Emily Gage

*The engagement is announced between Robin,
elder son of Dr and Mrs Nicolas Graeme of Crosbies,
Hampshire, and Emily, third daughter of Mr and
Mrs John Garden of Georgetown, Suffolk,
and widow of the late Mr John Gage.*

CHOOSING THE RING

When a friend of mine proposed to his wife, he hedged his bets by selecting three rings for his bride-to-be. Luckily for him she chose the first ring she was shown and the remaining rings were returned to the jewellers. I still think of that moment when she opened the velvet box to find the most beautiful emerald and diamond ring. A few years later we discussed this rather unusual approach by her husband. She said there was no way she would have wanted any other ring – as far as she was concerned that was the one and only.

I'm happy to admit I am rather old-fashioned in this respect and I still love the thought of the man down on one knee, slipping the ring on his fiancée's finger. It has been selected out of love and will be cherished for the rest of their lives together. However, on a practical note, most grooms should consult their bride as to the style of ring they prefer, because it will be worn almost every day.

So where do you start, with so many styles now available? You may be lucky and receive a ring that has been in a family for generations. The ring given to one of our brides had been in the groom's family for three or four generations. When her husband proposed he slipped the ring on her finger, only to discover it was far too big. However, it took her at least two years to have the ring altered, and this was only after a few panic-struck moments thinking she had lost the ring because it kept slipping off. If you are given a family ring, please make sure that you have it altered to fit by a reputable jeweller. This applies to all engagement rings. Remember that on hot days your hands swell and on cold days your hands shrink. Rings purchased in an auction house or antique shops are very good value for money. The important rule is to go to somewhere reputable. Choose carefully, as years of wear can weaken the settings. Do not let this put you off – simply take the ring to a trustworthy jeweller for any repairs and cleaning.

One of my oldest friends selected the most wonderful solitaire diamond for his bride's engagement ring and they then chose the setting together. Some brides are lucky enough to commission a design of their own choosing and select the stones for the setting. For most people, however, the choice will be a new ring or an antique from a retail shop, antique shop or even an antique market.

The first point to consider is to select a stone that will sparkle and catch the eye. Diamonds are the logical choice, representing purity and eternity. There are certain rules to follow when selecting diamonds. The value is determined by the four Cs: cut, clarity, carat and colour. The cut determines whether the stone is sparkling or lifeless. Clarity is the absence of any flaws. Carat is the weight of the stone and colour is rated on a scale from D to Z, with D representing the most perfect colour and also the most expensive.

Not everyone's choice will be a diamond. Some may prefer a coloured stone; my personal favourite is a sapphire. As with diamonds, the colour of the stones is very important to the value. Sapphires should be almost a cornflower blue, emeralds a deep green, rubies crimson. Although the most popular choice is a brilliant-cut solitaire diamond ring, if your choice is a coloured stone surrounded by diamonds, think about the shape of the coloured stone and setting. Remember the centre stone is the focal point of the ring, so the side stones should not detract.

Retail jewellers have vast selection of designs and stones. This is relatively good value because mass production of rings can keep costs low. Also remember that if you set your heart on platinum or white gold for the setting, this must complement the wedding ring as they are nearly always worn together. Some styles of engagement rings may be difficult to wear with a wedding ring, so take all these points into consideration.

'did you know that in ancient Rome, parents as well as the betrothed would exchange rings?'

One point to remember is styles go in and out of fashion. My advice is to select a style that will not date. You will always want to wear the ring you chose together. A further alternative to consider is a ring that doubles as an engagement and wedding ring. This is usually a simple band set with diamonds or other stones placed at intervals, or two bands connected with diamonds.

You may consider having your birthstone incorporated into your engagement ring. It is said to bring luck. Here is a list of stones and their meanings.

JANUARY – Garnet – *Truth*

FEBRUARY – Amethyst – *Sincerity*

MARCH – Aquamarine – *Courage*

APRIL – Diamond – *Purity*

MAY – Emerald – *Harmony*

JUNE – Pearl – *Wisdom*

JULY – Ruby – *Love*

AUGUST – Peridot – *Contentment*

SEPTEMBER – Sapphire – *Wisdom*

OCTOBER – Opal – *Good fortune*

NOVEMBER – Topaz – *Intelligence*

DECEMBER – Turquoise – *Success*

AN ENGAGEMENT PARTY

The announcement of your engagement is the start of celebrations with family and friends. As a couple you will be the centre of attention during the months leading to your wedding day. If you wish to arrange a party to celebrate your engagement, it can take any form you wish, from a small dinner party at home to a drinks party, usually hosted by the bride's parents with an informal speech given by the girl's father. Or, as the couple, you can host your own party and make an informal speech. Engagement parties are by nature small gatherings of friends and family, they are not meant to be large affairs. That will be your wedding.

getting started

Now you are engaged and things have calmed down, start discussing and making decisions on the date, budget and style of wedding you both would like. Most couples have limitations, mainly concerning the budget, but also over where and when the wedding will be held. Whatever you decide, you must be flexible and prepared to make compromises to achieve your wedding dreams.

Choosing the date of your wedding concerns not just you and your fiancé. It involves both sets of parents and the availability of your chosen professionals and venues. Diaries will have to be co-ordinated, taking into consideration the day of the week. Have alternative dates in mind, not only for the place of the ceremony, but also the honeymoon destination, the venue for the reception and the services of the floral decorator, marquee company, band, photographer, car hire and reception venue.

Choosing the time of year will make a difference to your options. If your choice is to marry at a traditional time of year or away from home, this will probably limit the number of guests who are able to attend. Most people think only of marrying in the spring and summer months, but do consider the autumn or winter months. You know that the weather may not be wonderful, so you can stop worrying about it. You will probably be able to have first choice on the time of day for your service and chosen venue. Most of your guests will be able to attend. Hotels for the honeymoon are also cheaper out of the high season. When planning the time and place you wish to marry, consider the guests who will have to travel a long way – do not expect your guests to arrive bright-eyed for an early morning wedding.

Discuss together the style of wedding you would both like and start working out your budget. Write a list of your wishes, trying to be practical and taking the not-so-obvious things into consideration. Everything you decide upon will affect the outcome of the next decision to be made, so you must understand fully the implications of all your choices before they are set into motion. For example, there is no point having your wedding at five or six o'clock in the evening when your budget will not allow you to have a large reception and dinner. If your budget is restricted and you would like a large number of guests, plan an early or mid-afternoon wedding followed by a reception serving canapés or afternoon tea.

Decide on your priorities. If flowers and music are what really matter to you, then allocate a larger proportion of your budget to these items. If sitting down to an amazing lunch or dinner with fine wines is your dream, then cut back in other areas. Keep priorities in perspective. If you are planning a large reception, remember you will not be able to spend time with your guests – a short hello will be the only few words you are able to exchange. Don't expect to do more than that as it's simply not achievable.

Another point to consider is not to plan a wedding that is outside your normal entertaining style. Weddings are a way for you to express your personalities. By tradition, a wedding involves many social and financial backgrounds, as well as ages. You are not there to shock and your guests must feel comfortable. Every wedding we have planned and catered for has always reflected the personality and style of the couple's families.

Investigate all these things before confirming the date. Most brides who contact us have alternative dates; they want to have the reception venue in place before they confirm the place of service because it is becoming increasingly difficult to secure popular venues and services. Bringing all the elements together can almost feel like a military operation. Keep your options open, be very practical. If the venue for your reception is not available until midwinter and you have set your heart on a summer wedding, it will need a little more research and compromise. When you have nearly all the elements in place, you can confirm the date. Do not even think of doing this before as you could be disappointed and you will probably have to start the hard work all over again.

the wedding planner

Planning a wedding can be a very complex affair, but this planner will prove to be invaluable. Tick off each item when it has been organised

SIX MONTHS OR MORE AHEAD

If your families have not met, arrange an informal get-together.
Place an announcement in a newspaper of your choice.

CHOOSE THE DATE Decide on what style of wedding you would like. If you are planning your wedding during the busy season, discuss alternative dates and try to be flexible as you may not be able to have your first choice of date. Arrange to see your minister, priest, rabbi or registrar to arrange the ceremony.

DRAW UP THE GUEST LIST When you have worked out how many guests you want to invite, plan your budget. Reserve accommodation at local hotels for your guests from out-of-town.

PLAN YOUR BUDGET AND YOUR PRIORITIES Now you can plan what style of wedding and reception you would like, within the budget you have set. Your dream may be to have the most amazing flowers, or food may be your passion, so decide now which elements are the most important.

ARRANGE THE RECEPTION Visit venues and hotels. If you are planning your reception in a marquee, arrange for at least three estimates from reputable marquee companies.

CHOOSE A CATERER The cost of the food and drinks served will depend entirely on the budget you have set. If you are using a hotel or civil venue, they may have deals that include pre-lunch or dinner drinks, canapés, three-course dinner, wines, soft drinks, wedding cake, a toast-master and sometimes music. Most caterers will provide sample menus. Ask them to include all the elements — food, service, hire of equipment, drinks, ice, etc. Don't forget to give timings. A good caterer will arrange for a tasting; this is usually held at their offices. Decide whether the caterer or florist will provide flowers for the tables.

CHOOSING YOUR FLOWERS Arrange to see florists who will understand the style you like. When you make your choice, confirm immediately in writing as good floral decorators are in great demand.

BOOK YOUR PHOTOGRAPHER Discuss with your photographer the style you would like. Ask what the price includes and the cost of prints. This also applies if you wish to have your wedding videoed. Check that the minister or registrar will allow photos to be taken or a video recorded during the ceremony.

THE WEDDING DRESS Order your dress, shoes, gloves, veil and accessories. Start to think about any special lingerie, stockings or other hair accessories that your dress design will require.

BRIDESMAIDS AND PAGEBOYS Start to think about who you would like.

HAIR AND MAKE-UP Book your hairdresser and make-up artist.

ENTERTAINMENT Arrange to see any bands or musicians you would like and book them as soon as you have made your choice.

HONEYMOON Plan and book your honeymoon. If you are marrying in the height of the holiday season, have some alternative destinations.

FOUR TO SIX MONTHS AHEAD

THE CEREMONY If you are marrying in a church or synagogue, arrange to see the minister to discuss the service, music and readings.

INVITATIONS AND SERVICE SHEETS Visit printers to choose your style of invitations. If you wish to have the invitations specially designed, start planning now. Also order place cards, seating cards, menus, service sheets and favours.

WEDDING GIFT LIST Make your lists and register with your chosen outlets.

WEDDING CAKE Choose the style and flavour of cake and place your order.

TRANSPORT Arrange any necessary transportation.

WEDDING RINGS Order or purchase wedding rings.

WEDDING NIGHT If you plan to stay in a local hotel for your wedding night, now is the time to make your choice and book the room.

GROOM'S AND GOING-AWAY OUTFITS Purchase or reserve the groom's outfit.

and always confirm all your arrangements in writing, keeping copies of the letters for your own file. Check that you are keeping to your

budget. If you have less than six months to plan your wedding, don't panic. Just start as soon as possible.

Arrange hire of best man's outfit and other male members of the bridal party. Start looking for the bride's going-away outfit.

ATTENDANTS' GIFTS Choose thank-you gifts for your attendants and best man.

NAME CHANGES If you are changing your name, remember to allow plenty of time for a new passport. Notify your bank and building society.

TWO TO THREE MONTHS AHEAD

INVITATIONS Send out invitations at least eight weeks before the day. Make a list of acceptances, refusals and any special requests. Confirm any hotel arrangements for guests who require accommodation.

HAIR AND MAKE-UP Make a separate appointment with your chosen hairdresser and beautician to discuss your requirements.

GIFTS FOR THE BRIDE AND GROOM Choose presents for each other and for parents of both parties.

ONE MONTH AHEAD

PRESENTS Start sending thank-you notes as gifts arrive.

WEDDING ANNOUNCEMENT Send wedding announcement to your chosen paper.

MARRIAGE LICENCE Obtain the licence.

TWO WEEKS AHEAD

SEATING PLAN This is probably one of the most difficult things to arrange, so start to think about it. Write seating plan and place cards.

WEDDING DRESS AND SHOES Arrange for final fitting. Most brides lose weight before the wedding day, so if you feel that you may lose a few more pounds, tell your designer or fitter. Start to break in the shoes at home.

SPEECHES AND TOASTS Start to write speeches.

CATERER Confirm final numbers.

BEAUTY TREATMENTS Have a facial and massage to relax, have a trial run with your headdress and make-up.

ONE WEEK AHEAD

WEDDING DRESS Pick up your dress or have it delivered. Try on your entire outfit including headdress, underwear and shoes, but don't forget to leave one item off – it's considered unlucky to try on the whole outfit before the day.

HONEYMOON Start packing for your honeymoon.

THE DAY BEFORE

REHEARSAL Have a rehearsal if possible.

BEAUTY Have a manicure and pedicure.

ON THE DAY

PRESENTS Give presents to your parents and bridal party with a note of thanks for their help and support.

BEAUTY Have a relaxing massage if possible.

FOOD Arrange to have a light snack and just one glass of champagne. It's important that you have something to eat before the wedding.

TIMING Allow at least two hours for hair and make-up, thirty to forty-five minutes for dressing and thirty minutes for photos at home.

setting the style

Most young girls have dreamed of what style of wedding they would like. The childhood fantasy often takes the shape of a fairytale princess in the most beautiful dress holding a bouquet of garden roses, surrounded by her friends and family, followed by dancing to romantic music under the stars with her groom. I think it has become increasingly difficult to define the traditional wedding as there are now so many styles and many more considerations apply, such as interfaith and interracial marriages, second and third marriages and marriage between couples who have lived together for a long time. What style of dress applies to a second or third marriage? Some brides remarry in white, others in cream or soft colours. Who is to say what is right or wrong? Only you can determine the style for your day.

Most of the couples whose weddings we have planned have definite ideas for their special day, but reality has to come into play. Our first question is always budget. Once this is determined, then you can plan the style you would like. Start by making a list of the priorities. Discuss in detail what you both would like. Take into consideration the time of year. Most couples think of early or late summer for their nuptials. Charlotte Barford, who works with us, married in February. She planned a winter wonderland style, her dress trimmed with white fur, the church decorated with frosted branches complete with icicles! And to complete the fairytale, during the afternoon reception, as guests gazed out of the windows, it snowed.

For a wedding we arranged in the autumn, we created a suitably seasonal style. The bride carried a beautiful bouquet of berries and foliage, and the lunch tables were decorated with sweet chestnuts still in their prickly shells, pears, dark purple grapes, walnuts, squashes and pumpkins.

During the spring and summer, on Saturdays I hardly pass a church without seeing signs of a wedding. Spring brings forth such wonderful flowers and fresh colours. Bouquets of snowdrops, white hyacinths and paper whites tied with simple garden twine. On dining

*'for most people, planning the
reception at home can bring a new
vitality to the house and garden'*

tables, a collection of small glass containers holding snowdrops and grape hyacinths complete the picture of spring. Marrying in summer means that with the wealth of flowers available you can create the most romantic style, choosing soft sweetpea colours for bridesmaids' dresses and for the bride, a bouquet of peonies. Dining tables can be draped in cloths the colours of sweetpeas and decorated containers filled with garden roses and peonies.

I know that not everyone's budgets will be able to accommodate some of the ideas presented here, but this does not prevent you from scaling down. Home – be it a large house or small flat – offers the most personal of all sites for the celebrations. It has its own warmth and character simply from being lived in, creating a feeling of comfort and familiarity for all, making it suitable for an intimate lunch for close family and friends, afternoon cocktail reception, barbecue or marquee in the garden for dinner followed by dancing. Decorations can take their cue from the style of the home. Some may dream of creating a style from the eighteenth century, but this won't work if the house is very modern. Some houses are just made for a wedding, with large flat lawns for marquees, wonderful gardens just right for photographs. Another house may require serious efforts to achieve this. But for most people, planning the reception at home can bring a new vitality to the house and garden through repairing, painting and replanting the garden with flowers that will be at their peak on the day. At one wedding where we provided the catering, the mother

of the bride planted a bed of white cosmos. On the day they were perfect, the tall, delicate plants swaying in the afternoon breeze, looking so soft and romantic.

spring is in the air

On a spring evening our reception takes place in a conservatory. Pre-dinner drinks and snacks are served in the garden. Inspired by the conservatory, the tables are decorated with hand-painted pots of variegated thyme. As the evening progresses the scent of thyme fills the air. Place cards are plant labels tucked into pots for guests to take away and plant in their herb garden or window box as a memento of the happy day. Placed on the plates are small favours filled with Provençal herbs for cooking. A cream cloth reflects the pots while green runners complement the natural colours of the herbs and also serve to mark the place settings. As the light fades, the tables are illuminated from above by simple glass lanterns, the chains on which they hang entwined with beautiful stephanotis. Blossoms are scattered around the base of the candles, adding to the scented air. Around the ledge small candles flicker. Herb-flavoured breads are baked in small terracotta pots and herb butter moulded into small wooden bowls. All these elements harmonise with the conservatory and the garden beyond to create a feeling of serenity.

(Left) Natural colours and materials – growing herbs, wooden bowls and terracotta pots – combine to create a calming and gentle scene. (Right) Herbs grown in pots make an interesting change from the more usual arrangements of flowers and can be taken home by guests at the end of the day.

(Left) Stephanotis petals scattered in the lanterns add the finishing touch.

(Right) Placing fabric runners horizontally across the table divides the table naturally into place settings.

(Below) The garden theme started by the growing herbs is continued in the plant markers, each inscribed with a guest's name.

twilight by a lake

This romantic setting by a lake is just perfect for an evening reception at twilight on warm summer's evening. Simple white linen covers the tables. In the centre of the tables, candles float in tall glass cylinders reflecting the light on the water and the wine glasses. Single Old English garden roses, musk mallow and miniature artichokes set in single tiny vases are the only flowers required to add to the cool romantic feeling. Clear glass lanterns hang from the trees and from shepherds' crooks. As night falls, the bridge is illuminated with candles. The atmosphere is one of mystery and the romance of candlelight, the setting cool and relaxing. When the dinner is over, the path back to the house is scattered with rose petals and marked with tall hurricane lanterns filled with water and floating candles.

Make the most of a natural setting such as this by using a simple colour scheme and flowers in keeping with the country setting.

NfB

Tony Mascólo

(Left) Linen napkins and
beautiful glassware add a
touch of luxury to the
simple colour scheme.
(Below) Frosted glass salt
and pepper pots are used
with matching bone spoons.

(Left) Even the bridge is co-opted into the wedding picture by placing candles all along its handrails. (Right) Spiky artichokes provide a contrast to the soft fullness of the roses. (Below) Groups of candles of differing heights look more inviting than a single candle placed in the middle of the table.

autumn bounty

Most of us think of weddings in the spring or summer, with soft colours and warm days. We tend to forget the wonderful Indian summers which continue until early autumn. Flowers and foliage are the bright jewels of autumn. The colours are magnificent – shades of cream, yellow, rust, orange, red, bronze and brown are all stunning. Our autumn wedding is designed to use all these colours. The tables are dressed with light brown top cloths, elegantly edged with a double satin ribbon. Pumpkins and squashes act as vases to hold flowers. Little squashes have been hollowed out and carved with hearts to become nightlight holders. The place card holders are golden and red pears with a green leaf attached with a dainty ribbon. Each place setting has a tiny vase of flowers. Napkins secured with ribbon complement the edge of the tablecloth. The light reflecting through the squashes and the warmth of the colours create a friendly atmosphere.

Make the most of natural seasonal produce when planning your theme. It will make a lasting impression on you and your guests who will be reminded of your special day every year when autumn arrives.

winter wonderland

Our winter wonderland reflects the season of Christmas. The inviting warmth seen through the doors welcomes guests. To make the entrance romantic, hearts made from white roses frame the doors; they are linked with a sage-coloured grosgrain ribbon. The box balls are wrapped with tiny lights.

As guests enter the house they are offered a welcome glass of mulled wine. The scent of spices pervades the air. An old mophead bay has been given new life as a favour tree. Sprayed silver, bunches are decorated with miniature stockings filled with mulling spices for guests to take home as a reminder of the celebrations. To solve the problem of constantly keeping logs burning, candles fill the hearth and give a warm glow, twinkling in the silver ornaments decorating the mantel. The tables sparkle with silver and candles; each guest has a posy of white roses to which their place card is attached. Silver bowls filled with white amaryllis complete the chosen theme of silver, sage and white. Silver hearts, crystal drops and lights decorate the tree. All these elements will remind the happy couple of their wedding day each year as December approaches.

A cool colour scheme of whites and silvers is given a warming and welcoming feel by the use of candlelight.

(This page) White candles used en masse make a stunning focal point.
(Opposite) Rose hearts frame the doorway and lead the way to the party.

who does what?

When planning a wedding – no matter how large or small – you will need supporters. This is the time to start making decisions together, learning to make compromises and to be tactful and diplomatic. Choose family or friends who will be a great source of strength, wisdom and good advice and who can be very practical. Choose carefully – you want to have the people who mean the most to you. There is no point in choosing someone who can only be there on the day as you will be working as a team. Sit down and discuss in detail whom you both would like as the chief bridesmaid and best man. Make your choices from friends and family you know you can trust. It's a good idea to have at least one person on your team who is married and can offer advice from personal experience.

THE BRIDE

As the bride you are the focal point, and your duty is to make yourself look wonderful. You make the choice of your dress, shoes, flowers, hairdresser and beautician, not only for yourself, but also for your bridesmaids, pages and attendants. Plan your trousseau and going- away outfit. Choose the flowers at the church and reception, your bouquet and the attendants' flowers. Organise the music for the service. Select a wedding present for your husband-to-be.

THE GROOM

As the groom, you appoint your best man and ushers, after discussion with your fiancée. You organise and pay for your wedding outfit, and pay for the wedding ring or rings. You are also traditionally expected to pay for your bride's bouquet and for those of the bridesmaids, plus buttonholes for yourself, best man and ushers.

The groom pays for all the church expenses, excluding the flowers and music. As well as selecting a wedding-day gift for your bride, you also give presents to the bridesmaids and pageboys. Although it is not traditional for the groom to give a present to the best man, I think it is rather unkind not to recognise all the hard work, kindness and effort he has contributed to make the day as seamless as possible not only for you but also the bride's family and guests.

So show your appreciation by giving a thoughtful gift with a letter of heartfelt thanks. The groom also pays for the hire of his car to the church or place of service and the car for leaving the reception, as well as organising and paying for the honeymoon.

THE BRIDE'S PARENTS

The bride's parents traditionally bear most of the responsibility and cost of the wedding. In consultation with the groom's parents and the engaged couple, they compile the guest list and pay for announcements in the press. The parents organise the wording, printing and posting of the invitations and the printing of the service sheets. The transport for the bridal party and flowers and music for the service are also their responsibilities.

The bride's dress and her going-away outfit are traditionally paid for by her parents. There is also a debate concerning who pays for the bridesmaids' and pageboys' outfits. They used to pay for their own outfits, but these costs now seem to be borne by the bride's parents. The mother of the bride has the wonderful task of selecting her outfit and sharing the hairdresser and make-up artist with the bride. The father of bride selects his outfit for the day, arranges a haircut and, as with the groom and best man, makes sure there is no polish left on his shoes, just in case he steps on the bride's dress.

THE GROOM'S PARENTS

They assume very few duties. They supply a list of guests and arrive on the day looking wonderful and are charming to all. One word of advice is not to upstage the parents of the bride, so try to ascertain the style and colour of the bride's mother's outfit well in advance. If the bride's parents live abroad or are deceased, I feel the groom's parents should take over the responsibilities of the bride's parents in helping the couple with the arrangements. If you feel the situation is appropriate, offer to help with the costs of the wedding.

THE BEST MAN

The best man is extremely important and being asked to take on the role is a great honour. The best man plays a major role in all arrangements and should be a very close friend or family member who can be completely relied upon. Traditionally he is a bachelor, but these days I feel this is of little importance, so long as he is very organised and can deliver an excellent and witty speech (after all, his speech is nearly always the highlight of the reception). He must be kept informed of all the arrangements, such as who is coming to the wedding and the chosen ushers, bridesmaids and attendants.

He must also be very presentable. He has to make sure that all aspects of the groom's requirements are cared for, such as his wedding outfit, haircut and grooming, so he looks just as well groomed as the bride. On the day, he is responsible for looking after the groom's going-away outfit, as well as the honeymoon suitcase and bags, including passport and tickets.

He will also be in charge of organising the stag night and making sure the groom makes no payment for the evening. If the wedding is taking place away from the groom's home town, he books accommodation and arranges a dinner the night before the wedding, making sure the groom doesn't stay up until the small hours. He is responsible for making sure the groom has everything he requires for the wedding day and the night before. If the wedding is in the afternoon, he organises a lunch for the groom and ushers.

A few days before the wedding, the best man checks the service sheets have arrived and makes final checks on the transport

The bride's parents make all the arrangements for the reception. This includes food and drink, flowers, photographer, music, toastmaster, wedding cake and calligraphy for menus, place cards and seating cards.

Weddings can be extremely expensive affairs and I see nothing wrong in asking for contributions from the bride, the groom and his family. No one should put himself or herself under any unnecessary financial burden.

inoculations if necessary. She arranges the hen night or bridal shower. She is literally the bride's 'maid' – there to help and support in all matters pertaining to her day.

On the wedding day, the chief bridesmaid prepares the bride's clothes and ensures her suitcase and going-away clothes are at the reception. She checks that the bridal flowers arrive and generally helps to keep the bride calm and insists she has a snack before dressing. At the church, she waits for the bride to arrive for the ceremony, checking that everything is correct. During the service she looks after the bridal bouquet and takes care of the smaller bridesmaids and pageboys.

BRIDESMAIDS AND PAGEBOYS

Once you have decided on the chief bridesmaid, think how many more bridesmaids you would like. Be practical about your numbers and choice. You really do not want an army. A chief bridesmaid and two others, not including pageboys, is a sensible number. If the groom has a sister then it is kind to include her. If you would like your bridesmaids to be children, make your choice from family or children of very close friends or your godchildren. Always ask the parents' permission before speaking to the child. Try not to choose children who are too young or over-excitable as they could be very disruptive during the ceremony. Think of the sizes too, as they will have to process down the aisle side by side and carry the train, so they should 'match' in height if possible. The bride is responsible for the attendants' outfits and they must follow what she would like to the letter. Bridesmaids carry posies of flowers, younger children baskets of flowers or petals.

USHERS

Choose the ushers from both sides of the family and from friends of the bride and groom. This is important as they will be able to identify guests from both parties. The ushers are the best man's 'army', and as with all the main players they must be well groomed and charming. Their main duty is to welcome guests on the day and hand out the service sheets. Allow one usher per forty

arrangements for the groom and himself and the going-away cars. He should check the ushers have a seating plan for the bride and groom's families at the service. In consultation with the bride's parents, he plans the timings of speeches and cake-cutting at the reception and knows the time of departure of the bride and groom. He may also act as toast-master.

On the wedding day, the best man prepares the groom's clothes and keeps the groom calm. He collects the buttonholes for himself, the groom and the ushers and double-checks he has the wedding rings. The best man accompanies the groom to the church and waits with him until the bride arrives, standing on his right-hand side. At the church, he ensures all relevant fees are paid and accompanies the chief bridesmaid to the signing of the register.

THE CHIEF BRIDESMAID

The chief bridesmaid is usually about the same age as the bride. She can be married, but these days I think it sounds so very dull to be called the matron of honour. She helps the bride choose her dress or outfit and those of the other bridesmaids and pageboys, selecting colours, veils, shoes and even the style of the bouquets, and arranging for any necessary fittings. The chief bridesmaid checks the bride has all she requires for her honeymoon including the correct visas and

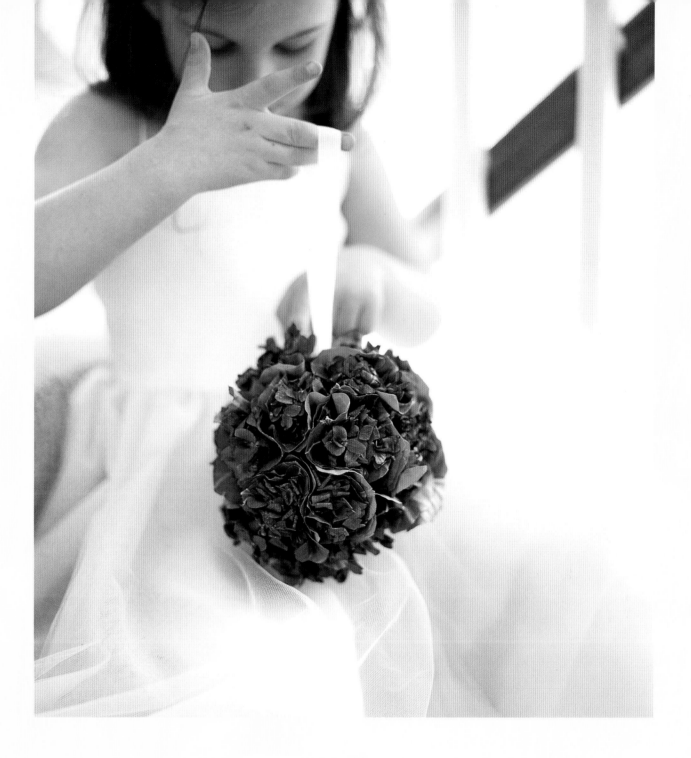

guests, but you can never have too many. It is advisable for the ushers to have an informal evening with the groom and best man, running through their duties on the day. On the wedding day, the best man usually arranges for the ushers to have lunch with the groom. On the day, ushers should arrive at the church at least forty minutes before the start of the service to check all of the final details.

They should also welcome the guests, directing them to either the bride's or groom's side of the church. Family members, in particular the bride's mother, and all unaccompanied female guests should be escorted by the ushers to their seats. After the service, the ushers must ensure that all guests have transport to the reception.

the guests

When thinking of your wedding, do you dream of a small gathering of close family and friends sharing an intimate lunch or dinner, where you are able to spend time with your guests? If a large party is what you have always longed for, you will probably only be able to have a brief time with your guests. If you have your heart set on a particular style and location, this will determine the numbers. The number of guests you wish to invite will be determined by the budget, so give yourself a maximum number. There are always different styles of receptions that will allow your budget to go further. An afternoon wedding followed by a reception of canapés and afternoon tea will make the budget go further, as will a buffet lunch or dinner. You may wish to have only close family and friends for the service, followed by a reception for the remaining members of your family and friends.

So you both have to sit down and start to draw up your lists, from friends and work and business colleagues. Parents of the bride and groom make their lists from family, friends, work and business colleagues. When the bride's parents are paying for the wedding, they are allowed to invite more guests; the same holds true if the groom's parents are paying. If you are paying for your own wedding and your budget becomes tight, I feel it's reasonable to ask parents for some financial help, particularly if their friends are on the guest list. If your parents are divorced and have remarried, then there will be more family and friends to invite.

Another thorny problem is those friends who think they are going to be invited and are not included in the guest list for reasons of your own. Be honest and say that you are having a small wedding and your budget is limited, as dealing with the problem honestly will head off any resentment. It is a courtesy to send invitations to the vicar and his wife, priest or rabbi and his wife or the officiant. It's also courteous to invite people you know will not be able to attend due to great distance or illness. The parents of the groom, best man, bridesmaids and ushers also receive invitations.

What remains most important is that you have the people you want to share your day with. So do not put yourselves under any more emotional pressure by feeling you are compelled to invite certain people, such as your boss or recent partners of your friends. Also consider whether you want so many business colleagues as this may make the occasion feel more like a corporate party than your wedding. You will have to consider some business and work colleagues, but the number is up to you, the budget and the space available.

Handling difficult situations such as recently separated or divorced couples if their ex-partners are invited calls for tact and diplomacy. My advice is to send each person an invitation. It's up to them to make up their minds whether they are going to attend. Don't do it for them by excluding one person, as this could cause bitterness and hurt.

You must set some limits – not only yourselves but also your parents. When you have compiled your guest list, if it is large, now is the time to edit. Within each family relationships are different, and both of you must be prepared to compromise. All sides must give and take when it comes to reducing the list. A good idea is to make an A and a B list. For example, there may be many courtesy invitations to families and friends who you know will not be able to attend. When you start to receive regrets, start sending invitations from the B list. However, do not do these weeks after the first invitations have been sent as they will definitely be perceived as an afterthought.

One problem that comes up time and again is whether or not to invite children to a wedding. This can be a delicate problem. All you can do is make a decision and stick to it. Once you have decided not to invite children, you must not make any exceptions. If you do, this is likely to cause offence to other guests. If, on the other hand, you decide that you will invite children, it's a good idea to arrange for child-minders and some form of entertainment. Make these arrangements clear on the invitation.

People love weddings. You can allow at least an 80 per cent acceptance rate. If the wedding is abroad, still send invitations and you may be surprised how many guests will attend. After all, it's a great excuse to have a holiday as well.

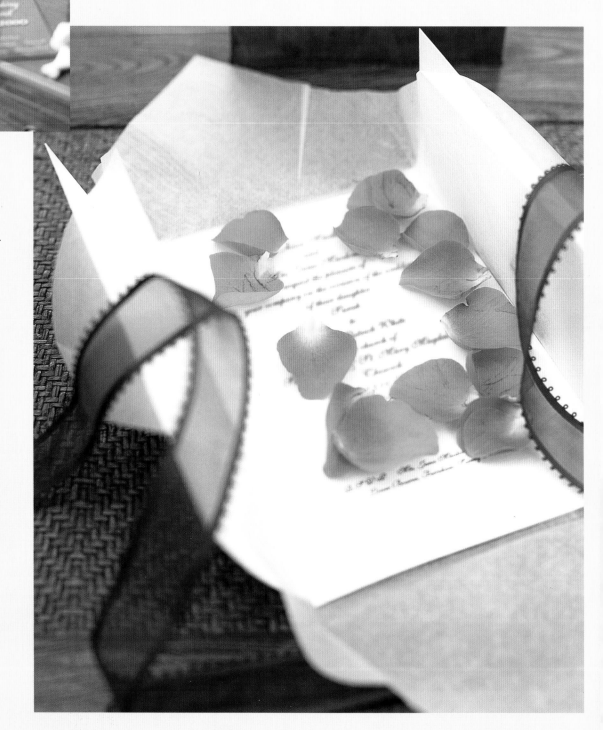

(Left) An etched glass invitation is a luxurious memento of the day.
(Below) Enclosing fresh rose petals with each invitation gets the celebrations off to a romantic start.

'the most important point to remember is that it is your day – invite people you will be happy to share it with'

SENDING THE INVITATIONS

Plan to send your invitations not less than six weeks before the wedding (I recommend ten to twelve weeks). The style of the invitation should reflect the family and couple. Any further information such as local hotels, maps and where the wedding list is held can be included. If your guests are from out of town and you are providing transport, coaches or cars, include these details as well. If you have chosen evening dress, this must be included on the invitation, otherwise there is no reference to dress. Make dress known by word of mouth.

If you are planning other celebrations, such as a dinner the night before the wedding or a lunch on the day after, these invitations are also enclosed. Some people like to enclose an RSVP card. All the enclosures should be printed on paper, apart from the reply card. The paper and card must match the colour of the invitation. The guest's name is always written by hand in ink in the top left-hand corner of the invitation. Some people like to employ the services of a calligrapher. They will need the correct names and titles of the guests. Decorations and prefixes are not included on the invitation, but are on the envelopes which are written in black ink.

Wedding invitations have retained their traditional form over the years. If you intend to change from the traditional style, it is important that etiquette is followed.

Traditional-style invitations are usually printed on heavy white or cream card with copperplate engraved script. This style of printing can be quite expensive. Another printing choice is thermography which resembles copperplate but you do lose the subtlety. It is a cheaper, quicker way of printing. Black is the preferred colour of ink.

You may wish to have your invitations designed to suit your style of wedding and both your personalities. I have known couples who have made their own invitations, purchasing paper and cards from specialist suppliers, creating something unique. When you have found your printer, you will need to discuss in detail the style and how many you require. It is important to ask how long it will take to print. Some printers quote six to eight weeks. While you are discussing the invitations, you may wish to include service sheets and thank-you cards. Ask to see samples of cards and textures of papers.

Find out precisely what costs are involved. If you are not collecting the invitations from the printer, you will need to know the cost of postage or courier, plus any taxes such as VAT or sales tax. Always ask for a written quote. The printer will supply you with proofs. You must check every detail carefully as mistakes cannot be rectified later. It will be very costly to reprint and cause a delay. Confirm your approval or changes in writing. Ask the printer for the envelopes before the invitations are ready, so you can start addressing them. You must remember the busy times of year – if your wedding is in the popular season, allow plenty of time for the printing.

The choice of wording is governed by the hosts of the nuptials and their relationship with the bride. Let us start with the parents who are still married. The wording is as follows:

Mr and Mrs William Smith
request the pleasure of your company
at the marriage of their daughter
Lauren
to
Mr John Brown

at Holy Saviour Church
Chelsea
on Tuesday 21 October
at 4.00 o'clock
Afterwards at
The Dorchester

RSVP
The Manor
Little Manor Farm
Manorshire

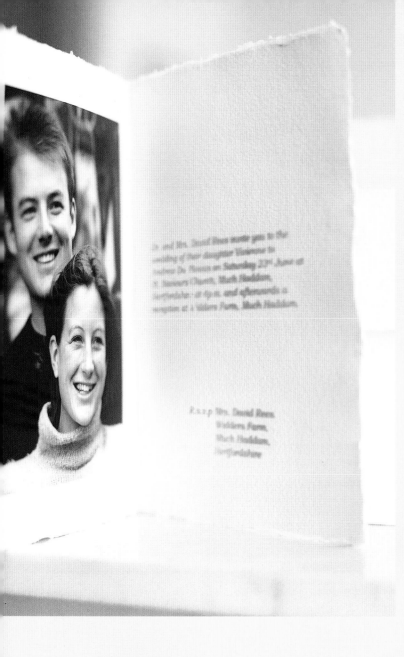

If the bride's parents are divorced and the mother has remarried the wording is as follows:

> Mr William Smith
>
> and
>
> Mrs Helene Bailey
>
> request the pleasure of your company
>
> at the marriage of their daughter
>
> Lauren
>
> to
>
> Mr John Brown
>
> etc.

If the bride's father is deceased:

> Mrs William Smith
>
> requests the pleasure of your company
>
> at the marriage of her daughter
>
> Lauren
>
> to
>
> Mr John Brown
>
> etc.

Bride's parents who are separated or divorced but still share the same surname:

> Mr William Smith
>
> and
>
> Mrs Helene Smith
>
> request the pleasure of your company
>
> at the marriage of their daughter
>
> Lauren
>
> etc.

For divorced couples who are having a blessing in church, the invitation should read:

> *Mrs Sophia White and Mr Patrick Churchill*
> *request the pleasure of your company*
> *at a service of blessing, following their marriage*
> *etc.*

If the bride is hosting her own wedding, the invitation should read:

> *Miss Lauren Elliott*
> *requests the pleasure of your company*
> *at her marriage*
> *to*
> *Mr John Brown*
> *etc.*

The church may not be large enough to accommodate all the guests so invitations may be for the reception or a dance only.

> *Mr and Mrs William Smith*
> *request the pleasure of your company*
> *at a reception following the marriage*
> *of their daughter Lauren*
> *to Mr John Brown*
> *on Tuesday 21 October*
> *at The Dorchester*
> *6.00pm*
>
> *RSVP*
> *The Manor*
> *Little Manor Farm*
> *Manorshire*

'ask the printer for the
envelopes before the
invitations are ready,
so that you can start
addressing them'

wedding presents

Are you having problems deciding whether or not to have a wedding list? I fall into the category of a guest who likes to know the present I am giving is something the couple have chosen. It makes it a lot easier for me and for the couple. My advice is always to have a list. Do you really want presents that you will probably dislike and leave in a drawer or cupboard? Or receive ten lamps?

The list you plan must be in proportion to the number of guests you are inviting. Remember to think carefully about the price range so the list will suit all your guests. The details of where your wedding list is held must be ready to send with your invitations.

If your wedding is at a popular time of year, remember that the bridal registry of a department store or a specialist wedding list shop will also be busy so start planning early. It can be a real pleasure to sit down and put together ideas and styles you like. This will take time so do not try and achieve all this in one evening or a day. The gifts are to help you establish your new home together. If you already have a home, then look at upgrading items you already have. Check that what you are choosing is not about to be discontinued as you will not be able to replace items. Think about how practical certain items will be. Do you really have the time to hand-wash very delicate glassware?

The most practical way of starting is to visit several large department stores and perhaps a specialist wedding list shop. Take time to walk around the stores and get a feel for what you would like. When you have some ideas, talk to the store's bridal registry consultant. Some stores like you to make an appointment, while at others you can just turn up, so make a phone call before to check. If you do have to make an appointment, remember they are usually very booked up, so allow for alternative dates and times. Large department stores will give you a workbook. Write down the description and price of the items. Labels can be quite complicated so ask sales assistants

for guidance. If possible, visit the store during quieter times. You must be very focused: most shoppers tend to browse and this does waste a lot of time. Make it easy: give yourself a time limit and then stop, perhaps for lunch so you can discuss what you have chosen.

When planning your dining table, a good place to start is with your china, cutlery and glassware, as these items will guide your choice of linen and other accessories. Concentrate on the most essential items, only later adding those luxuries. Think about what you will use every day. These will probably chip or crack so add extra to the numbers you require. Also look to the future. You may not want certain items now, but in a few years' time this could change – ask friends and relatives which items they have found invaluable. When you are planning bed linen, allow four sets for the master bedroom and two sets for guest bedrooms. For bathroom linen, allow as for bed linen. If you select hand-painted or hand-made items, bear in mind that they may not be immediately available. On the other hand, if you choose items from what I would call a high fashion store, remember that they may not be able to supply the same articles in six months' time as the stock can change rapidly.

There are small specialist wedding shops that offer a very personal service. They can be a lot more flexible when it comes to making appointments outside working hours. This way of choosing your list is easy as it eliminates trawling around large busy stores. Large or small bridal registry shops or stores will spend more time getting to know you and your style. They will be in contact weekly, keeping you informed. And about two days before your wedding expect a phone call to wish you good luck and happiness.

When you have completed your list, the store will probably take up to ten days to register the items. As presents are bought, the store will update you weekly and this is a good prompt to send thank-you notes. Stores will send the gifts to the address you have given on the forms you have completed. Some stores do this before the wedding while others wait until the couple has arrived home from honeymoon. As you have so much to think of before your wedding, it can be nicer to arrive home from your honeymoon and receive your guests' presents then.

the honeymoon

If asked my ideal honeymoon destination, the place that would come to mind is a lovely cottage on the banks of the Essequibo river in Guyana. On the edge of a tropical rain forest, it has everything required for a honeymoon: tranquillity, an exciting location, warmth, surrounded by the most beautiful flowers, birds and views. The only transport is by boat. The nearest town is seven miles away and the closest neighbours two miles up river. Total peace and quiet.

A honeymoon is extremely important for the newly married couple. After all the months of planning, tension and hard work, it's time for you both to have a complete rest. Planning the honeymoon has always been the responsibility of the groom and by tradition the destination should be a surprise for the bride. Even if you do not want to tell your bride her final destination, I feel it's fair she should have some idea of when and where as she will want to know what to pack.

As unromantic as it sounds, honeymoons must be planned within your budget and other considerations, such as the time you can reasonably take away from your professional life. A century ago the honeymoon often lasted a month to give the couple time to get to know each other. Today times have changed. As much as you would like to take a month, few couples are lucky enough to be able to.

You will feel ecstatic on your wedding day, but at the end of the day and after months of planning you will probably both be exhausted, so plan a restful time. Consider spending your first night in a hotel and then travelling the following afternoon. If you want an active honeymoon, take a few days' rest at the beginning and again at the end. If you have only a short time, don't take a long journey by plane as jet lag is debilitating and will add to your exhaustion. Plan for time that you can spend together in peace. Don't forget to allow for time at home when you return, before starting back at work.

Booking the airline tickets in your married name may become a problem with the bride's passport. You can either book the tickets in her maiden name or take the marriage certificate with you for identification. You will definitely require this for airport security.

If you are travelling to countries that require visas, these need to be applied for as soon as you have confirmed your destination. If you require inoculations, most doctors or airlines will be able to advise you what is required and the timing. Don't leave this until the last moment as some inoculations have side effects. Travel and medical insurance cover must be taken when travelling abroad. If you are travelling within your own country, some home insurance policies cover you for loss of baggage and personal effects. This will need to be confirmed with your insurance company.

If for some unfortunate reason you have to claim on your insurance, most companies will expect you to pay the cost. You retain all the bills and invoices and are then reimbursed when you make your claim on return to your home country. About a month before your wedding, order any foreign currencies and traveller's cheques. Credit cards are now used world-wide, but it is wise to make enquiries about which card is most widely accepted at your destination.

Where do you start to plan your perfect honeymoon? You will probably have some ideas on where you would like to go. Take time to visit a bookshop that specialises in travel or a bookstore with a good travel section and make notes. Remember seasons and weather patterns. If you are planning your own honeymoon, find a very reliable travel agent that can tailor your requirements specifically for you. Finding the right one for you will take as much planning as some elements of your wedding. When you have confirmation of all your arrangements, don't forget to check the tickets and hotel bookings. Make sure you have any vouchers required for hotels, car hire or other trips planned and paid for.

When you have found your ideal destination, you will need to plan the clothes you require. Start to do this as soon as you have made your confirmation. Try and travel as light as possible. That's almost impossible for me. I always take hand baggage when flying. In the bag I carry a wash bag, a change of underwear and a change of clothes, so if my luggage is lost or delayed I have something with me to change into. Bear in mind that you may arrive in a completely different climate to the one you have left behind at home.

Plan the books you would like to take with you, not only for the flight but also for reading on your honeymoon, including the guidebooks. If you are planning a beach holiday, take your sunscreen and a sun hat with you; also cream or gel for any sunburn. Also pack a small first-aid kit which should include plasters, pain relief, antihistamine creams and tablets, medicine for stomach upsets and mosquito repellent. Buy travel-size toiletries. If you take medication, check you have a sufficient supply. Don't forget film and batteries for your cameras and buy adapters for any electrical equipment you are taking. If the exchange rate is complicated, take a mini calculator.

Photocopy the following honeymoon planner and tick off each item when completed or confirmed.

HONEYMOON PLANNER

- As soon as you have confirmed the date of your wedding, start to plan your honeymoon, taking into account the busy times of year.
- When you have booked your flights, confirm your seats and order any special dietary requirements.
- Hotels should be informed you are on honeymoon and the time you are expected to arrive. Ask for any requirements, such as a quiet room, non-smoking, a sea view. If your flight arrives in the early morning, you may have to wait until after midday for your room. Ask if there are any alternative arrangements for checking in early.
- Any car rentals should be reserved and confirmed at the time of booking your flights and hotels.
- Apply for new passports and the bride's passport in her married name.

THREE MONTHS BEFORE

- Start to plan what you are going to pack and buy any clothing required.
- Arrange visas if required.
- Arrange for inoculations if required.
- Check you have travel and health insurance.
- Check the cameras you are planning to take with you are working properly and buy spare batteries.

ONE MONTH BEFORE

- Confirm all your travel arrangements.
- Your tickets and vouchers will probably be posted to you. Check all details are correct.
- Buy traveller's cheques and foreign currency.
- Buy toiletries, sunscreen, film for cameras, put together a small first-aid kit.
- Buy the books you will be taking.
- Finish planning and buying outfits for your honeymoon.

WEEK BEFORE

- Cancel any deliveries.
- Check travel arrangements to and from the airport.
- Confirm with your bridal registry that they will not be sending any gifts while you are away.
- Make sure that someone close has your complete itinerary with hotel addresses and telephone numbers.
- Make a final check that you have confirmed all the arrangements and have everything required.

DAY BEFORE

- Pack your suitcase.

the big day

Every element, large or small, contributes to the success of your celebrations. At first, the list can seem

endless and it may be difficult to see the wood for the trees. Concentrate on getting the major elements in

place first and, when those are arranged, you can focus on the details that will make the day a perfect one.

the run-up to the day

As the day of your wedding comes closer, there are arrangements and duties to plan. These include arranging the bachelor night or hen night, writing speeches, confirming final numbers for the reception, planning the wedding rehearsal and the dinner the night before your wedding. Make a planner to ensure everything runs smoothly, giving clear instructions for the duties of your supporters (refer back to page 34 for more details on who does what on the day).

THE WEEK BEFORE

Most couples stop working during the week before their wedding as there are so many last-minute details that require their involvement. It's important that you share these responsibilities. What you must not do is start to panic if you think you have forgotten anything. Sit together in a quiet room and go through your checklist to reassure yourself that all the arrangements have been confirmed to the caterers, floral decorators, transport company, photographer and

You can write the place cards in advance, but someone will need to be on hand to attach the fresh flowers and put them in position.

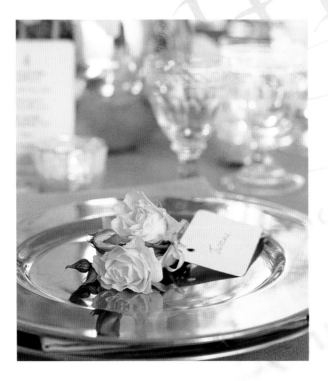

videographer and that service sheets have been printed and given to the best man. Domestic details, such as paying household bills, have to be addressed before you depart on honeymoon.

Plan and write your timetable for the day. The groom should also do one for his family and supporters. Write a checklist for the best man and chief bridesmaid. If you are arranging your own flowers for the church, these should be collected and prepared ready to arrange the day before. If your family is arranging and catering for the reception, all the duties and staff briefings should have been finalised. Make sure you have the telephone numbers of the contractors on a separate list for any last-minute changes. You will need to confirm the number of guests attending the reception. If the number of dining tables has increased, inform the floral decorator that you require an extra arrangement. It's the little details that are easily overlooked, not the large ones.

Arrange to have beauty treatments and haircuts about three days before. Do not have a facial the week of your wedding. As luck would have it, you will break out in spots. Collect your wedding clothes. Try on your whole outfit, leaving off one item to ensure good luck, then store your clothes and accessories somewhere safe. On the day before your wedding, gather together your shoes, underwear, veil, jewellery and make-up in one place and check you have everything. Hang your dress so it will not crush.

Make final checks on the seating plan for the reception and service. Rehearse your wedding vows, but don't try to learn them as you may be nervous and forget them on the day. Speeches need to be written and rehearsed. Check you have everything for your honeymoon. Arrange for your going-away outfit and suitcase to be taken to the reception, if it is not being held at home, and finish packing your suitcase the night before. Make sure you have all your documentation for travelling in a safe place – it's a good idea for the best man or chief bridesmaid to look after this.

Arrange separate dinners with your families the night before. Some couples may wish to include guests who are from out of town. There are no hard and fast rules whether to invite them. It's really up to you. Have an early night.

If you are having a morning wedding, check that you can have access to the church or other venue the night before to arrange the flowers.

THE REHEARSAL

One of the most important arrangements is the rehearsal. This normally takes places during the week before your wedding, ideally a few days before the actual day.

The bride and groom and the bridal party should all be present. If your dress has a long train, take fabric and pin this to your clothes so the bridesmaids can practise. Locate the loo as you may need it on the day. The ushers are given the family seating plans to familiarise themselves. During the rehearsal, you should also discuss which ushers will escort members of the bridal party to their seats. This is normally the bride's mother, groom's parents and grandparents of the bride and groom.

Follow the rehearsal with a lunch or dinner, depending on the time of day. It's a nice time for the families to be able to relax and talk about the wedding and any final details that require addressing. Driving to the rehearsal is a good opportunity to check the timing of travel to the place of your service, allowing extra time for any delays due to roadworks or road closures. One other detail you may like to consider is practising your walk to the processional and recessional music at home, just to get the rhythm and timings right.

YOUR PARENTS

Arranging a wedding can be a rollercoaster of emotions. During this time of looking forward to your new life together, do consider your parents. They have cared and supported you all your life and this is also an emotional time for them. We hear parents saying they have not lost a daughter but gained a son. Think of the meaning behind that statement. You should spare a thought for them. It is very comforting and caring to tell them how much you care for and love them and to thank them for helping you to achieve your goals in life. You might even write a letter thanking them and leave it with a small gift for them to find on the day.

THE DAY FINALLY ARRIVES

At long last the day dawns. All the plans you have made will, of course, work with military precision. All you both have to do is relax and enjoy the whole day.

If you are marrying late in the afternoon, arrange to have a pampering massage during the day or a relaxing bath with scented oils, but do this before you have your hair and make-up done. Arrange for the delivery of the bridal flowers at least two hours before they are required. Store them in a cool, shady place. If you are having small bridesmaids and pageboys, don't dress them too early as this is almost inviting accidents to happen. The chief bridesmaid helps you to dress. If your mother is there, you can ask her to make sure all the arrangements are running to time.

Before you leave for the church, make sure you have your veil down and your bouquet in hand; place your engagement ring on your right hand. Try to be completely ready before your mother leaves for church with the chief bridesmaid so they can check that you and your father are ready. Don't forget to give your mother or other reliable person a mirror and make-up so you can make one final check before you enter the ceremony. Take time to have a chat with your father. You are probably both feeling nervous and this is the time to try and relax. If you are marrying from the family home, this is the last time you will leave it as a single woman, so turn and take a last look at yourself before you go.

THE CEREMONY

When the bride arrives, the chief bridesmaid will be waiting and she will check that the bride is looking perfect. As the music starts, the bride, on her father's right arm, takes slow steady steps to the chancel steps and stands to the left of the groom and best man. Don't forget to smile as you walk down the aisle. When you reach the groom, turn and hand your bouquet and gloves, if you are wearing them, to the chief bridesmaid. If you do not have a chief bridesmaid hand them to your father who will pass them to your mother.

After the service, walk down the aisle slowly on the groom's left arm followed by the bridesmaids and pages, the best man and chief bridesmaid, the bride's mother with the groom's father and the groom's mother with the bride's father. It is the best man and the chief usher's responsibility to see that the bridal party take the correct transport to the reception. When you arrive at the reception, take a moment to check your make-up and dress and await the arrival of your guests.

THE RECEPTION

You will have made a decision before your reception whether or not you are having a receiving line. Some families choose not to as family marital relationships can prove too complicated. A receiving line does ensure that the couple are congratulated and the parents are introduced to the guests. If you have engaged the services of a toast-master, one of his duties is to announce the guests. The line-up is the bride's parents, the groom's parents and the happy couple. Some people like to include the chief bridesmaid and best man. If you have a large number of guests, take into consideration that the line can take a long time so offer drinks from trays to your guests as they wait. Keep the greetings to a minimum, otherwise you will find that you spend more time in the line than attending the reception. If you do not wish to have a receiving line, then the bridal party should stand somewhere prominent so they can greet their guests.

After you have received your guests, then the photographs are taken. Try not to take more than twenty minutes. Little bridesmaids

Cones of handmade paper filled with rose petals can be handed out to guests as an alternative to confetti.

and pageboys become restless and other people you want in the photograph may disappear into the reception. Don't try to have the photographs taken before the guests arrive – they will probably have arrived while you are being photographed and be wandering around, wondering what is happening.

THE SPEECHES

Speeches require to be properly planned with rehearsals and timing. Whatever style of reception you choose, the speeches and cake-cutting are two of the main highlights. If you are having a reception followed by a dinner, for the sake of the bridal party who are giving the speeches, do this before you start dinner. The waiting staff will know the time of the speeches so they can ensure the guests' glasses are filled ready to toast the happy couple. The toastmaster, head waiter or messages are read out, avoiding very personal ones. There is no formal toast, but the guests will raise their glasses to the bride and groom and absent friends.

CUTTING THE CAKE

The other highlight of the wedding is the cutting of the cake. The toastmaster or best man announces this. The bride and groom hold the knife, make a wish and smile for the assembled cameras. The cake is taken away, cut into small slices and offered to the guests. Some cakes may require a small plate and pastry knife. If the cake is a traditional fruitcake, the top tier is saved as the christening cake for the first child.

DEPARTURE OF THE BRIDE AND GROOM

Shortly after the cutting of the cake, the time comes for you to depart. The best man will have found you at the arranged time so you can change your clothes. Arrange for some champagne and maybe a snack to enjoy while you are changing. The best man will have placed your cases in the car; he also makes sure you have everything with you, such as passports, tickets and money.

Then everyone gathers round to see you off. The bride says goodbye to her parents and other family members, throws her bouquet into the crowd and then waits to be covered in confetti. I do not advise throwing rice as it can be painful – fresh rose petals are much nicer. Have several large baskets so guests can take handfuls. Be careful when using paper confetti if it is raining, as the dye from the paper could run and ruin an outfit. One other point to remember is that it's unfair for guests to go totally over the top decorating the going- away car. If you are being driven, then the driver should be briefed. There is nothing wrong with a few harmless decorations, balloons or streamers. Anything else can be deemed very tacky.

When you have departed, it is time for the guests to leave. One good way of doing this if you are holding the reception at home is for your parents to remain outside near the door or on the doorstep. If you are at a hotel or venue, the bride's parents can leave any time after the bride and groom.

best man will ask for silence and introduce the first speaker. There are three speeches, the first given by someone who has known the bride for a long time. This is usually an uncle, godfather or an old family friend. This speech about the bride is best kept short and sweet. If one or both parents are deceased, then a mention of how proud they would have been on this happy day is appropriate. Then comes the toast to the bride and groom.

The groom gives the second speech. There are thank-yous to make, in particular to his new in-laws for allowing him to marry their daughter and for the reception. He thanks the guests for attending the wedding and for their presents. It's much better to keep the speech short and full of feeling than to ramble on. The speech ends with a toast to the bridesmaids and pageboys.

The best man makes the final speech and this is usually the highlight. The speech should be witty and fun and delivered with confidence. There are usually a few anecdotes about the bridegroom, which should be light-hearted and never embarrassing. Some

stag parties or bachelor nights

In the not-too-distant past, stag parties were often held the night before the wedding. I am glad this has changed. The thought of marrying when feeling tired and probably suffering a hangover is not really the way to start married life. Today they are more likely to be held at least two weeks before the nuptials, with all the groom's friends and members of his family gathering to celebrate his last days of being a bachelor.

The arrangement and organisation of the stag night are the responsibility of the best man. The party is kept a secret from the groom to make the evening a great surprise. It should reflect the groom's personality and his likes and is usually a dinner followed by other forms of entertainment. The cost of the evening is borne by the guests attending rather than the groom. The best man also has the responsibility to ensure the groom arrives safely and departs with dignity and is not placed on a train to a strange town. As funny as this may seem, it is hardly a friendly gesture.

hen nights or bridal showers

Hen parties or bridal showers have become very popular in the last twenty years. The chief bridesmaid has the responsibility of the planning and organisation of the party. The guests may arrive with a small personal gift for the bride. Aim to make the whole evening a very memorable affair but don't be tempted to arrange anything embarrassing. Don't forget to take photographs and present them in an album when she returns home from honeymoon. The party can be arranged at home or in a restaurant with other entertainment. The chief bridesmaid should make sure the bride arrives safely and departs in dignity. The guests, not the bride, should pay for the party.

the ceremony

We have to be practical when it comes to the marriage service because it is legally binding. If you are marrying in the Church of England, the minister is also the registrar. Other religious denominations require the services of a registrar at the service. If a registrar is not present, it may be necessary for the couple also to have a civil ceremony for the marriage to be legal.

The law in England states that marriages can take place only between the hours of 8.00 am and 6.00 pm. The reason for this rather strange and quaint law is that by marrying in daylight there can be no case of mistaken identity! So if you wish to marry as the moon rises over Land's End, you would have to have a civil ceremony during the hours of daylight first so the marriage is legal. Certain licences can override this rule. For instance, Jewish, Scottish and Quaker weddings can take place at any time, but not on Saturdays for Jews as that is their Sabbath or on Jewish holy days. In the Church of England it would be very rare to be married on Good Friday, Holy Saturday or Easter Day. Marrying during Lent is allowed, but you must be aware that flowers are not usually allowed in the church.

You have to decide on the type and style of wedding that is suitable for you and your circumstances. A traditional wedding in a place of worship should be for those couples who uphold the values of religious views on marriage. A close friend of mine who is a Church of England minister says if he meets a couple who do not have strong religious views, he would give them time to think about what they want and why and then counsel them to come to the right decision.

However, no Church of England clergy can refuse to marry any couple who meet the legal requirements of residence and haven't been previously married. If the bride or groom have been widowed, remarriage in church is allowed. If one or both of the parties has been divorced, they may be allowed to be married in church, depending on the circumstances. You will need to discuss this with your minister. The Church does offer a Service of Prayer and Dedication after a civil marriage. You must bear in mind this is not a marriage ceremony and does require a civil ceremony first. The tradition is for the couple to enter the church together and a blessing takes place in front of the minister with hymns and readings. Although you will not take vows, you can make a dedication to each other in front of the congregation if you wish. No banns are read in the church.

One of the most important things to remember is not to enter into any financial arrangements with reception venues etc until you have a date booked for your wedding. You must be flexible with your dates and times, remembering the busy times of the year.

CHURCH OF ENGLAND

Tradition dictates the wedding takes place in the bride's church. There are instances where you can marry in a parish other than the one the bride or the groom lives in. If you wish to marry in another parish, you may need to go on the parish electoral roll and become a regular worshipper for a minimum of six months. Alternatively, you could apply for a special licence or a bishop's licence to marry in that church. If you choose a church simply because you think it is very pretty and will look lovely in the photographs, the Church of England will take a dim view.

Outside every church is a noticeboard displaying the name, address and telephone number of the vicar. Telephone the vicar and arrange an appointment to meet. This will usually take place at the vicarage. Some churches may display a notice specifying a particular time for wedding enquiries, perhaps one evening a week when the couple can call into the church, introduce themselves to the vicar and check they can marry in that parish. You can also find out if the date and time you would like are available.

At the second meeting with the vicar you will be required to complete various forms and show your birth or adoption certificates. If one of you has been married before, a death certificate of the late spouse or a divorce decree absolute must be provided. The vicar will be able to give you details of what the church can offer regarding choirs, organist, pianist, bell ringers and flowers. Some churches offer none of these services. You will be told what fees are payable, not only to the church but also for the organist, bell ringers and choir. Make it clear what you would like.

The third meeting is pastoral, where you will discuss why you wish to marry, why you wish to marry in church and how those decisions apply to you as a couple and your married life. The pastoral obligations of the clergy are to make sure the couple understand their commitment to each other and to God.

During the second and third meetings you will have the opportunity to discuss prayers, hymns and readings. You are going to take time to choose the menu for your wedding reception; it's just as important to choose the right prayers, music and hymns for your wedding service. Read the words of the hymns and make sure they are appropriate for your wedding, expressing the feelings you and your partner share. The vicar will gladly lend you a hymn book. At one of the meetings, you will have the opportunity to discuss the possibility of a wedding rehearsal. This usually takes place during the week before your marriage.

One point that needs to be handled with diplomacy is if you have a family member or close friend who is a member of the clergy and you would also like them to officiate at the service. You must consult your clergy and discuss how this could work. On the day they both conduct the service, with the visitor taking the marriage section address and blessing. Alternatively, the visiting clergy can conduct the complete service.

Most Church of England clergy will not allow the couple to write their own vows, but after the service you can, if you wish, turn to the congregation and say 'I am doing this because ...' and your partner can respond.

Before the marriage can take place, it must be announced in the church of the bride and in the church of the groom on three Sundays within three months of the wedding. Like marrying in daylight hours, the reason for reading the banns dates back a very long way. It was to stop rogues, vagabonds and bigamists going from village to village, marrying several times.

Other types of licences are available under special circumstances and these are best discussed with your vicar. Remember that your vicar 'attends' more weddings than the most socially minded person. They are there to guide you through the practicalities of the day as well.

THE ROMAN CATHOLIC CHURCH

The approach to the priest is much the same as to a Church of England vicar. The Roman Catholic Church tends to require up to six months' notice so the priest can spend time with the couple and instruct them in their commitment to each other and the sanctity of marriage. There are also courses for the couple to attend. The priest is there to guide up to and after your marriage. You will require birth, baptism and confirmation certificates, also a death certificate if relevant. The choice of readings, prayers, hymns and music are chosen to reflect the sanctity of marriage and the couple's personalities.

There are two services to choose from. The first is the rite of marriage during mass. This is for couples who are both Roman Catholics. This service lasts about one and a quarter hours and usually includes a nuptial mass. The second is the rite of marriage outside mass and is for occasions when either the bride or groom is a non-Catholic. This ceremony lasts about forty-five minutes. Roman Catholic services are longer than Church of England ones. Couples are discouraged from marrying during the penitential seasons of Advent and Lent, but this is no longer forbidden. Dress code is the same as for a Church of England wedding.

JEWISH WEDDINGS

These normally take place on a Sunday during the afternoon or early evening. They are never held on the Sabbath or holy days. Most weddings take place in a synagogue, although law or tradition do not require this. The wedding can also take place in a hotel, outside if the weather permits, or in a hall or banqueting suite.

The customs of the traditional Jewish wedding date back several thousand years and the service combines religious law and symbolism. The couple must contact their synagogue to confirm the date they have chosen is free. Normally the reservation will not be confirmed until the rabbi has been contacted, so they can confirm their availability to officiate and make an appointment to meet both of you. As soon as the date is confirmed, arrange an appointment to obtain the chief rabbi's authorisation for your marriage. Up to twelve months before your wedding you must each visit your local register office and give notice of your intended marriage.

For your first meeting with the rabbi, if you are getting married for the first time, you will need to bring the following: the Jewish marriage lines of your parents or the date and place of their marriage, your birth certificate, the registrar's certificate and a letter from a close parent or close relative stating that you have not been married before. You will also need documentary evidence if there has been a change of name since your parents' marriage. If you have been married before, bring your previous *ketubah* or the date and place of your previous marriage, the death certificate of your late spouse or where applicable your *get* (Jewish divorce) and civil decree absolute, the registrar's certificate, and a letter from a close relative confirming that you have not remarried since becoming widowed or divorced. There are regular workshops organised by the Jewish Marriage Council for those intending to marry. If your partner is not Jewish, the orthodox synagogue will not marry you unless the partner considers becoming Jewish.

Your synagogue will be able to give you information regarding the cost of the choir. When you first contact the synagogue you will be given the list of fees that are payable. The marriage of the bride and groom takes place under a *chupah* (an open-sided canopy) that parallels the union of Adam and Eve in the Garden of Eden and the union of God (Adam) with the Jewish people (the 'bride'). The chupah also represents the couple's new home together. Before the service starts the groom is asked to read and accept the terms of the Jewish marriage contract, after which he raises a handkerchief with the officiant, which confirms his acceptance and empowers the officiant to read to the bride later in the service. Officiating ministers witness this part of the service.

When the bride arrives she is escorted into the bride's room where the groom lifts the veil over his bride's face (traditionally to satisfy himself he is marrying the right woman). The rabbi gives a

(Above) A bride walks toward her future husband, who stands beneath a traditional Jewish *chupah*.

blessing on the bride. The service begins when the groom stands under the chupah and awaits his bride. She enters with her father and stands on the right of her groom. During the service the bride walks around the groom seven times, followed by the betrothal, which is a blessing over wine, followed by the betrothal blessing recited by the rabbi and groom. The marriage itself follows the reading of the *ketubah* and seals the union, permitting the couple to live together as man and wife. The seven blessings are recited over a second cup of wine. The breaking of a wine glass by the groom ends the ceremony and this is followed by the signing of registers. The couple return to the bride's room where they can enjoy their first moment of privacy together.

It is a religious requirement for guests to do their utmost to make this a very happy celebration. What guests wear depends on the time of the wedding. For a late afternoon wedding followed by a dinner and dancing, men wear black tie and women wear evening dress. If the ceremony is at lunchtime, men wear lounge suits and the women smart day clothes and hats.

CIVIL CEREMONIES

If you choose to have a civil ceremony, there are now many more options available to you than there were ten years ago.

A wedding in a register office is usually a very short affair, lasting only about ten minutes. Some offices can accommodate large numbers of guests, others only a small gathering. The bride and groom stand in front of the registrar and two witnesses, make a declaration that they are free to marry and wish to be man and wife. The registrar declares they are man and wife. The service does not include the exchange of wedding rings, but this can usually be performed at some point.

Each party to the marriage will need to attend the register office to give notice of their intention to marry. Each party will be required to declare their nationality and bring with them passports, birth certificates, ID card or a Home Office travel document or acknowledgment showing nationality. The bride and groom do not have to attend together, but it is preferable if you do. You will need to satisfy the residential qualification of seven days in the district and then wait a further fifteen days before you are eligible to marry. If you would like to marry sooner, you must apply to the Registrar General and they will consider each case on its merits.

Unlike the reading of banns in the church, the register office will display a marriage notice in the register office for fifteen days before the wedding date to ensure there are no objections to the marriage. A certificate is then issued and the marriage can take place.

Do not be late for a register office wedding as the bookings for the offices are timed and you may lose your spot. It is very important to bear in mind that this is purely a legal service. It is not a church. Long white dresses, morning suits and top hats and bridesmaids are inappropriate. A smart suit with a buttonhole is the correct attire for the groom and a suit or dress with a hat and a small bouquet for the bride. Guests who attend should compliment the couple on their choice of dress. Depending on the time of day, a small celebration is normally arranged. Some people marry a few days before and follow with a larger celebration or church blessing. Normally the service is followed by a luncheon party or if late in the

afternoon a drinks party, hosted by the couple or a close friend.

A register office wedding can be rather cold and clinical. However, with the recent change in the law, there are now a lot more options available. If you do not wish to marry in a register office, there are many interesting venues from hotels and grand country houses to boats and barns that are licensed for weddings. As an alternative to a register office, it is not surprising these new secular civil weddings are gaining in popularity.

Make a choice of venue that is suitable for your style and budget, ensuring it will give a sense of the occasion. The marriage service will be as at a civil ceremony, but you probably will be able to have a separate area set aside for the service. You can set up chairs so you will have an aisle to walk down. Flowers, music and bridesmaids are permitted, but anything religious is totally inappropriate and is not allowed. You can have music as you enter the room, singing and music during the ceremony and when walking back down the aisle.

One other benefit of having a civil wedding at a venue that has a licence is that the reception will be in the same place. The reception can follow the same structure as a church wedding reception, with cake-cutting, speeches and the bride and groom going away. The style of dress for your guests is determined by the time of day you have chosen for your ceremony. For an early evening wedding followed by a dinner, I would suggest black tie for the men and evening dresses for the women, but for a lunchtime or afternoon reception, lounge suits for men and smart dresses or suits with hats for the women. Morning dress is inappropriate.

HUMANIST SERVICES

You may be one of the increasing number of people who have ideas on marriage that have no religious affiliations, but would like to mark a committed relationship with a service that includes family and friends. The most important consideration is that a humanist wedding has no legal status, so you must enter into a civil ceremony, followed by the service. The humanist service takes place at a different location. The wedding is conducted by a celebrant who is trained by the Humanist Association. For couples who are divorced and wish to remarry although their Church forbids remarriage or for those who have no religious views, the humanist ceremony is ideal. Gay couples who wish to commit to a long-term relationship can have an affirmation.

The service is totally different from any traditional wedding service. Couples can write and exchange their own vows; music can be played, rings exchanged and readings given – the service can include anything the couple feels is appropriate to the occasion and reflects their commitment to each other. The service can take place at any time and anywhere, so if you wish to have a service on a romantic summer evening by a lake you can. There are really no dress codes; this also applies to the style of invitations too. Presents can be given if the couple feel it is appropriate.

(Left) Your wedding should reflect your personality and beliefs. This could mean that your wedding will take the form of a pagan 'handfasting' ceremony that culminates in the ancient tradition of 'jumping the broom'.

SECOND TIME AROUND

Remarriage tends to be lot more low key. Although divorce is on the increase, remarriage seems to take on different styles. If the bride and groom are older, long white dresses and bridesmaids are not really appropriate. The couple usually host the celebration and this could be a lunch, drinks party or a small dinner. Speeches are not really appropriate, but a close friend would normally toast the bride and groom. A few days later, the couple may like to host a larger party. Invitations to the wedding are in the bride and groom's names. Dress is elegant, with a hat for the bride and a small bouquet.

This style of wedding is also ideal when one of the parties has been married before and the unmarried side would like a celebration. A civil service usually takes place in the morning, attended by close family and a few friends. In the afternoon a Service of Prayer and Dedication is held followed by a reception, dinner and dancing, speeches and cake-cutting

If you are widowed and wish to remarry in church, long white dresses, bridesmaids and large bouquets are not really the correct thing to do, although you can be given away by a member of your family or a friend and have a matron of honour. If you have children from a previous marriage or marriages, they must feel they are involved on the day. They can be ring bearers or if the bride or groom has young children and it is deemed appropriate, they could be bridesmaids and/or pageboys.

Should you inform your previous husband or wife that you are going to remarry? I feel you should and this also applies to the families of both sides as well. However, if you have been divorced for a long time, I feel it is not necessary. What you really need to avoid is them hearing through a third party or, worse still, from the children of that marriage. No announcement in newspapers should be made until each party is free to marry legally.

Who pays for what? If you are divorced and remarrying, then the couple pay for all the expenses. If the bride is unmarried but the groom divorced, then the bride's parents take on the traditional role. Widows are also expected to pay for the wedding, but these days it is usually a shared expense.

Dress in the case of a bride who has not been married before would normally be as for a first-time marriage; the same goes for the guests. For other remarriages, morning dress is not appropriate. For evening services, black tie for men and evening dresses for women is fine. Widows or widowers should wear a suitable dress or suit.

As far as a wedding list is concerned, if the bride has not been previously married, a wedding list can be compiled as for a first-time couple. I do not feel this is appropriate for widowed couples or second or third time around. Small gifts from friends as a gesture of the new marriage are much more suitable.

AWAY FROM HOME

Your heart's desire may be to marry on a beach on some tropical isle as the sun sets, surrounded by a few close friends or just yourselves and the celebrant. The idea of marrying in this way is becoming very popular.

If you are planning to marry abroad, make as many enquiries as possible as there are now so many companies offering wedding packages. I would advise you to use a reputable agency that specialises in overseas weddings and is able to help with all the international legalities. You will need to fulfil the legal requirements of this country and the one you are marrying in. If you want to do it yourself, then the embassy or consulates of the country you are choosing will be able to give you the relevant information.

(Below and opposite) From Las Vegas to the deep blue sea (or local swimming pool), possible locations for your wedding are limited only by your imagination. If a quirky and original wedding is what you've always wanted, then maybe you should consider these options.

SERVICE SHEETS, HYMNS AND READINGS

I always keep the service sheet as well as the invitation as a memento of any wedding I attend. The service sheet is a guide to the ceremony and you can either simply list the prayers, service and readings or also include the words to all the hymns. I prefer to have the complete ceremony on the service sheet as it is far easier than juggling with hymn books, a prayer book and an order of service sheet.

When you have decided the order of service with your clergyman, you need to decide on the design. There are many options. By tradition they are printed on white or cream paper and generally match the style of the invitation. On the front are either the Christian names or initials of the bride and groom, the date and the name of the church. Other options are booklets covered with fabric or ribbon or a plain service sheet with ribbon bindings. I have seen the most beautifully elegant order of service booklets covered with fabric and bound with ribbon, which would always remain a treasured memento.

(Above) If you are marrying in a church, the choice of wedding music need not be limited to the traditional marches. There are plenty of other less familiar options.

MUSIC

My friend the Rev. Frank Mercurio writes in his booklet about music at weddings: 'Music plays a very important part in a wedding service. If you have hymns, you will obviously want them to be appropriate to the occasion and for guests to be able to join in singing them. You will want to decide whether to have the traditional bridal and wedding marches or have something different, but still suitable. You may like to have a particular anthem that you wish them to sing.' This is very sensible advice.

Music before the service
This is usually played for about ten minutes before the service starts.

Air on a G String – Bach

Sheep May Safely Graze – Bach

Air (Water Music) – Handel

Minuet (Berenice) – Handel

Prière à Notre Dame (Suite Gothique) – Boellman

Behold a Rose is Blooming – Brahms

Air and Gavotte – Wesley

Allegretto in E Flat – Wolstenhome

Cantilena Romantica – Dunhill

Toccatina – Yon

Romance Sans Paroles – Bonnet

Tuba Tune in D – Lang

Romance (Eine Kleine Nachtmusik) – Mozart

Meditation on Brother James' Air – Harold Duke

Improvisation on 'O my Soul Rejoice with Gladness' – Karg-Elert

Canon in D – Pachelbel

Andantino in D Flat (Moonlight and Roses) – Edwin Lemare

Ave Maria – Bach/Gounod

Jesu, Joy of Man's Desiring – Bach

Adagio (Clarinet Concerto) – Mozart

Salut d'Amour – Elgar

At the entry of the bride

Only a short piece is required, just sufficient for the bride to proceed down the aisle.

Bridal March (Lohengrin) – Wagner

Trumpet Voluntary – Clarke

Trumpet Tune and Air – Purcell

The Arrival of the Queen of Sheba – Handel

Hornpipe (Water Music) – Handel

March (Scipio) – Handel

Fanfare for the Bride – Bliss

Coro (Water Music) – Handel

Trumpet in Tune – Carpentier

Minuet (Royal Fireworks Music) – Handel

Concerto in A Minor – Vivaldi

Sonata No 3 in A – Mendelssohn

Hymns

Allow for three hymns.

Praise My Soul the King of Heaven

Morning Has Broken

Lead Us Heavenly Father

Lord of Hopefulness

The Lord's My Shepherd

Praise to the Lord the Almighty

Father Hear the Prayer We Offer

O Perfect Love

O Jesus I Have Promised

Now Thank We All Our God

Come Down, O Love Divine

O Holy Spirit, Lord of Grace

The King of Love My Shepherd Is

Fill Thou My Life

For the Beauty of the Earth

Love Divine All Love Excelling

O Praise Ye the Lord

O Thou Who Camest From Above

O Worship the King

Crown With Love, Lord, This Glad Day

Give Me Joy in My Heart

Anthem during the signing of the registers

If you have a choir to sing, here are some suggestions. If you do not have a choir, the organist could play from the list for music before the service.

Jesu, Joy of Man's Desiring – Bach

Brother James' Air – Jacob

Love One Another – Wesley

God Be in My Head – Walford Davies

Lead me, Lord – Wesley

Ave Maria – Bach/Gounod

Music as you leave the church

If you have bells. the music will last only until you reach the church door. Then the bells will start to peal.

Wedding March (Midsummer's Night's Dream) – Mendelssohn

Toccata in F (Symphony No 5) – Widor

Grand March (from Aida) – Verdi

March on Now Thank We All Our God – Karg-Elert

Final (Symphony No 1) – Vierne

Carillon-Sortie – Mulet

Wedding Day at Troldhaugen – Grieg

Choral Song – Wesley

Sonata in G (first movement) – Elgar

Fantasia in G (slow section) – Bach

Grand Coeur in D – Guilmant

Toccata and Fugue in D Minor – Bach

March Pontificale (Symphony No 1) – Widor

Readings and Psalms

Psalms 67, 121 or 128

Genesis 1:26 – 28

Romans 12:1 – 2

1 Corinthians 13

John 2:1 – 11

Matthew 7:21

1 John 4

planning the reception

Wedding receptions were traditionally held in the bride's home. In times gone by, the bride lived at home until her marriage. She would leave for her local church and return to her parents' home for the reception. Times have changed and receptions now take place in hotels, restaurants, grand country houses, galleries, riverboats, museums and marquees. We have catered for weddings based on themes as diverse as an autumnal woodland scene to an ancient Greek temple complete with Greek dancers and statues of gods. At one of the first weddings we organised, the bride wanted to recreate Miss Haversham's table, right down to the cobwebs! All these themes suited the personalities of the couple. When it comes to planning your reception, budget is the first priority followed by the type of celebration you both would like to have.

WHAT DO WE WANT?

Everything stems from the time of day your wedding will take place. By tradition, the wedding ceremony took place at about 2.00 pm, followed by an afternoon reception with champagne, wines, soft drinks and canapés, lasting for about three and a half hours. The bride and groom's departure would then be closely followed by that of the guests. In the evening, the bride's family would host a small dinner for close relatives.

The other celebration after a morning wedding is the wedding breakfast, a formal lunch with top tables and all the formality the occasion requires. The bride and groom depart in the afternoon followed by the guests. Again the bride's parents would host a small family dinner. These days many couples prefer to have a late afternoon wedding, followed by a two-hour reception that carries on to dinner followed by dancing. They depart after midnight followed by the guests. Another option is to have a lunchtime wedding followed by an afternoon reception. The happy couple leave and guests depart, only to return three hours later for a dinner and dance. This works two ways. You can have a large reception including everyone in the afternoon and the evening can be a smaller affair. Or vice versa – hold a small afternoon reception and a larger evening party including guests who were not invited to the service. Remember, also, that the reception does not have to be a seated lunch or dinner. Buffets work extremely well, allowing guests to circulate, but remember to have seating otherwise it's a long time to be on your feet.

You have to decide what you both would like. This really depends on where you are getting married. If you cannot hold the reception at home, look at local hotels, restaurants, venues, houses, etc. What you do not want is to have your guests driving for more than half an hour from the ceremony to the reception, otherwise people will rush away from the ceremony, worrying about being held up in traffic, parking and being late.

There are a few other considerations to remember. One is parking for guests. If it is difficult, you must make your guests aware of this – a note with the invitation will suffice. If you are planning to hold your reception at home, it will generate a lot of garbage and it may be worth hiring a skip. Security must also be addressed. Homes left open, cars parked in fields, and marquees set up the day before with equipment could be a target for thieves. You may like to consider security guards. We do this for every large party held in a home and/or marquee. They are not conspicuous and will give you peace of mind.

PLANNING

Now here comes the planning. Whatever you choose, make a provisional booking; most photographers, transport companies, caterers, florists, entertainers, venues or hotels will hold the date for twenty-eight days. Remember the busy times of year and book early. However, do not feel forced into confirming anything until you are sure it is what you both like and want.

HOUSE AND GARDEN

Let's start at home. If at all possible, I feel the reception is best held at the bride's parents' home as it is so much more personal. Take some time to work out the space that is available. This may not be readily obvious and will involve a critical eye. Take a good look at familiar usable spaces; see how they could be arranged differently and how guests could be accommodated comfortably. Look at where you could install a bar, store coats and place a buffet or set up dining tables. Do you have enough loos to cope with the number of guests? Is the kitchen large enough for the caterer? Or can you turn the garage or another suitable area into a kitchen for the day? If the time of year is suitable, gardens can be made to look heavenly with some forward planning. Plant flowers that will be at their best on the day. Bars can be placed under trees and large calico umbrellas can cover buffets and tables seating guests. Blankets placed on the ground are ideal for guests to relax on.

MARQUEES

Some houses and gardens are just right for marquees. If you are marrying in winter, remember that receptions can be very cosy in a well-heated and carpeted marquee. First consider whether you have the space to accommodate the number of guests you wish to invite. Will the marquee company be able to gain access? How long will it take to erect and dismantle? Will you require extra loos? Do you have enough power in the house for lighting, heating and caterers? (You may need to hire a generator.)

Armed with all these questions, the next step is to find marquee companies. As with everything, personal recommendation is the best. You will have been to many weddings and seen what you like and dislike. Marquees come in all shapes and sizes. You should look at them as an extension to your home. All marquee companies will make a site visit – and you must discuss with them the number of guests, the time and style of the reception. Discuss the number of tables required, the number of buffets and bars and the size of dance floor. If you are planning to hold a reception before lunch or dinner, how much space will be required? Try not to be fobbed off with using the dance floor – it's never large enough. Afternoon receptions must allow space for bars, small tables and chairs and a focal point for the speeches and cake-cutting. Service marquees must

be large enough for the caterer to operate safely. If you are planning a very large wedding with lots of staff, entertainers and support staff, a separate area must be taken into consideration for storage, changing and eating.

Ask to see samples of linings, photographs of recent constructions and arrange a visit to a marquee under construction. Some marquee companies also supply furniture, lighting, heating and organise the loos. The area you are planning to use may not be flat, so will require scaffolding to create an even floor. If you know it's going to be a very hot day or evening, choose a marquee where the sides can be removed to give a feeling of space. Another nice feature is to have no sides and a clear ceiling at night, but don't think of doing this during the day when the sun is at its height as it will be too hot. If this is the style of marquee you would like, ask the company to wrap the support frames in lining fabric. The marquee can come straight off the house if windows and doors open onto a terrace or garden. If your marquee is a distance from the reception area, you may require an awning, in case of rain or snow.

When it comes to lighting the marquee, this really depends on the time of day and what theme or mood you wish to create. This can include a night sky, tables pin-spotted with tiny lights, bars and buffets bathed in pools of light, decorative features spot-lit to bring them to life and interesting lighting for the dance floor and the band. Don't forget the garden – enhance trees, shrubs and flowers with decorative lighting. Lanterns hung from trees and candles lighting pathways add to a romantic atmosphere.

Everything you discuss with your chosen marquee company must be confirmed in writing. Make sure every detail is included: size of dance floor, colour and type of lining, size of service tent, right down to the time they will have completed their work so other contractors can have clear access. This should be at least twenty-four hours before the wedding, if not sooner. Large marquees really need to be finished two days before. How long will it take them to dismantle? Do they have insurance against damage? All other contractors must remove their equipment before the marquee is dismantled. When you have checked every detail carefully, sign the contract and pay a deposit. If you have been dealing with one person from the company, insist they make regular visits during the construction to make sure all is as it should be. Marquee companies differ in price and quite frankly you get what you pay for. It's not always cheaper for a local company to do the work, so be aware of this when making your enquiries.

HOTEL RECEPTIONS

If you do not want to have your reception at home, there are so many alternatives. The first choice is often a hotel. Hotels offer a wide range of services, such as recommending a florist and entertainment. Your first point of contact will be the banqueting manager. If your chosen date is available, make an appointment to discuss your plans in detail. Large hotels will have more than one space, so make sure you see all they have to offer.

Talk through every element of the day: the style you like, are you allowed to bring in party designers to change the look, can you bring your own florist, wedding cake, entertainment, photographer and lighting designer? Can you supply your own tablecloths and different style of china and cutlery, or will they only allow recommended suppliers? If you can bring in your own suppliers, at what time will

(Below) The glory of Glamis Castle would be a memorable place for a wedding. Be sure to check carefully the options and services offered by civil venues as they differ greatly from place to place.

they have access to the rooms? If you are planning a large party and the rooms have to be decorated in an elaborate style, 3.00 pm on the afternoon of the party will probably not be enough to time, so check what fees are payable for access at the time required.

Ask for sample menus. If there are favourite dishes or foods you like but are not included on the menus, ask if you can have alternatives. Look at the wine list; if you are booking a long time in advance, check they will still have the same wines and vintages. Ask to see samples of linen, china, cutlery and chairs. Most hotels will have photographs of the rooms when they are dressed and ready for parties. Take a good look as there may be designs and ideas you like. Discuss the timings of the day. If the party overruns in the evening, what, if any, are the charges? Is there a room for the bride and groom to change?

You will need more than one visit and your florist and other contractors will require a planning meeting at the hotel. After you have chosen your menu, a tasting will be arranged. If you are planning an afternoon reception, see how they propose to present the canapés. For a wedding breakfast or dinner, request to see the table set and ask the florist to provide a sample of the proposed table flowers. If cocktails are to be served, ask to taste these when tasting the food. Check how they charge for the drinks consumed. Some establishments may charge for opened bottles of spirits that are not consumed. If for some reason you wish to supply your own wines and champagne, ask about the corkage charge.

If there is any element you are not happy with, then say so. Things can be changed and corrected at this stage, but not on the day. When you have all the details in place, the hotel will write to confirm everything. When you are satisfied all is correct, reply to confirm the booking, enclosing the deposit.

OTHER GREAT VENUES

For a grander or more unusual venue, start by looking at country houses, barns, galleries and museums. Most of these venues will have a very experienced function manager who is there to be as much or as little help as you would like. You may come armed with all your ideas and contractors, or require a lot of help. Some venues may only let you use their approved contractors. My advice is to make an appointment to discuss all your requirements. If you are not happy, then say so. Help is always available. Visit more than one style of venue. Also go and take a look on a grey day to see if you still like it.

When you start to consider where to have photographs taken, choose an area away from the main reception. Check the access is good for older guests, where the coats are stored, whether there are stairs or lifts. Establish the quantity (and quality) of the loos. Find out at what time the hire period starts and finishes. Does the time include set-up for florists? Kitchens are of the utmost importance. Will they be large enough for what you are planning, and if there is no kitchen where do the caterers set up? Is there a separate area for the bride and groom to change? Can you have music? If so does it have to finish at a given time so the residents of the area are not disturbed? If you are having a band, can they arrange for a sound check before the guests arrive? Check the parking. Some venues may not allow candles or smoking. All these questions must be answered before you are satisfied.

YOUR CARRIAGE AWAITS

On the day of your wedding, most brides will make three journeys. You must choose the right form of transport for your style of wedding. Finding your ideal transport will probably need some research. For years the large black limousine was the car of choice. These days more original transport is available.

So plan your budget, then choose a style to suit you and your personality. When you are choosing the transport to take you to the service, make sure it will be large enough for your dress as you do not want to arrive looking creased. You must be sure the company you have chosen is reliable and takes care of their cars. Ask to see the cars – some companies will bring them to you. If you would like ribbons on the car, these should be the same colour as the bride's dress. Ask to see the driver's livery. Normally the contract is for three hours. The number of cars required depends on the size of the bridal

party. You will need a car for the bride and her father, one for the bridesmaids and bride's mother, another if you have close family. Also allow for transport if you want your hairdresser or dressmaker to arrive at the church before you do. These cars will take the bridal party on to the reception. Send the company maps before the wedding so they know the route. If you live in an area where parking is difficult, it may be wise to reserve spaces.

You may wish to arrange a different style of transport for arriving at the service and leaving the reception. These come in many styles. A couple I met one summer were marrying ten miles from the bride's home. By road it was a long and difficult journey, but there was a quicker route to the bride's home from the church. The couple took a horse-drawn carriage to the river where a family friend kept a boat. This small, pretty boat was decorated with hoops of white and cream flowers and ribbons, fluttering in the breeze and the happy couple were ferried across the river to the delight of a crowd of holidaymakers who applauded them.

Transport we have arranged includes old London taxis, vintage cars, horse and carriage. When leaving the reception, couples have been very inventive, from quad bikes to hot air balloons. But do remember if you are being driven from the reception, have a bottle of champagne on ice in the car with a snack. The chances are you will not have had the time to eat properly. Over a glass of chilled champagne, you can reflect on the day.

MAGNIFICENT FOOD

Many caterers have good contacts with marquee companies, florists, entertainment, transport, printers, lighting companies, photographers and venues. They are an excellent starting point for helping you to find many other elements of your wedding. You must include your caterer at every site visit to a venue or meetings with other contractors such as the marquee company, lighting, entertainment and florists. They will be running the event on the day. I cannot stress enough how important it is to keep the caterer informed on all the details and timings.

Weddings go hand in hand with entertaining and food. The time of day you are getting married will dictate the style of food you will serve to your guests. Like all the plans you are making, you have to decide what is the most important element. The parts of the wedding most guests will remember are the bride, the flowers and the food and drinks served. There are many combinations to choose from. I have put together ideas from the most popular styles of entertaining your guests. Chapter 3 provides sample menus and recipes.

If you are marrying in the morning, plan a lunch. This could be one of two different styles: a seated wedding breakfast or a buffet lunch. You must remember that a lot of your guests will probably have been up early and will be hungry by lunchtime. Afternoon weddings are followed by a canapé reception as most of your guests will have had a light lunch. Canapés should be an interesting mix of meat, fish and vegetarian options; we also like to include interesting bite-sized tea sandwiches and miniature afternoon teacakes. As well as alcoholic drinks, tea is available for guests.

For a reception of three and a half hours allow at least sixteen canapés per person. Later afternoon weddings would have a reception of about two hours followed by dinner, so allow six to eight canapés per person followed by a three-course dinner. You can approach the dinner with several styles. The first option is a served three- or four-course dinner followed by coffee. If you do not like the idea of formality, serve the first and main course and continue with a dessert and cheese buffet with coffee served from bars. This will allow movement of guests and the buffet can be replenished during the evening. If you have dancing, a dessert and cheese buffet works extremely well. Another option to consider is a buffet dinner. This is an informal way of entertaining and very economical when there are a large number of guests. Whatever your preferences are, the food served should be interesting, with a combination of flavours and textures. Always offer vegetarian alternatives.

When looking for a caterer, personal recommendation is always best. Ask family, friends and work colleagues. You will have been to other weddings and will have ideas of what you want and do not want. My advice is if you do not have a favourite caterer, meet at least three.

Make an appointment at home or the venue you have chosen to discuss the whole day, the style you are planning, your likes and dislikes. Ask to see samples of linens, china, cutlery and glassware. Discuss sample menus and wine lists. If they are providing the waiting staff, ask what uniform they usually wear and if there any alternatives. Do the staff regularly work together or do they contact an agency for casual waiting staff?

Ask for a tasting at their offices. The table should be dressed as you would expect for the wedding reception, complete with a sample arrangement from the florist. If you have asked for the waiting staff to be dressed in a different outfit from their normal style, ask to see these as well. Canapés should be presented in the style discussed. Wines or special cocktails and fruit coolers should also be tasted. Go over the timings for the day in detail (not only your timing but also what time they will set up). Check whether the staff charges for the whole day, or if you run into overtime how much an hour do they charge. Is staff transport included? If you do not have a master of ceremonies, can their head waiter make the announcements? Every detail must be covered. When you are satisfied, ask for a full estimate, detailing every point; then write and confirm with a deposit.

entertainment

The style of music for your reception will probably be decided when you have agreed on the main elements. Hotels and venues will normally be able to make suggestions and recommendations and there are many agencies specialising in music and entertainment for weddings and parties. If planning a lot of entertainment, an agency should send a representative to oversee the arrangements and timings for the reception.

As a couple you will probably have your favourite style of music, but this must be in harmony with the surroundings. In a grand country house a band playing barn dance music will not be quite right. Music is very important during the reception as your guests will have left the service full of music to arrive to silence. Some hotels and venues may have a time limit on when the music must end. Check the acoustics in the area where you are planning to dance, so the sound is just perfect on the day. When planning your reception, arrange the timings so you will have time for dancing.

String quartets and jazz bands are the obvious choices, if a little predictable. Wind quintets, steel bands, even jazz violins make a change and seem a little less corporate. A harpist will be lost in the conversation; a piano can be too overpowering. If possible, the music should not be in the main reception room, but just as the guests enter. Other reception entertainment we have encountered are one-man bands and barber-shop quartets.

CHOOSING A BAND

Finding a dance band has to be researched very carefully. Guests will remember a good band, as they will a bad one. The number of guests will determine the size of the band. Dance bands come in all shapes and sizes and styles. Your thoughts may be for a salsa band, but can you realistically dance all evening to that style of music? I would advise a good mix of modern and old favourites. The band must be able to encourage all ages to dance.

Take into consideration that musicians will require breaks. What are you going to do when the music stops? Some bands will rotate

their players, so there is continuous music. No music for twenty or so minutes will lose atmosphere and it could be difficult to get your guests to start dancing again. One seamless way is to have a discotheque between the sets. You will need to discuss with the bandleader the music for dancing. Do some research into the music you would like to dance to. Think of the old favourites, such as Gershwin and Cole Porter, as well as modern composers. Add a touch of salsa, samba, as well as waltzes, fox-trots, rock and roll. As the couple you will open the dancing. Some couples we have catered for have taken dancing lessons to surprise their guests. One couple learned how to dance the most amazing tango and completely wowed their on-lookers.

When making your enquiries into choosing the music, consider the following important points. Ask the band for cassettes and if possible a video so you have some idea of their sound and look. Find out their style of dress. If possible, watch the band playing before you make your booking. Ask how long they play for and how they manage their breaks. You will be expected to supply refreshments and this will depend on the time of day and how long the band is booked for. You will need to let the caterer know about this and plan for the extra costs. Does the quote include transportation, hotels if required, VAT, amplification? Not all bands have their own equipment. Do you have to provide chairs? You will need to know what they require for changing and storage, when they want to set up and do a sound check (not, of course, in the middle of the reception). Plan the play list with a good balance of music and specify this in the contract. Sign the contract and return with a deposit. Popular bands can be booked as long as a year in advance during the busy season. Take this into account when making your plans.

BOOKING A DISCO

Discotheques are probably the first choice of many couples today. As with finding the right band, you will need to do the same for your disco. Play lists have to be planned as it's very important to have the correct mix of styles so everyone wants to dance. Being a disc jockey is not as easy as it may seem. They need to be able to judge the mood of the party. You do not want one who is continually talking over the music and misjudges what people want. Some discotheque operators can offer lights, smoke machines and lasers; others just bring their music and equipment. What you do not want is music so loud that guests cannot have a conversation. Like all the elements you are planning, ask if you can see them in operation so you can be sure their style is what you like. You should also make enquiries into their style of dress for the evening.

OTHER ENTERTAINMENT

Also consider other forms of entertainment as well as music. Magicians can wander from table to table, doing close-up magic tricks. Caricaturists can do cartoons for guests. Palm readers, fire-eaters, dancers, jesters, mime artists and circus acts all add to the atmosphere. You may also want to book a children's entertainer.

Fireworks can be a spectacular end to the day. Professional companies can arrange displays set to music and these can be tailored to most budgets. Only have fireworks if your guests can leave the reception area to watch. It could also be cold and many ladies will be wearing thin evening dresses – space blankets work a treat to keep guests warm. If you are planning a firework display and your reception will be near any livestock, such as cattle or horses, it's very important to inform the persons concerned as the noise can be disturbing.

photographic memories

Finding the right photographer for you is as much about personality as it is about being an excellent wedding photographer. The approach must be professional and an understanding of the bride and her wishes is of utmost importance. You want to be able to recall all the moments of the day. With meticulous planning, this should be achievable.

Start with a list of what you would like recorded. Think not only of the obvious, but also consider informal shots of the preparations for the reception, florists and caterers working, the wedding cake being set up as well as the band's preparations. Firstly, find the person you feel is right for what you want. There are many wedding photographers out there, so start by asking friends and family. Make an appointment to see at least three photographers who are known for their wedding work. Discuss where you are marrying and where the reception is being held. Ask to see samples of their work.

Discuss the charges as they can vary enormously. Some photographers make an all-inclusive charge for the day, including contact sheets, but prints are extra. Others will charge for about three hours and include an album and a certain number of photographs. Ask the charges for extra prints. If you know how many

sets of reprints you would like, it is often less expensive to have them developed together. The copyright of the photographs remains the property of the photographer. They keep the negatives, unless you have come to any other arrangement. Discuss what would happen if you lost your photographs due to any unforeseen circumstances over the years and come to some agreement. It's important you have a full understanding of the amount of time and the costs involved from the very beginning.

You will need to arrange for your photographer to visit your home, place of ceremony and reception so they see where they can make use of the space and areas available to them. Discuss the style you would like. They will have ideas of what is required.

You will want to have photos taken of the bridal party getting ready; the groom, best man, ushers and guests arriving at church; the bride and her father arriving; the wedding party leaving the church. Have consideration for your guests and don't make them wait around for too long while family photos are being taken. By all means have some photos taken outside the church, but then it is much better to arrive at your reception and disappear for about twenty minutes to have the family photographs taken. Now this is where you become bossy. Instruct the members of your party you wish to be photographed to be nearby, so you are not trying to find them. Informal shots of guests during the reception are a real treasure. You will want the general atmosphere captured on film, with photos of the cake-cutting, the speeches and leaving the reception.

Most photographers will have an assistant who will take the photographs at the church and preparations at the reception. You must be very clear about what you want recorded on the day. A good photographer is so unobtrusive you may wonder if any photos have been taken. If you are

(Left) The most successful wedding photographs are not always carefully posed. Capturing the joy of the day is often best achieved in a more relaxed picture.

giving a seated lunch or dinner, consider a disposable camera for each table so guests can take their own candid photos. Don't forget to instruct the waiting staff to collect them at the end of the reception. When you return from honeymoon, you will have photos of all your guests enjoying your wedding.

Many places of service do not allow photography. If you want to have photographs taken during the ceremony, you must ask the minister or registrar if this is possible. Flash photography is not allowed. Some couples may want to have a record of signing the register and certain times of the ceremony.

When you are totally satisfied you have all the details covered, request a detailed estimate. Some photographers ask you to sign a contract. Check that all the details and times are correct. Write and confirm with a deposit, including the agreed timetable of the day. Some photographers, especially the good ones, can be booked as much as a year ahead.

When you receive your wedding photos, one current trend growing in popularity is to set up a special website and post a selection of the shots there. This means that friends and family who live some way away can see the pictures and order prints for themselves. As the copyright remains with the photographer, you may need to check this with him first.

VIDEOS

You either love or hate them. As with a good photographer, a good videographer is just as unobtrusive. Do you really want the reception ruined by bright lights and cameras in guests' faces? You will need to do a lot of research to find a good one. Ask to see samples of their work. Give clear details of what you would like recorded. You will want to know how many videos are included in the quote. As with the photographer, the master video remains the property of the video company. You will need to discuss this and establish the cost for extra copies. My feeling about videos is they are wonderful to send to family and friends who were unable to attend your wedding due to distance, illness or age, but I doubt you will play a video as much as you will look at your photographs.

wedding flowers

When you are planning the flowers for the service, reception, your bouquet and those for the bridal party, try to choose flowers that are in season. They are at their best and least expensive. Even in the depths of winter there are some wonderful flowers available. A large bouquet of peonies at that time of year looks completely wrong, but a bouquet of snowdrops and grape hyacinths is magical. Balance is the right description. You want try and carry the theme through all the elements of the day. Now how do you find the right person to do all this for you?

Like all things, ask friends, family and work colleagues. Don't choose someone who may have a very modern style if you are planning a traditional country wedding. There are an enormous number of florists and their ways of working and costs differ. It may take time to find the right person for you, but when you do you will know they are right. Make an appointment, allowing at least an hour. Take along as much information about your dress, hairstyle, timings for the day, where the ceremony and reception are being held. Ask to see photos of their recent work. If they are decorating a church and reception for a wedding in the near future ask if you could visit to see the work. You will need to arrange a site visit to the place of your service and the place of the reception. There may be more than one wedding per day at the place of service which may require a meeting with the other couple or couples to discuss how you could all work together when organising the flowers.

If you are planning to have a marquee, the florist will require a plan of the layout. If you are having a tasting with a table set up, ask for a sample table arrangement. Discuss in detail the style and type of flowers you like. Check there are no hidden charges, such as if the church and reception require the flowers to be removed.

At the reception flowers should be bold and noticeable. Marquee poles can look very unattractive, so wrap these with garlands of flowers and foliage. You could also scatter dried lavender flowers on the floor — as guests walk on them and the marquee warms, the scent will fill the air and banish any mustiness. If you are having a seated lunch or dinner, tables must have arrangements. The wedding cake table, buffets and bars should also be decorated with flowers, perhaps either flower runners or garlands. Tall, slim vases placed on buffets and filled with summer rose petals or autumnal hydrangea heads make a bold statement.

The entrance to the reception is a natural place for flowers. You may feel this is a waste because your guests will only pass by when arriving and leaving, but the flowers make a nice welcome and goodbye, especially if they are scented. If your reception area has large blank walls, there are many ways to make the area a lot more cheerful. Large arrangements in urns or wrought-iron floor-standing candelabras (with non-drip candles) will make the space more welcoming. In marquees fill these areas with plants or make a small flower border or woodland scene. Consider adding fruit or even some vegetables to the arrangements. Frosted fruits look wonderful in the winter. Don't forget herbs as they complement flowers and help to scent the room.

You must take into account the size of your tables. If you have a two-metre (six-foot) round table, a small table centre will look lost. If you are having a lot of tables, consider having some arrangements that are tall as this looks very attractive. Guests' eyes are not drawn to a large space and the tall arrangements give a feeling of intimacy. Don't place them so it is difficult for conversations to be held across the table. The arrangement should be on a tall stand with the flowers and candles above the seated guests' heads, with more candles and flowers around the base of the stand. If you are planning an afternoon reception with small tables, don't forget the flowers for these.

You must have the flowers specified in the quote; you will not want them to be replaced by a flower that is three times the cost. The quote you receive will have all the details of flowers, containers, style of bouquets, buttonholes. Confirm in writing and pay a deposit if necessary. Some florists may offer a visit to a flower market so you can see what is available. This will give you an idea of how different flowers go together to create your perfect day.

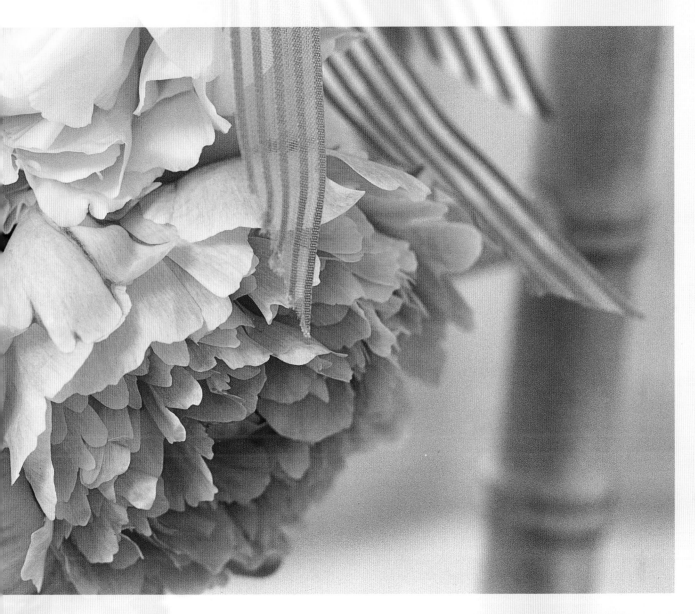

flowers for the service

Flowers for your ceremony must complement the place of worship. For religious ceremonies, there are many focal points. There should be an arrangement in the entrance to welcome guests. Pew ends or chairs look wonderful decorated with posies of flowers. Depending on the scale of the chosen site, large urns can be filled with seasonal flowers. If possible, it is best to decorate the church the day before the service. The day of the wedding a member of the floral decorator's team should check the flowers and top up any containers. The flowers are left in the church after the wedding. Do bear in mind, however, that many churches do not allow any flower arrangements during Lent (see page 56).

If you are planning a civil wedding in a register office, it is almost impossible to decorate the office because the ceremony is short and many couples are married in the same place in one day. There is usually already an arrangement on the table. If you are planning a civil wedding in a licensed venue, you can decorate the area with flowers as you wish, but remember nothing religious is allowed. If your budget is tight for flowers, opt for one large statement rather than small offerings which can seem lost.

pink flowers

At this summer lunch we have created a table of pink, silver and white with clear glass vases holding bunches of bold peonies. In early summer these wonderful flowers are available in many colours and tones. The table is designed to complement and enhance these abundant flowers.

The blowsy blooms of summer peonies take centre stage in this flower scheme and are complemented by tones of pink and silver used in the place setting and the favour box.

Boldness pays dividends, as proved by this unusual colour scheme. Its understated elegance is carried through from the bride's bouquet right through to the place card attached to a dramatic single lily.

purple
calla lilies

At a late winter evening reception bunches of violets and pots of green helxine complement the deep purple tones of the bride's calla lily bouquet. The table design was created to add warmth and a touch of mystery. Amethyst water glasses, jewel-coloured overcloths and candleholders in shades of purple remind guests of the bride's choice of bouquet.

country church flowers

This lovely Saxon church in the middle of the Suffolk countryside is the setting for a country wedding. The style is very simple and the flowers could have been picked from the gardens, cornfields and hedgerows. The design of the flowers sits well with the simplicity of the church. Glass jars filled with cottage garden flowers are tied to alternate pew ends with fine fishing wire, tall wooden candlesticks stand proud at the remaining pew ends, adding a touch of elegance. The bridal chairs are linked together with a garland of flowers and ivy. The main lighting in the church is metal chandeliers with candles with ivy and trailing foliage to soften them. The frame supporting the flowers over the main entrance door was made by the local blacksmith. The flowers reflect the designs on the chairs. On the path outside, a carpet of dried lavender flowerheads and fresh petals has been scattered while the service is taking place. When the bridal party and guests leave the church the lavender scent is released into the air. The simplicity and elegance of this wedding is carried through to the lunch which is served on long tables, dressed with blue and white checked cloths, wooden platters and simple white china, adding to the charm of the occasion.

Above: Streamers like maypole ribbons hark back to more innocent times.

The style of the flowers complements the age of the church, conjuring up images of bygone weddings. When choosing your flowers you can either choose a style that chimes perfectly with the location or one that contrasts boldly. Here the former most definitely applies.

The country theme is carried through from the church flowers to the flowers for the reception. Cheery vases of country flowers reflect the bride's bouquet (seen on the previous spread) and are complemented by the checked tablecloth and wooden platters.

Menu
~
Terrine de Foie Gras
Asperges Anglais
~

Carré d'Agneau
Jus de Menthe
Petits Légumes Nouveaux
~

Symphonie de Desserts
Café, Petits Fours

Guiraud 1986, Sauternes
Château La Louviere,
Graves Pessac Ledgnan 1993
Château Ducru Beaucaillou 1988
Pol Roger Brut 1988

Wrotha
29 Ja

tables

Whatever style of reception you choose, the tables must be attractive and welcoming. Small tables for an afternoon reception must have decoration. The same applies to the tables used if you are giving a buffet. Candles are never used for a lunch or afternoon reception, unless the wedding is late in the afternoon and it becomes dark early. In the evening lots of candles on the tables give a warm, sensuous and romantic atmosphere.

Candleholders come in many shapes and sizes. They can be made by cutting patterns in hollowed-out fruit and vegetables, such as apples, oranges or pumpkins. Square glass vases wrapped with coloured tracing paper give a warm diffused light, with the candle secured in place by standing in a couple of inches of sea salt or fine white sand. Candles floating in clear glass containers reflect the shimmering light. Lanterns suspended over tables also work well. Hanging clear glass lanterns on transparent fishing line looks magical, even better if you hang flowerheads as well. Consider paper lanterns with the light inside provided by battery candles – a very safe and effective alternative to candles.

The design of your table must be in keeping with the surroundings. If you have a blank space, you can create whatever look you like. China, cutlery, glassware and linen are available in so many styles today. Design a table setting that is creative and memorable. Napkins can be tied with ribbons, ivy, string, garlands of flowers or herbs. Banana leaves are inexpensive and work well for tying napkins folded to hold cutlery or menus.

A colour theme can be created. Colours such as oranges, browns, creams and yellows work extremely well for an autumn wedding. In winter white, dark green and ruby colours are inviting. A summer colour scheme should be cool and crisp. Spring pastel shades harmonise with the colours of spring flowers. Consider graduated colours from

red through to pink or a single colour for a lunch. If you are restricted to plain white tablecloths, make a top cloth from an organza or similar fabric and place flower petals under the semi-transparent layer to soften the look. Place mats made from three colours of grosgrain ribbon woven together are simple but extremely effective, especially if used with a clear glass presentation plate. Placing leaves or flowers under a clear plate is also very attractive. Butter will look appetising decorated with a few flowerheads or herbs. Flowers can be very grand or a small statement.

Chairs can be decorated with small bunches of flowers tied to the backs, but make sure that pollen or sharp foliage will not damage clothing. If you want to hide the rather unsightly chairs available from catering hire companies, make slip covers for the backs.

Transparent plates are laid on place mats made of ribbon threaded in a chequerboard pattern and the menu is framed by ribbon in a toning shade of yellow.

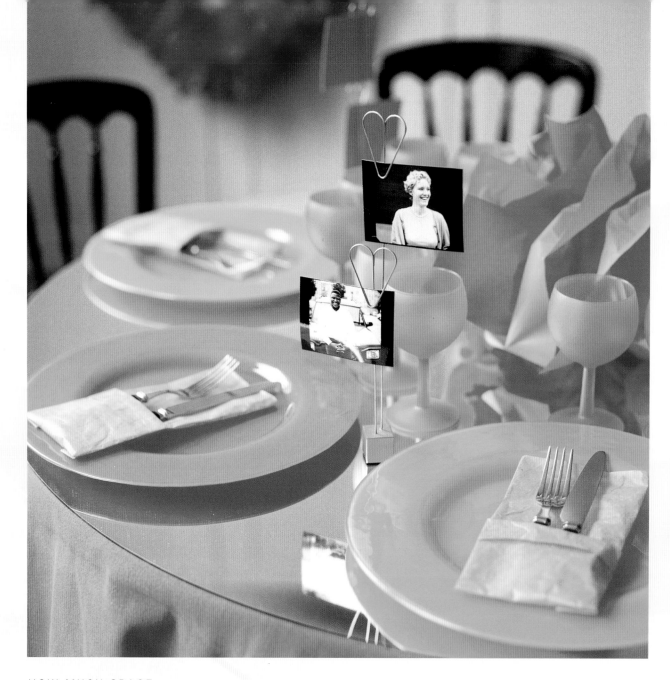

HOW MUCH SPACE

Planning the space for your wedding reception requires some time to work out how to arrange the area to maximum advantage. At home, if space is tight, remove some furniture and store in an area which will not be in use, such as a cellar, garage or garden shed. There are numerous removal companies that will take away furniture for the day, and return it the next, but you will not want to leave the house completely empty.

Before you decide where you wish to hold your reception, it's a good idea to work out the space required for the number of guests you are inviting. For an afternoon reception where guests are standing, you will only need some small tables with chairs, bars and a cake table. You should allow 3 square metres (10 square feet) per person. For a stand-up buffet allow 3.6 square metres (12 square feet) per person.

For a seated lunch or dinner allow 30 square metres (100 square feet) for each 1.8 metre- (6 foot-) round table that seats ten guests. This will allow space for the staff to serve, bars and buffet tables, but not a reception area, stages or dance floor.

The band or disco will be able to tell how much space they require. For a dance floor allow 1 square metre (3 square feet) per person. A dance floor 5.5 metres (18 feet) square will be able to accommodate up to 150 guests. You must remember not everyone will be dancing at the same time.

To work out how many guests you can have in an area that is empty of all furniture, take the measurements, multiply them together and divide by the number of guests to find the capacity. For example, a room 18.2 metres (60 feet) long by 10.6 metres (35 feet) wide will give you 193 square metres (2100 square feet). Using the figures given above, you will be able to work out how many guests it can accommodate. You must allow for fireplaces, furniture that cannot be removed and doors that open into the room (if space is at a premium consider removing them). Ensure windows are accessible so they can be opened.

If you are giving a seated lunch or dinner the following chart lists table sizes and the number of guests they can seat.

ROUND TABLES

Diameter	Number of guests
1 m (3 ft)	4–6
1.2 m (4 ft)	6–8
1.5 m (5 ft)	8–10
1.8 m (6 ft)	10–12

RECTANGULAR TABLES
(Based on 1.2m (4 ft) wide table with a guest either end)

Length	Number of guests
1.2 m (4 ft)	8
1.8 m (6 ft)	10
2.4 m (8 ft)	12
3 m (10 ft)	14
3.6 m (12 ft)	16

(Opposite above) Paper napkins and flower decorations and plastic glasses can look as effective and dramatic as a far more expensive table setting.
(Above right) An original twist on a place card – insert photographs of your guests in wire holders at each place setting.

Remember that rectangular tables take up more space than round ones, so if you are trying to fit the maximum number of guests into an odd shape, use a combination of different-sized round tables to utilise corners.

For an afternoon reception allow seating for at least one-third of your guests. You must take into consideration the elderly and infirm. For a fork buffet reception, allow seating for half the guests. At a buffet lunch or dinner, allow seating for all your guests (you may need a seating plan if you have a lot of guests).

THE SEATING PLAN

If you are planning a seated lunch or dinner, you must organise a seating plan. Out of all the arrangements you have made, without doubt this can be the most difficult task. But on the day you will be so pleased you have made the effort. I find by far the best way of organising this is to hand out seating cards when guests arrive. On the envelope is the guest's name, inside a card saying 'you are seated at table A'. You can make changes right up to the last minute, thus facing the guests: chief bridesmaid, groom's father, bride's mother, groom, bride, bride's father, groom's mother, best man. These days the 'high table' is unfashionable and is being replaced by round tables. This is a very good way of making extended families feel a lot more comfortable. For comfort, if you are planning a round table, use one that measures 1.5 metre (5 feet). The seating plan remains the same.

It is best to seat little bridesmaids and pageboys with their parents. Step-parents, unless they have brought up the bride or groom from a child, are not seated at the top table. Second husbands and wives are not included in the bridal party. Close family tables are placed near to the top table. Friends' tables are further away.

avoiding crossing out on a board which looks awful. Number, letter or name your tables. Make sure the tables are easily identifiable when guests enter the dining area.

Place cards are normally a white or cream tent card with the guest's full name. You can have some fun and make place cards from photographs of your guests. Or use fruit with a label, favours (see page 92) with the guest's name on or biscuits with the guest's name piped in chocolate. The menus can also have your guest's name on the top. Leaves and large stones also make interesting place cards.

There is a traditional order for seating the bridal party. If rectangular, the top table seating is in this order, from left to right

Seating cards, place cards, menus – all are ways of organising your guests with a minimum of fuss. The day will run much more smoothly if everyone knows exactly where they are supposed to be and when.

(Left) Lush roses are reflected in the patterned table cloth.
(Above and right) This table has an Oriental feel thanks to its exotic fruits and laquered boxes.

The traditional favour is the box of five sugared almonds, but use your imagination to think of a favour which will have some significance to you and your guests.

FAVOURS

Wedding favours are becoming increasingly popular. They have their roots in Europe, where five sugared almonds representing health, long life, happiness, wealth and fertility are presented either in small lace bundles or small boxes. These symbolise hospitality. In France they are called bonbonnières and Italy confetti. They are not meant to be gifts. They are a token of thanks to your guests for taking part in the celebrations, but this does not mean they cannot be something interesting and a reminder of the happy day.

A small box makes an ideal container. It could be filled with a souvenir from the city of your marriage, some home-made sweets or heart-shaped biscuits, flowers, dried herbs or herb seeds, even small soaps. If you want your guests to see the gift, consider a clear box tied with ribbon or coloured cellophane tied into a bundle. Alternatively, choose boxes tied with string then finished with sealing wax stamped with the couple's initials. Allow yourself time, filling and tying over a few days or evenings. Store them in a cool dark place. I think it is a special treat for your guests to receive a favour that has been designed and prepared by the bride and her family.

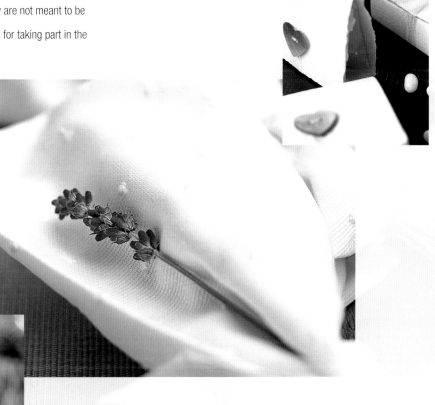

Plan how you will present them. Arrange them on a table near the door with a sign for guests to help themselves as they leave. At the dining table, they could double as the place card with the guest's name tied to the ribbon or placed in piles in the centre of a dining table.

the bride's outfit

Every bride should wear the dress of her dreams and with careful planning you will be able to. It's a wonderful feeling to try on a wedding dress for the very first time. Although your wedding is months away, when you look at yourself in the mirror, you will feel like a bride for the first time.

Shopping for the dress of your dreams can be a daunting affair. Firstly, make a list of designers and specialist wedding dress retailers located in your area. Think about the fabric you would like. The huge choice includes silks, duchesse satins, silk chiffons, organzas, velvet trimmed with fur for winter, hand-embroidered fabrics and taffetas. Natural fabrics look and feel wonderful, while synthetic fabrics can look shiny and the colours are not as natural. Delicate embroidery and beading on the bodice of a dress can look beautiful.

Do some research into the style you would like. Buy magazines, chat to your family and friends. If it's a historical style you are after, visit museums and art galleries to get ideas on styles and colours used. There are retailers specialising in original Victorian and Edwardian dresses that would be suitable as wedding dresses. A friend of mine, Clare Signy, chose an Edwardian lace tea dress for her wedding gown with an antique lace veil. It was absolutely perfect for her in so many ways. It suited her slim figure and her personality, and I could not imagine her wearing any other style of wedding dress. She simply looked amazing.

If you can afford the luxury of having your dress made exclusively for you, there are obviously many advantages. An expert dressmaker will make sure her dress fits you perfectly. If you are asking a dressmaker you have known for years to create a style you would like from a pattern, she may be able to adapt or add some ideas and styles of her own. Remember that most dressmakers have had years of experience in making wedding dresses. Don't be talked into using someone who only makes dresses for themselves and, for some reason best known to themselves, would like to make it for you. You do want to wear your dress with confidence on the day, knowing that it feels right and fits like a glove.

The time you should allow for making the dress really depends on the time of year. Some dressmakers require at least six months' notice, others may need longer. You will probably be required to attend at least four fittings. One of the most important points to remember is that most brides lose weight, especially the last few weeks before the wedding, so make sure the dress can be altered right up to the last week.

If buying a made-to-measure dress, there are many shops selling designer wedding dresses. You choose a design from their collection and they have it made up specially for you.

If you are buying an off-the-peg dress, you will have a range to choose from. Some shops take orders and will measure you; when the dress arrives from the manufacturers, alterations are made. Some shops offer a service where they can make any dress from their range to fit you. If you are on a tight budget, sales are a good time to buy old samples or end-of-season dresses. It is likely they will be shop-soiled, but a good dry cleaner should be able to restore it to pristine condition. They may also offer an alteration service.

However you choose your dress, for each fitting you must take with you shoes and underwear, even if they are not the same as you will wear on the day, but they must be similar.

When you feel you have researched your options as thoroughly as you can, contact your chosen designer, retailer or dressmaker. Most will ask you to make an appointment. This is not for any reasons of grandeur. It's purely practical because they will be able to spend time with you to discuss styles and fabrics in detail. Remember they are there to make your dream dress come alive and they have the experience that this requires.

THE DRESS

Although wedding dresses are not considered to be a fashion statement, styles, fabrics and colours do change from season to season. White can be a very hard colour for most people to wear, whereas ivory, light cream or off-white are far more flattering. When it comes to choosing the style that is right for you, remember that the dress must be very comfortable to wear. You do not want to feel it's too tight to walk, sit down or even to stand up in. The style must suit you and your personality.

A designer wedding gown (opposite) and a rack of sumptuous dresses (above) illustrate the wide range of styles available.

Think of your size and shape when choosing a style. If you are short, a full dress with large puffy sleeves will swamp you. If you are tall and slim, you can probably wear any style you like. If you are on the large size, choose a style that is understated with not too many frills. One of the most flattering styles for most figures is a fitted

(Left) A traditional dress, with full sleeves and exquisite detailing. (Right) A more contemporary, sleeveless gown. Both dresses are appropriate to a modern-day wedding.

can be slipped over the wrist, to prevent anyone stepping on it.

If you are having a civil wedding in a register office, a bridal dress is the wrong choice. Instead, opt for a very smart suit or dress with a hat. When it comes to older brides, choose a style that is fitting for the occasion. You want to look and feel wonderful. So no white veils or long trains.

Your wedding dress will probably be the most expensive item of clothing you ever purchase. It's important you feel happy with your choice. A beautiful dress will give you bags of confidence on the day. Knowing you look truly wonderful, you will radiate happiness. If you are not happy with your choice, this will also affect you on the big day. You will feel uncomfortable and probably hate looking at the wedding photographs afterwards. The other point to keep in mind is that we are not all super-models. Whatever size and shape you are, you will know what suits you. Don't try to disguise a style that you know is wrong with additions that will serve only to make the design even more unsuitable.

bodice, dropped waist and scoop neck. Add touches such as beading or embroidery to the bodice, and pearl, bone or fabric-covered buttons. Don't forget some services last up to or beyond an hour and the guests will spend that time looking at the back of your dress, so details are important.

There are also other factors to take into consideration. If you choose a design with very thin shoulder straps, perhaps you should consider having a jacket or a wrap to cover your shoulders during the service. You may have one of those complexions that reacts in small red patches when you become nervous. If this happens to you, I would advise covering your neck and back, perhaps with a thin, translucent fabric such as lace.

Most dresses look wonderful with a train. Long trains will require the help of several little maids, whereas you will be able to cope with a short train with your chief bridesmaid to make sure it is adjusted before you walk up the aisle. If your train is long, it would be sensible to make it detachable for the reception; otherwise attach a loop that

TRADITIONS AND SUPERSTITIONS

It's bad luck for the bride to make her own wedding dress.

It's bad luck to try on your complete outfit – even during the fittings – until you leave for the service.

The dress should not be finished until your wedding day; the last stitch should be sewn just before you leave for the service.

Something old, something new, something borrowed, something blue: perhaps you could wear an old veil, your dress is new, borrow some jewellery, and sew a small blue ribbon into the lining of your dress.

Did you know that the Armenian tradition is for the groom to deliver the bride's dress in a beautifully decorated box on their wedding day?

ACCESSORIES

Now you have chosen your dress, it's time to plan the accessories. All really will depend on the style, time of year and the type of wedding you are planning.

Our traditional image of a bride is a beautiful dress, her face slightly hidden and mysterious behind a veil. You will need to match your veil to your dress. This can be done with help of your dressmaker or the shop which is supplying your dress. You will want your veil to drape gently, so choose a fabric that will not stick out. There are many ways to secure your veil: a tiara, a feathered headdress, veil sewn to a hair band, or a flower headdress. It must be comfortable and securely positioned. The veil could be embellished with beads, fake jewels or embroidery.

No wedding dress is complete without jewellery, but you shouldn't choose any that will detract from the overall look. Pearls are the obvious choice. If your dress is very plain, consider wearing a single-strand necklace of light semi-precious stones. Earrings should match the chosen style of your necklace, but make sure they are not too long and dangling or they could become caught in your veil. The only jewellery to wear on your hands is your engagement ring (transfer the ring to your right hand before you leave home); avoid anything on your wrists or arms.

You will be standing for most of the day, so common sense tells you that your shoes must be comfortable, easy to walk up and down the aisle in, dance in and complement your dress. As soon as you have decided on the final design of the dress, start to investigate shoe styles. As with finding the right dress, there are many specialist shoemakers and shops for bridal wear. Spend time deciding on the shoes. Remember your feet will swell so they must be a perfect fit. Fabric should be your choice of shoe, preferably the same as your dress. Leather looks wrong. Choose a heel height you are used to wearing. Once you have found your pair, break them in at home, by wearing them for about half an hour a day for about two weeks. By the time your wedding day arrives, they should be comfortable. Use a specialist spray to protect the fabric on the shoes.

Choosing your underwear is equally important. The type and style will depend on the design of your dress. Start by finding a specialist lingerie shop. You will certainly benefit from the experience of the staff. If possible, take with you a copy of the design of your dress. If you have a strapless dress, you need to find a good strapless bra that is cut low enough at the back not to show. There are many pretty bras on the market, but you may need to choose a flesh-coloured bra in a plain design that will not show through clothing. Nothing worse than seeing a bra through the dress. You could consider the possibility of wearing a corset. This may sound old-fashioned but it will hide any lumps or bumps and will give you a smooth outline throughout the day.

Unless you particularly want to wear stockings, buy a good pair of sheer tights with a cotton gusset which can double as pants and thus avoid the horrors of a visible panty line. Always buy a spare pair of tights just in case you ladder them when getting dressed. Add a garter to wear just above the knee. Save the sexy underwear for your honeymoon – you want to be comfortable and cool on your wedding day.

Satin (above) or feathered (below), slippers such as these help seal the beauty and elegance of a bride's appearance.

bridal flowers

Your bouquet is your most important accessory. The bouquet must complement the colour and style of your dress. If your dress is multi-layered and full, a small bouquet would be lost. If the style of your dress is fitted and slim, an elegant long bouquet would complement the design, as would a simple hand-tied bouquet.

You must also think about your size. If you are petite, you do not want to look overwhelmed by a large bouquet. If you are tall, long-stemmed flowers look balanced. Also take into consideration the comfort factor. The bouquet must not feel too heavy. If you choose a style that drapes over your arm, the stems must be protected to prevent damage to the fabric of the dress. Pollen can stain clothing, so if you decide to have flowers that are likely to cause this problem, make sure all the stamens are removed before you pick it up.

Choosing flowers is very personal as certain flowers may be symbolic in your relationship, such as the first flowers your fiancé gave you or flowers you both love. Seasonal flowers represent the most sensible choice, as they are at their best and most economical. Although you will probably have ideas of colours, shape and style, you must be practical as well. Very soft, easily bruised flowers will not last through the service. The time of day and season are also important. A daytime spring wedding suits pale, fresh colours, while a dark winter's day demands rich, jewel-coloured roses with their intense warmth. In summer, consider garden flowers such as peonies and sweetpeas. Early summer brings lily of the valley, which makes the most stunning yet simple bouquet. Sunflowers wrapped with golden corn reflect the colours of late summer. Autumn brings berries, crab apples and rose hips. Don't forget to have a little rosemary for remembrance and myrtle for love.

You will probably want to preserve some or all of your flowers. Before you throw your bouquet to your female guests, remove the flowers you wish to keep. They can be pressed or preserved. There are companies who specialise in preserving flowers from bridal bouquets. If you are considering this, ask someone whom you know to be reliable to carry out your wishes as you will be on honeymoon.

Flowers for your hair must be chosen with care. If the hairstyle you are planning is elaborate, it will not require flowers. A floral headdress could present problems with a veil, and thorns, spikes and pollen could damage the fabric.

Flowers for your attendants should complement your bouquet. Small bridesmaids with floral headdresses, carrying decorated baskets filled with roses petals, present a charming picture. Don't forget to tuck some sweets into the basket, choosing only non-sticky, non-

A striking, densely packed bouquet of vibrant red roses (far left), a springtime bunch of grape hyacinths, lily-of-the-valley and hellebores (below left), an autumn arrangement of berries and foliage (above left) and a contemporary bouquet of steel grass and white phaleonopsis orchids (above). Each is suited to a different season and style of dress.

staining ones! Pomanders of violets or small roses are also dainty. Older bridesmaids and the maid of honour carry small bouquets, normally a scaled-down version of the bride's.

The groom, best man, ushers and fathers of the bride and groom usually have a simple single buttonhole for their jackets. If the mothers of the bride and groom care to wear a corsage, the design must be only a little larger than a buttonhole and match the colour of the chosen outfit and the bridal flowers.

hair and make-up

Your wedding will be the most important day of your life. More photographs are taken of you than at any other time. You want to feel and look absolutely wonderful. Your dress and accessories have been chosen with great care. Now for want the finishing touches.

You are spending a lot of time and money on the whole day so it really is worth spending that little bit extra to have your hair and make-up done by a professional. You know how the hand of fate works. If you do your own hair and make-up on the day, you can almost guarantee it will go wrong, especially if you feel nervous. If you are really confident that you can manage it, then congratulations.

You have to choose whether to have a hairdresser and make-up artist come to your home or whether to visit them in their salons. I feel there are very good reasons for having them both with you on your wedding day. You will feel more relaxed at home or in a hotel. You do not have to drive anywhere, have the problems of parking, perhaps visiting two different salons or battling with the weather. You may have to struggle with your headdress and veil. You may even have to make an appointment hours before your wedding. The following advice is given by well-known hairdresser and make-up artist Derek Thompson, known as the 'Wedding King'. He has looked after many brides on their wedding day.

With your hairdresser with you in a relaxed atmosphere, you will feel pampered and well looked after, but whatever your choice you will need to make an appointment with your hairdresser to discuss the style you would like. If possible, take with you a sketch or photograph of your dress with a sample of the fabric and your headdress or hat. Much will depend on what time of day you are getting married and where. Is it a grand wedding reception or a simple country wedding? Spend time discussing the look you want. Do you want to look chic, natural or glamorous? However, you do not want to look radically different from normal – just a subtly enhanced version. If possible, wear your hair up and choose make-up to suit your style and personality. You must feel very confident and, above all, radiant and beautiful.

When having a trial hair and make-up session, do not allow yourself to be talked into anything you know is not right. We all know that when we look in the mirror it is either instantly right or wrong, so keep that in mind. So if it's not you, if the hair is wrong or the make-up too heavy, it will always be wrong. When you look at yourself it should feel comfortable. You may require more lipstick or a little more eye shadow but it will feel right. You must communicate now if you don't like what you see.

When you have chosen your hairdresser and make-up artist, remember to confirm the booking in writing. Make sure you tell them in advance if they will also be expected to attend to bridesmaids or any other female relatives.

If you would like to wear fresh flowers in your hair, speak to the florist. The flowers have to complement your bouquet, but make sure they are robust enough to stand up to the rigours of the day and will not flop within twenty minutes.

Your hairdresser should arrive at least two hours before you need to put on your dress. Allow at least one hour for your hair and thirty minutes for your make-up and fifteen minutes for a gossip! Wash your hair when you are bathing. If you want to wear your hair up, wash it the day before. This is a very calming time. Do not allow anyone in the room with you; they will be seeing you for the rest of the day.

When dressing, cover your face to protect the fabric, then lift the dress over your head. You may need help with this manoeuvre. Your make-up may require a little adjustment, so drape a cloth over your dress to protect it. Some dresses come with what can only be described as a large mesh bag to slip over your dress and protect it from make-up when you are dressing.

If you are doing your own hair and make-up, sit down at least three times and practise with styles of hair and make-up. Apply your make-up before you do your hair. You do not want to spoil your hair by scraping it back. Your headdress might take some time to get right so make sure you practise this. Some beauty salons will give you make-up lessons in advance of the big day. Do not be talked into wearing extra make-up for the photographs. Use a matt foundation as this is much more flattering in photographs. When properly applied, make-up will last all day so give yourself time. Stay calm and do this in a very relaxed atmosphere, even if it means pinning a 'do not disturb' note to the door.

Remember to take make-up such as lipstick or powder with you to touch up later on – ask your mother or a close friend to carry it in their handbag for you.

A sparkly tiara (left) will look glamorous, or you can opt for elegant arrangement of fresh flowers in a simple hairstyle for an understated look.

clothes for the groom

Although all the eyes will be on the bride as she arrives for the service, it's just as important that the groom is as immaculately turned out as the bride. Somehow it seems to be easier for the man.

The traditional morning suit of black coat, grey waistcoat and pinstripe grey trousers looks very elegant and dashing. If you wish to change details, then a wing collar with a stock can replace the white shirt with a stiff collar and tie. Try to have some idea of the colour of the bride's dress so you can match the stock. If you choose to wear a tie, chose one that is not too loud but is jolly. Waistcoats are grey or buff colour, single or double breasted. A brocade waistcoat adds style. If you are planning to wear a stock it should match the waistcoat. – Stock pins, cuff links should be elegant and not too loud. Plain, highly polished black leather lace-up shoes with grey socks complete the suave groom. Don't forget to remove all traces of shoe polish – if you inadvertently step on your bride's dress, you do not want to leave polish marks. No handkerchief is worn in the morning jacket pocket as it would conflict with the buttonhole. With morning suits comes the top hat. They are very cumbersome to carry, the groom never wears it and it is just an accessory – my advice is not to bother.

If you are marrying in the evening, followed by a dinner and dancing, traditional black tie is the correct dress. Worn either with a wing collar or Eton collar, the choice of tie can add a little colour and, depending on the style of the wedding, some humour.

If you are marrying in a register office, wear a formal dark suit with suitable accessories or maybe some other form of dress that suits your personality – and you know you can carry off with style and humour. Morning or evening dress is not really appropriate.

the supporting cast

The best man and ushers must be as smart as possible, since they are greeting and looking after the groom and the guests. The ushers are always the first contact and looking immaculate sets the tone for the day.

The best man and ushers wear morning dress without hats as they are cumbersome to carry and never worn. They may like to theme the waistcoat with a stock. If morning dress is not the order of the day, opt for a dark lounge suit with white shirts and matching ties. This also applies to evening dress – choose matching bow ties. Shoes worn with morning dress are plain black, polished lace-ups, with black or dark grey socks.

As most men will need to hire their outfits, arrange to do this as soon as you have set the date, especially if you are getting married at a busy time of year. You will be measured and fitted and asked to pay a deposit. Don't forget to return all the items of clothing in order to have the full deposit repaid. If the groom has also hired his outfit, the best man is responsible for collecting and returning it and reclaiming his deposit.

When you have chosen your wedding dress, think about your bridesmaids and pageboys. By tradition their parents pay for the outfits, but you must give thought to the costs as it is very unfair for you to expect the parents to pay a fortune. If you want to have a certain style and fabric, offer to pay for some of the costs. It's much better to have the outfits made by a friend or someone you know would like to help. Bridesmaids' dresses should be made to ensure they fit correctly. Have the dresses made as late as sensibly possible; children grow very quickly. Don't have long dresses as the children can trip over or step on and tear the fabric. Girls look charming in three-quarter-length dresses and after the wedding they can be made into party dresses. Don't choose strong colours or patterns as they can overwhelm the child. Little bridesmaids look sweet in ballet shoes and they are comfortable. The colours of the shoes can easily be made to match the fabric of their dresses.

Older bridesmaids' dresses must be elegant and understated. It's rather unfair to put them in an unflattering design full of bows, frills and layers of fabric.

When choosing on your pageboys' outfits, there are many styles to choose from, but they must be in harmony with the bridesmaids. The sash of the bridesmaids' dresses can match the sash of the pageboys' outfits or the colour of their knickerbockers. Other outfits are military, kilts, sailors, or whatever style you want to develop. Shoes depend on the outfit, but are usually black patent or a plain shoe with buttons. Break the shoes in a few weeks before the wedding.

The most important person after the bride is her mother. The outfit should be chosen with care so as not to upstage the bride in any way. After all, it's the bride's day. Choose an outfit that is comfortable, a style that is classic and elegant. One colour always works well. Team the dress or suit with a hat. Shoes are so important for comfort as you will be on your feet most of the day. Choose a handbag that is not too large, but can carry the bride's lipstick and a small make-up bag and mirror. The groom's mother nearly always worries about what the bride's mother has chosen. After the outfit is decided, tell the groom's mother so she can avoid choosing a clashing colour.

food & drink

The food and drink at your wedding reception represent one of the most important elements of the day, so take the time to decide what you really want. Champagne and wedding cake may be the most traditional elements of a wedding feast, but there are plenty of other options.

celebratory drinks

A wedding and champagne go hand in hand – one's first thought of celebrating is to toast the bride and groom with a chilled glass of champagne but of course there are plenty of other choices.

WHAT TO SERVE AND WHEN

Planning the drinks you wish to serve is as important as deciding on the menu. The time of day and your budget are important considerations. For a late morning and lunchtime wedding reception consider serving champagne, as well as something light such as Bellinis (puréed fresh peaches mixed half-and-half with Prosecco) or sparkling white wine with fresh raspberry juice. These two drinks are particularly delicious during the spring and summer when the fruit is inexpensive and readily available.

Fresh fruit coolers, punches and cocktails, displayed in large jugs, are wonderful to look at and taste divine. Displaying them in this way makes it easy for guests to serve themselves from the bar. With so many mouthwatering fruit drinks available today, to serve plain orange juice is very unimaginative. Pitchers of ice-cold Bloody Mary made with tequila or flavoured vodkas are perfect for a late morning reception, followed by an early lunch or brunch. I personally do not like serving Bucks Fizz as I feel it is a waste of good champagne and fresh orange juice.

For an afternoon reception, champagne and sparkling wine mixed with fresh fruit purée is refreshing, as are jugs of white wine punch garnished with fresh fruits and flowers. Remember if you are planning an afternoon reception that there may be guests who would welcome a cup of tea so set up a tea bar just before they leave. In winter,

(Left) An inviting bar for guests to serve themselves at an informal outdoor reception.

glasses of mulled wine with lots of spices and citrus peel, or hot buttered spicy rum, warm the coldest of hands. Chilled beers and soft drinks, including water, should also be available for your guests. At a large evening reception, a cocktail bar is lots of fun. Many cocktails can be made up in advance and stored on ice or in a fridge. When there is dancing plenty of soft drinks and water must be on hand. If your budget does not stretch to serving champagne during the reception, white wine or sparkling wine such as good Prosecco are also very good.

If children will be present, have plenty of fresh fruit drinks and water on hand. Children are notorious for not eating very much at a wedding as they are so excited. To tempt them we have started to serve interesting-flavoured and layered thick milk shakes made with lots of ice-cream.

HOTELS, VENUES AND CATERERS

Discuss in detail with your chosen hotel, venue and/or caterer what you would like. If you are selecting your wine six to eight months in advance, enquire if the same vintages will be available. All drinks will probably be on a sale or return basis. Discuss quantities, and be generous in the calculations – it's better to have more than to run out. Another point to consider is to ask for a bottle count at the end of the evening. They will be quite used to people asking, so do not be embarrassed. If you wish to supply your own champagne, wines and soft drinks, some venues and caterers will have a corkage charge. Determine how much this charge is and allow for it within your budget. Some caterers do not have corkage charges but may charge for removing the empty bottles and taking the leftover drink back to their base for you to collect or they may deliver for you.

DESIGNING A BAR

If you are arranging your own bar for drinks there are a few important points to remember. Your bar or bars should be inviting, convenient for guests to serve themselves and easy to keep uncluttered and clean. Place the bar in a convenient position, so that it is easily accessible for guests to serve themselves. Place a waterproof protection on the floor, taping down the edges to prevent accidents. The bar table should be at least 2 metres (6 feet) long and 1 metre (3 feet) high. Cover with a cloth to the ground, so storage of ice bins and glasses is hidden. If you are serving cocktails, make sure you have a supply of electricity to the bar for the blenders. Tape down the flex. On the bar place snacks so your guests can nibble while waiting for a drink. Fill tall vases with fruits in season. Place garnishes and ice in glass containers. Make garlands of flowers to decorate the front of the bar. Large cookie jars or jugs, labelled and filled with fresh fruit coolers or cocktails with a ladle by the side can stand ready for guests to serve themselves. Write a menu and place on the bar. Arrange the glasses in matching rows. I like to use attractive and fun glasses. Tie ribbon or ivy around the stems of champagne glasses. In summer use French lavender for stirrers in fresh fruit coolers. This is unusual and looks very pretty placed in the glass ready to be served. Fruit or flower ice cubes look particularly lovely in glasses of mineral water and white wine punches.

COOLING DRINKS

Use large, waterproof containers to cool champagne, wines, beers and mineral water. A new dustbin, a smart galvanised container, plastic toy box, a large cooler or half-wooden barrel are all suitable. When using ice bins, place them in large rubbish bins to protect the floor from condensation. Cover the bottom of the container with ice, place the bottles in the bin and cover with more ice. For large receptions, use separate ice bins for champagne, wines, beers and soft drinks. To make serving easier, before chilling down, remove the foil from around the champagne corks. Remove and replace the corks in the white wine bottles. Allow at least two hours for the drinks to cool. When serving beers for guests to help themselves, tie the bottle opener to the ice bin so it does not go missing.

QUANTITY OF ICE REQUIRED

For a lunchtime reception (4 hours) with 100 guests, allow 10 x 3.6kg (30lb) bags of ice.

For an afternoon reception (5 hours) with 150–200 guests, allow 18 x 13.6kg (30lb) bags of ice.

For an evening reception (6–7 hours) with 100–150 guests followed by dinner and dancing, allow 25 x 13.6kg (30lb) bags of ice.

This allows ice for chilling the drinks and ice cubes for placing in drinks. If the weather is very hot, allow for another delivery of ice about halfway through the reception. Remember to store the ice out of direct sunlight.

HIRING GLASSWARE

It's unlikely that, unless you are planning a very small lunch, dinner or reception, you will have the quantity of glassware required. There are many wonderful styles available for rental these days and for your wedding it is worth spending just that little bit more. For a small extra charge, you can return the glasses unwashed. When buying your drinks, some suppliers offer free glass hire. Make sure they are sparkling clean before use and just as sparkling when you return them.

QUANTITY OF DRINK PER PERSON

LUNCH
¼ bottle champagne
¼ bottle white wine
¼ bottle red wine
1 litre bottle mineral water
½ litre fresh fruit juice

AFTERNOON RECEPTION
⅓ bottle champagne
¼ bottle white wine
¼ bottle red wine
1 70cl bottle mineral water

EVENING RECEPTION FOLLOWED BY DINNER AND DANCING
½ bottle champagne
½ bottle white wine
½ bottle red wine
2 bottles beer
½ litre fresh fruit juice
1 litre mineral water

EQUIPMENT FOR SETTING UP THE BAR
Bottle openers
Cloth for mopping up spills
Cocktail shaker
Containers for garnishes and ice cubes
Corkscrews
Crushed ice
Cutting board and knife
Drink napkins to wrap around glasses
Ice bins
Ice cubes
Jugs
Large containers for chilling drinks
Serving trays
Spoons, ice tongs or scoop
Stirrers
Strainer
Straws
Tin opener

cocktails and soft drinks

COCKTAILS

CANALETTO

Many years ago I had the great pleasure of drinking one of these delicious cocktails at a fiftieth birthday party at the Gritti Palace in Venice. Made with puréed fresh raspberries mixed with very cold Prosecco and garnished with fresh raspberries and mint, this is a wonderful alternative to the classic Bellini. We have served these drinks on many occasions and they are extremely popular. They are also easy to prepare in jugs, ready for serving.

SERVES 100 IN 100ML (4FL OZ)
GLASSES

4 kilos (8lb) fresh raspberries (this yields 4 litres (7 pints) of fresh raspberry juice)
10 bottles of chilled Prosecco
130 raspberries, variegated mint leaves and viola flowers, to garnish

Place the fresh raspberries in a blender and blend until smooth. Sieve the purée through a strainer set over a large jug or bowl, pour into an airtight container, seal and place in the fridge until ready to use. To serve, place the juice and Prosecco into a large container, mix well and pour into jugs. Serve in glasses garnished with raspberries, mint and viola flowers.

CHOCOLATE MARTINI

A very popular cocktail. For a fun look, add a few Smarties.

SERVES 10

500ml (17fl oz) chocolate vodka or a good Polish vodka
250ml (7¹/₂ fl oz) chocolate liqueur
Ice
Smarties, to garnish (optional)
Cocktail shaker

Mix the vodka and liqueur together. Cover and place on ice or in the fridge. To serve, pour about 75ml (3fl oz) into a cocktail shaker filled with ice. Shake until very cold, pour into a cocktail glass and garnish with the Smarties.

RASPBERRY MARTINI

Refreshing on a summer day and very different.

SERVES 10

500ml (17fl oz) raspberry vodka or a good Polish vodka
150ml (¹/₄ pint) fresh raspberry juice
100ml (3¹/₂ fl oz) raspberry liqueur
100ml (3¹/₂ fl oz) crème de mûre
Ice
Frozen raspberries, to garnish
Cocktail shaker

Mix all the ingredients except the ice and the garnish, and stir well. Place on ice or in the fridge until required. To serve, fill the cocktail shaker with ice, pour in one-tenth of the mixture, shake until ice-cold, pour into a cocktail glass and garnish with a frozen raspberry.

(Left) Canaletto. (Top right) Mango Berry Coolers (see page 122). (Bottom right) Chocolate Martinis.

WHITE WINE PUNCH

White wine with a kick which looks very inviting.

MAKES 9 x MEDIUM-SIZED WINE
GLASSES
2 bottles good white wine (not sweet), well
  chilled
100ml (3¹/₂ fl oz) brandy
100ml (3¹/₂ fl oz) vodka
Ice
Berries and flowerheads, to garnish

Pour the wine, brandy and vodka into glass
jugs with an ice lip. Add the ice and stir. Place
the garnish in the glasses, pour in the punch
and serve.

PLANTERS PUNCH

My friend Stephen Camacho is the best drinks-
mixer and cocktail-maker I have ever known.
This is his family recipe for planters punch.
Rather than the sweet and sticky variety, this
version is made with fresh fruit juices and
matured for 36 hours.

SERVES 10
1 litre (1³/₄ pints) light rum (Mount Gay or
  Cavalier)
1 litre (1³/₄ pints) fresh pineapple juice
250ml (7¹/₂ fl oz) fresh passion fruit juice
250ml (7¹/₂ fl oz) fresh lime juice
Grated nutmeg
Ice
Slices of mango and pineapple, to garnish
Straws

Place all the ingredients except the ice and
garnish in a large airtight container. Stir well
and place in the fridge for 36 hours to mature.
To serve, pour over ice in tall glasses, add a
straw and fruit to garnish.

**(Top left) White Wine Punch. (Bottom left)
Mojitos. (Right) Planters Punch.**

MOJITO

This is an extremely refreshing drink to serve
on a hot summer's day.

SERVES 8
200ml (7 ¹/₂ fl oz) white rum
120ml (4fl oz) fresh lime juice
60ml (2fl oz) sugar syrup
240ml (¹/₂ pint) sparkling water
Ice
A good handful of mint leaves, washed
Stirrers

Place all the ingredients except the water, ice
and mint in a container and place on ice or in
the fridge. To serve, place about 8 mint leaves
in the bottom of each tall glass, crush the mint
with a long spoon, add the mix to three-quarters
of the way up the glass, fill with ice and top up
with water. Place a stirrer in the glass.

SOFT DRINKS

MANGO BERRY COOLER

When mangoes and raspberries are in season,
this makes a delightful drink, served ice-cold.
Lavender is in season at the same time and a
stalk of lavender acts as an unusual stirrer.

SERVES 10
1 liltre (1³/₄ pints) fresh mango juice
500ml (15fl oz) fresh raspberry juice
500ml (15fl oz) still mineral water
Ice
Lavender stirrers

Mix the juices and water together, stir well.
Place in a container on ice or in the fridge. To
serve, fill the glasses with ice, pour over the
juice and add the lavender.

THE BIG APPLE

This is a classic combination of apple juice and ginger beer.

MAKES 5 x 250ML (8FL OZ) GLASSES
1 litre (1³⁄4 pints) organic apple juice (choose
   a sharp variety)
1 x 330ml can of Old Jamaican ginger beer,
   or a good old-fashioned brand
Ice
Fresh mint, to garnish
Straws

Pour the apple juice and ginger beer into a jug and mix. Fill the glasses with ice and drink, garnish with the mint and straws, and serve.

COOL VANILLA CHERRY

Vanilla and cherry work so well together. If you don't want to serve just juice, a shot of vodka or grappa makes a great cocktail.

MAKES 5 x 140ML (¹⁄4 PINT) GLASSES
500ml (15fl oz) dark cherry pulp
200ml (7¹⁄2 fl oz) sparkling mineral water
1 teaspoon vanilla essence
Ice
Cherries, to garnish
Straws

Mix the cherry pulp, water and vanilla essence together, stir well, and pour into jugs. Fill the glasses with ice, pour over the juice, garnish with the cherries, add a straw and serve.

PEAR AND APPLE CRUSH

A refreshingly different fruit cooler for your guests who enjoy soft drinks. This is very easy to mix ahead of time and leave on ice or in a fridge. Try to find a good brand of organic juice; the apple will be nicer if you can use a fairly sharp variety.

SERVES 100 IN 200ML GLASSES
20 x 980ml (1³⁄4 pint) bottles organic apple
   juice (such as Bramley)
5 x 980ml (1³⁄4 pint) bottles organic pear juice
1 litre (1³⁄4 pints) fresh lemon juice
   (squeezed from approximately 20 lemons)
Ice
Thinly sliced whole apples, to garnish
Stirrers

Mix together all the ingredients apart from the garnish. Store in an airtight container on ice or in a fridge. To serve, stir well and pour into jugs. Fill the glasses with ice, garnish with whole apple slices, add a stirrer and pour over the juice.

SUMMERTIME PEACH

Like the berry cooler, it's wonderful to use fruits when they are plentiful to create delicious, refreshing drinks like this one.

MAKES 10 x 200ML (7$^{1}/_{2}$ FL OZ) GLASSES

500ml (15fl oz) fresh mango juice
1 litre (1$^{3}/_{4}$ pints) fresh peach juice
500ml (15fl oz) still mineral water
Ice
Slices of peach or mango, to garnish

Mix the juices with the water, stir well, store in a container on ice or in the fridge, until ready to serve. To serve, fill the glasses with ice, pour over the juice, garnish with the fruits and serve.

CAPE CRANBERRY

I created this soft drink for the wedding of Ming Veevers Carter who married on Cape Cod this year. It combines two loves in her life: the Cape and the tropics.

MAKES 5 x 250ML (7$^{1}/_{2}$FL OZ) GLASSES

1 litre (1$^{3}/_{4}$ pints) cranberry juice
250ml (7$^{1}/_{2}$ fl oz) fresh mango juice
Ice
Fresh cranberries, to garnish

Mix the juices together and stir well, place in a container on ice or in the fridge. To serve, fill the glasses with ice, pour over the juice and garnish with cranberries.

MILK SHAKES

I first had one of these delicious three-colour milk shakes eighteen years ago in Boston. This year I returned, looking forward to enjoying another one. Alas the ice-cream parlour had been replaced by a coffee shop. Great for children (and adults) at an afternoon wedding.

SERVES 6

Place six glasses in the freezer. If you have the luxury of being able to use three blenders, all the better. If not, fill each glass with a layer of shake, then place in the freezer, wash the blender, and repeat the process until the milk shakes are complete.

VANILLA LAYER

100ml (3fl oz) full-fat milk
1 litre (2$^{1}/_{4}$ pints) vanilla ice-cream
Seeds from a vanilla pod or a teaspoon of
 pure vanilla essence

STRAWBERRY LAYER

100ml (3fl oz) full-fat milk
1 litre (2$^{1}/_{4}$ pints) strawberry ice-cream
4 fresh strawberries, washed and chopped

CHOCOLATE LAYER

100ml (3fl oz) full-fat milk
1 litre (2$^{1}/_{4}$ pints) bitter chocolate ice-cream
2 tablespoons Ovaltine

FOR THE VANILLA LAYER:
Place the milk and half the ice-cream in a blender, add the vanilla seeds or essence. Blend until smooth. Add the remaining ice-cream, blend until smooth, pour into glasses; place in the freezer for about half an hour.

FOR THE STRAWBERRY LAYER:
Place the milk, half the ice-cream and the strawberries in a blender, blend until smooth, add the remaining ice-cream and blend until smooth. Pour into the glasses and place in the freezer for about half an hour.

FOR THE CHOCOLATE LAYER:
Place the milk, half the ice-cream and the Ovaltine in a blender, blend until smooth, add the remaining ice-cream, blend till smooth. Pour into the glasses and serve immediately with long spoons and straws.

wedding food

Planning the style of food for your reception is dictated by the time of day you are marrying. There are four options: a seated lunch, an afternoon wedding with canapés, an evening dinner or a buffet for lunch or dinner. If you are thinking of catering your own reception, forward planning is essential.

Planning the style of food within your budget is not too difficult. Instead of canapés served before lunch or dinner, place snacks on tables for guests to help themselves. You could hire a chef or chefs to do the cooking, along with waiting staff to set up the bar and tables as well as serve and clear away. If you are considering providing your own ingredients for someone else to prepare, I would advise having a trial run. You will need to be detailed in your instructions and what you like and dislike. What you cannot do is spend your wedding day in the kitchen, or expect your family and friends to do the same. Plan to use seasonal foods as they are at their best in flavour and price.

Kate Dyson, who owns the Dining Room Shop in London, decided she would cater for both her daughters' weddings. At the first wedding she entertained 150 guests with a barbecue supper; for the second a year later, she organised picnic baskets for 350 guests. Armed with a Victorian afternoon tea cookbook, they set about planning the contents of the baskets for adults and children. While they were at the church, twelve people at home filled the baskets, ready to hand to guests as they arrived. This idea inspired our picnic on the lawn (see page 147).

I have put together five styles of wedding receptions, all developed from menus we have served at weddings. The food should be memorable, a feast for the eye and a combination of flavours and textures. At weddings people will remember bad food as well as excellent creations. Balance the menus and think of the age range of your guests. Children and more elderly guests would probably not eat hot and spicy foods. Chocolate is always a winner for dessert and lamb is the most requested main course. The food you both like becomes part of the menu. Don't forget the vegetarians and don't simply offer the vegetables that are served with a main course. Whatever the style of reception you are hosting, the food must be presented in an elegant way.

This chapter contains a grand five-course dinner, a simple three-course menu that could be served for a lunch or dinner, canapés for an afternoon reception, a buffet inspired by the flavours from the Mediterranean and a summer's afternoon picnic for adults and children. Some elements can be prepared in advance and stored in the freezer.

(Left and below) Simple or sophisticated, appetisers are important ingredients of the wedding reception. (Right) Tower of Asparagus.

informal lunch

This light summer lunch for 20 is an interesting mix of modern and traditional styles using seasonal ingredients full of flavour. Fresh asparagus is tied neatly into bundles that are filled with artichokes and wild mushrooms. Succulent scallops are lightly grilled and drizzled with a sweet chilli dressing. For dessert there is a classic fruit fool with pretty heart-shaped cookies sparkling with sugar.

FIRST COURSE
Tower of Asparagus

MAIN COURSE
*Scallop and
Langoustine Salad with
Sweet Chilli Dressing*

DESSERT
*Gooseberry and Elderflower
Fool, served with Sugared
Heart Biscuits*

TOWER OF ASPARAGUS

These towers can be prepared and stored in the fridge 6 hours before they are required.

FOR THE TOWER:

60 red cherry tomatoes, halved

8 shallots, peeled and finely chopped

2 cloves garlic, peeled and finely chopped

2 tablespoons soft thyme leaves

Olive oil, for frying

600g (1lb 4oz) wild mushrooms, brushed

20 artichoke hearts, cooked and chargrilled

*160 green asparagus spears, blanched and cut
into 8cm (3$^1/_2$in) lengths*

*160 white asparagus spears, blanched and cut
into 8cm (3$^1/_2$in) lengths*

*2 large leeks, washed, cut into 20 1cm ($^1/_2$in)
strips, blanched and dried*

FOR THE DRESSING:

200g (6¹/₂oz) goat's cheese, outside ash
  removed, cut into small pieces
300ml (¹/₂ pint) warm water
2 tablespoons good sherry vinegar, warmed
300ml (¹/₂ pint) balsamic vinegar, reduced by
  half
Sea salt and freshly ground black pepper

SPECIAL EQUIPMENT:

20 metal rings, 6.5cm wide x 4cm deep
  (2¹/₂ in x 1³/₄ in)

Preheat the oven to 100°C/210°F/gas mark ¹/₄.
Place the cherry tomatoes cut side up on a
metal baking tray. Sprinkle with half the
shallots, the garlic and thyme; season. Place in
the oven for 6–8 hours. Remove from the
oven. Cool and carefully store in an airtight
container in the fridge.

Heat a sauté pan with a little olive oil, and
sauté a few mushrooms at a time with the
remaining shallots. Season and place in a
colander to drain. When cooled, place in an
airtight container in the fridge.

Cut a 3cm (1¹/₄in) disc from each
artichoke. Place the discs in a bowl, cover and
set aside. Cut the remaining artichokes into
small pieces and place in a large bowl. Add the
tomatoes and wild mushrooms, season well,
cover and set aside.

Place the rings on a metal tray. Put
an artichoke disc on the base of each ring.
Season. Place the asparagus in two
separate bowls and season well. Arrange
the spears around the rings in alternate
colours. Fill the centres of the rings with the
tomato and mushroom mixture. Place the
blanched leeks around the top edge of the
rings and tie tightly in place. Cover and place
in the fridge.

TO MAKE THE DRESSING:

Heat a pan of water. When warm place a metal
bowl over the pan, add the goat's cheese and
slowly melt. Do not over-heat the cheese or it
will split. Remove the bowl. Whisk in the warm
water a little at a time, then whisk in the
vinegars. Check the seasoning. Do not place in
the fridge.

To serve, place the towers in the centre of
the plates, remove the rings and drizzle around
the dressing.

SCALLOP AND LANGOUSTINE SALAD WITH SWEET CHILLI DRESSING

FOR THE DRESSING:

6 tablespoons sweet chilli sauce
5 tablespoons fish sauce
2 tablespoons light soy sauce
Juice of 3 large limes
3 cloves garlic, peeled and finely chopped
3 tablespoons peanut oil

FOR THE SALAD:

40 medium-sized scallops, roes removed
100 langoustine tails, poached and peeled
Vegetable oil
400g (13oz) spring onions, finely sliced
400g (13oz) red onions, peeled and finely
  sliced
400g (13oz) bok choy leaves, washed and
  dried
800g (1lb 10oz) carrots, peeled and cut into
  strips
500g (1lb 1oz) French beans, split and
  blanched
400g (13oz) snow pea shoots, washed and
  dried
2 cups coriander, washed and dried
1 cup Thai basil, washed and dried
1 cup mint leaves, washed and dried
2 radishes, washed and cut into strips
Sea salt and freshly ground black pepper

FOR THE GARNISH:

1kg (2lb 2oz) cashew nuts, roasted
40 crayfish, poached and cooled

**(Above) Scallop and Langoustine Salad with
Sweet Chilli Dressing. (Right) Gooseberry and
Elderflower Fool with Sugared Heart Biscuits.**

In a bowl mix the sweet chilli sauce, fish
sauce, soy sauce, lime juice and garlic. Whisk
in the peanut oil and set aside. Heat a chargrill
plate; slice the prepared scallops in half
lengthways, brush with a little oil and season
with salt and pepper. Chargrill the scallops for
approximately 15 seconds per side, then leave
to cool.

Place the langoustines and scallops in a
bowl. Place all the other salad ingredients in a
separate bowl. Lightly dress the langoustine
and scallops and the salad with the dressing.
In a serving bowl, layer up the langoustine,
scallops and salad, seasoning between the
layers. Scatter with cashew nuts, garnish with
crayfish, drizzle over any remaining dressing
and serve.

GOOSEBERRY AND ELDERFLOWER FOOL

2.5kg (5lb 5oz) gooseberries, trimmed
900g (1lb 14oz) caster sugar
120ml (4fl oz) elderflower cordial
1 litre (1³⁄₄ pints) double cream, lightly
    whipped
Elderflowers, to garnish

Place the gooseberries, sugar and cordial in
a heavy-bottomed saucepan, slowly bring to
the boil, cover and simmer until the fruit is
tender. Remove from the heat. Place into a
bowl, cover and leave to cool. When cold,
place into a food processor and purée until
smooth. Sieve into a bowl. Fold in the cream.
Cover and place in the fridge. To serve, fill
200ml (6¹⁄₂fl oz) glasses with the fool and
garnish with the elderflowers.

SUGARED HEART BISCUITS

FOR THE DOUGH:
240g (8oz) unsalted butter
400g (13¹⁄₂ oz) caster sugar
2 large free-range eggs, beaten
560g (1lb 3oz) plain flour
¹⁄₂ teaspoon salt
1 teaspoon vanilla essence
Zest of 2 lemons

FOR THE ICING:
2 free-range egg whites
300g (10oz) icing sugar
Juice of ¹⁄₂ lemon
Various food colours and sanding sugars

Preheat the oven to 170°C/325°F/gas mark 5.
Line a baking tray with nonstick baking
parchment paper or a silicon baking mat.
Cream the butter and caster sugar in an
electric mixer until light and fluffy. Add the
eggs gradually and beat until smooth. Carefully

fold in the remaining ingredients. Place the
dough on a floured surface and knead until
smooth. Cover with cling film and rest in the
fridge for 1 hour or until firm. Remove and
place on a floured work surface. Roll out to
5mm (¹⁄₂in) thickness. Cut out with a heart
cutter and place on the tray. Bake in the oven
for 15–20 minutes or until golden brown.

Remove from the oven and cool on a wire
rack, then store in an airtight container in a
cool place.

To make the icing, place the egg white
and icing sugar in an electric mixer and beat
until stiff. Add the lemon juice and beat until
smooth. Colour as required and decorate as
desired.

afternoon reception

The dishes chosen for this afternoon reception for 50 people provide an interesting mix of flavours and styles of food.

Rillettes of Salmon with Caviar and Crème Fraîche

A Selection of Sushi

Little Spoons of Lobster with Avocado

Heart-shaped Quesadillas with Smoked Chicken

Sesame-crusted Tuna with Mango and Chilli Salsa

Banana Leaf Cones filled with Noodle Salad

Chinese Duck Wrap

Parmesan Baskets filled with Butternut Squash Risotto

Toasted Bread Boxes filled with Creamed Wild Mushrooms

Crab Cakes with Corn Chowder Dip

Red Pepper and Ginger Soup Sip

Muffalata

Sandwiches

Heart Pavlovas

Passionfruit Heart Tartlets

Little Heart Fruit Tarts

Ginger Chocolate Box

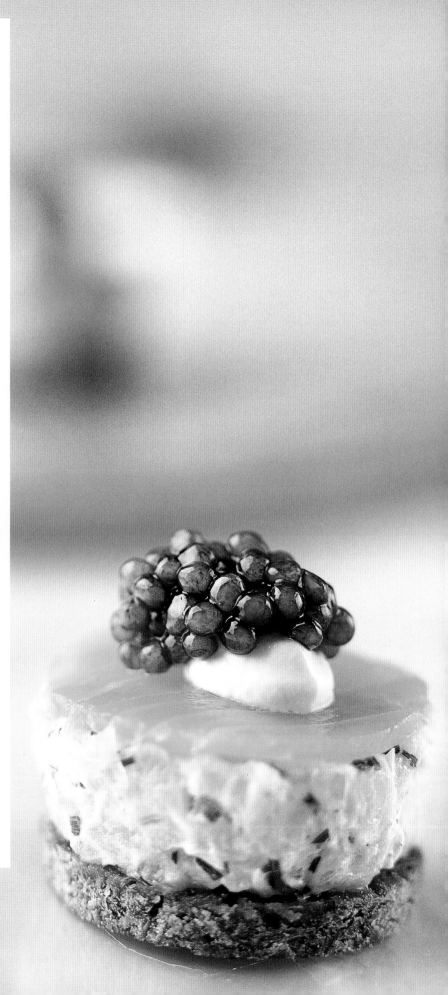

RILLETTES OF SALMON WITH CAVIAR AND CRÈME FRAÎCHE

FOR THE SALMON POACHING LIQUID:

1 leek, washed and sliced

1 onion, peeled and sliced

1 bay leaf

2 sprigs of thyme

10 whole black peppercorns

1 glass of white wine

2 litres (3 1/2 pints) fish stock or water

FOR THE RILLETTES:

500g (1lb 1oz) skinless salmon fillet

120g (4oz) gravlax, finely chopped

2 shallots, peeled and finely diced

2 tablespoons chives, finely chopped

2 tablespoons dill, chopped

Juice and zest of 1/2 lime

Juice of 1/2 lemon

3 tablespoons crème fraîche

Salt and freshly ground black pepper

FOR THE GARNISH AND BASE:

250g (8 1/2 oz) packet pumpernickel bread

500g (1lb 1oz) oak-smoked salmon, thinly sliced

4 tablespoons crème fraîche

120g (4oz) Sevruga caviar

Place all the ingredients for the poaching liquid in a large saucepan, season and bring to the boil. Place the salmon fillet in the pan, bring back to the boil, then remove the pan from the heat and leave to cool. Once cold, drain and flake the fish into a bowl.

Combine the rest of the ingredients apart from the crème fraîche with the salmon, mix well, season and fold in the crème fraîche. Once all the ingredients are combined, place the mixture into a piping bag with a 2.5cm (1in) nozzle, and pipe a long 'sausage' onto cling film. Roll up the cling film and twist the ends tightly. Repeat this until all the mixture is used. Place in the freezer.

Cut out 50 discs of pumpernickel bread with a 2.5cm (1in) cutter; repeat this with the smoked salmon. Place in separate airtight containers and refrigerate.

To serve, remove the salmon from the freezer and leave for 5 minutes. Lay out the pumpernickel bread on a serving plate and slice the salmon rillettes into 1.5cm (1/2in) slices, remove the cling film and place on the pumpernickel bread. Top with smoked salmon discs, a swirl of crème fraîche and caviar.

A SELECTION OF SUSHI

1kg (2lb 2oz) sushi rice

300ml (1/2 pint) seasoned sushi vinegar

200g (6 1/2 oz) very fresh fillet of salmon, skin and brown flesh removed

200g (6 1/2 oz) very fresh loin of tuna, skin removed

20 large Mediterranean prawns, shelled with the tail on

7 sheets of nori

60g (1oz) tube wasabi

120g (4oz) salmon roe (keta)

5 tablespoons white sesame seeds

5 tablespoons black sesame seeds

1 x 500g (1lb 1oz) lobster, cooked, shell removed and cut into strips

1 cucumber, deseeded and cut into strips the length of the nori sheets

1/2 daikon radish, cut into strips the length of the nori sheets

1 avocado, peeled and cut into strips the length of the nori sheets

juice of 1/2 lemon

600ml (1 pint) Kikkoman soy sauce

SPECIAL EQUIPMENT:

Japanese rice cooker

Fan (uchiwa)

Rice cooling tub

Wooden paddle

Bamboo rolling mats

Heavy chopping knives

(Left) Rillettes of Salmon. (Above) Sushi.

TO COOK THE RICE:

Place the rice into a fine sieve, wash well. Leave to drain, then wash again and leave for about 1 hour in a cool place. Place the washed rice into the cooker, pour over 1.3 litres (2 1/2 pints) water and cook to the packet instructions. When cooked, drain the rice and place in the cooling tub or on a large plastic tray. Toss the rice with the wooden paddle and add the seasoned vinegar, fanning the rice all the time (you will need someone else to help with this). The best way is to lift the rice with the paddle as you add the vinegar. When all the vinegar is absorbed, cover the rice with a damp cloth and leave in a cool place.

Take a clean plastic tray lined with cling film. With large teaspoons, make 60 quenelles with the rice (the remainder of the rice is for the sushi rolls). Place on the tray, cover and place in the fridge.

TO PREPARE THE FISH:

Cut the salmon and the tuna into rectangular blocks, and slice thinly to the width and length of the rice quenelles. Place on a tray, cover and place in the fridge. Cut the prawns along the underside, open out to a butterfly, leaving the tails on. Cover and place in the fridge. Cut 20 5mm (¹/₈ in) strips of nori. Place into an airtight container.

TO MAKE THE SUSHI:

Remove the rice quenelles and prepared fish from the fridge. Spread a little wasabi on the top of the rice. Top the rice with the fish. Place the prawns on the rice and place a strip of nori around the prawn.

TO MAKE THE SALMON ROE
SUSHI ROLLS:

When handling the rice, it is important to moisten your hands with sushi vinegar to prevent the rice sticking to you. Also have a clean cloth by your work area to clean your hands between each handling of the rice.

Lay a nori sheet on a bamboo rolling mat, rough side up. Spread the nori with the rice, leaving a 2cm (¹/₂in) edge on the far side. Roll the mat away from you, pressing the rice to keep it firm. Wet the far edge of the nori with water, so on the final roll the nori will stick together. Repeat with another 2 sheets of nori. Cut each roll into 10 even pieces, place a dot of wasabi on the top, and top with the salmon roe.

TO MAKE THE INSIDE OUT ROLLS:

Cover the bamboo rolling mat with cling film. Place a nori sheet on top. Spread the nori with the seasoned rice. Sprinkle with sesame seeds, covering the rice. Turn the sheet over and spread a little wasabi down the centre of the nori side, then place the lobster, cucumber, radish and avocado down the centre. Squeeze over the lemon juice. Make the roll by holding the base of the mat and pressing the ingredients with your fingers, roll up tightly, then gently mould into a square. Repeat with another 2 nori sheets and cut each roll into 10 even pieces.

TO SERVE THE SUSHI:

Arrange the sushi on a black lacquer tray. Pour a little soy sauce into dipping bowls and serve.

LITTLE SPOONS OF LOBSTER WITH AVOCADO

3 x 500g (1lb 1oz) lobsters, poached and
cooled, all the meat removed
10 red cherry tomatoes
1 Hass avocado
1 lime, halved
1 large bunch of coriander leaves, washed and
dried
2 chillies, deseeded and cut into 3cm (1¹/₂ in)
strips
50 crayfish, poached and peeled
150ml (¹/₄ pint) good quality lemon olive oil
Sea salt and freshly ground black pepper

Cut the lobster meat into 5mm ($^1/_8$in) round slices. Using a sharp serrated knife, cut each cherry tomato into 5 slices. Cut the avocado in half, peel and cut into 5 segments lengthways and slice each segment into 20. Squeeze the juice of the lime over the avocado, season.

To serve, lay out the teaspoons. Layer the avocado, lobster, cherry tomato, coriander and chilli strips, seasoning each layer. Top with the crayfish and drizzle with a little lemon olive oil and serve.

HEART-SHAPED QUESADILLAS WITH SMOKED CHICKEN

FOR THE SALSA:
6 large plum tomatoes, blanched, peeled, deseeded and finely diced
1 small red onion, peeled and finely diced
1 red chilli, deseeded and finely diced
$^1/_2$ cup chopped coriander, washed and dried
Juice of 2 limes
2 tablespoons extra virgin olive oil

3 x 30cm (12in) flour tortillas
150ml (5fl oz) crème fraîche
2 smoked chicken breasts, thinly sliced and cut into strips
3 large pickled walnuts, sliced
60g (2oz) Manchego cheese, cut into small dice
Coriander leaves, to garnish
Sea salt and finely ground black pepper

To make the salsa, place all the ingredients into a bowl, season, cover and place in the fridge.

To make the quesadillas, preheat a deep-fat fryer. Cut the tortillas into hearts using a small heart-shaped cookie cutter. Deep-fry

(Left) Little Spoons of Lobster with Avocado.

until golden, drain on absorbent paper. When cold, layer in an airtight box. Store in a cool place.

To serve, place the hearts on a work surface. Pipe a little crème fraîche into the centre of each heart, spread it slightly but do not go over the edges. Place a few strips of chicken on each heart, followed by the walnuts and cheese. Season, top with the salsa, garnish with the coriander and serve.

SESAME-CRUSTED TUNA WITH MANGO AND CHILLI SALSA

3 large free-range egg yolks
3 tablespoons runny honey
6 tablespoons black sesame seeds
6 tablespoons white toasted sesame seeds
800g (1lb 10oz) loin of tuna cut into squares, 2.5 x 2.5cm (1 x 1in)
Unscented vegetable oil
Sea salt and freshly ground black pepper

For the salsa:
1 large ripe mango, peeled and finely diced
1 red chilli, deseeded and finely diced
1 small red onion, peeled and finely diced
1 clove garlic, peeled and finely diced
Juice of 1 large lime
2 tablespoons fish sauce
2 tablespoons coriander, washed, dried and chopped

Whisk the egg yolks in a bowl with the honey. Place the sesame seeds into a bowl and season well. Coat the tuna in the egg and honey, then in the sesame seeds, coating well. Heat a large sauté pan with a little oil. Seal the tuna on each side for 20 seconds, remove and leave to cool. When cold, place in an airtight container in the fridge.

To make the salsa, place all the ingredients into a bowl, mix well, pour into a container, cover and place in the fridge.

To serve, remove all the ingredients from the fridge. Cut the tuna into 2cm ($^1/_2$in) thick slices, top with the salsa and serve.

BANANA LEAF CONES FILLED WITH NOODLE SALAD

TO MAKE THE CONES:
6 whole banana leaves

FOR THE NOODLE SALAD:
Vegetable oil
1kg (2lb 2oz) thin fresh egg noodles
4 cloves garlic, peeled and finely chopped
1 walnut-sized piece of ginger, finely chopped
500g (1lb 1oz) carrots, peeled, sliced on a mandolin and cut into triangles
500g (1lb 1oz) spring onions, finely sliced
500g (1lb 1oz) shiitake mushrooms, finely sliced
10 red peppers, quartered, deseeded and cut into diamonds
500g (1lb 1oz) mangetout, cut into triangles
1 cup coriander leaves, washed and dried

FOR THE DRESSING:
450ml ($^3/_4$ pint) light soy sauce
3 tablespoons sweet chilli sauce
Juice of 3 limes
3 tablespoons caster sugar
3 tablespoons peanut oil

FOR THE GARNISH:
2 tablespoons black sesame seeds
2 tablespoons white sesame seeds

Place a large dinner plate approximately 25cm (10in) across on the banana leaves, cut out 25 circles the size of the plate, cut each circle in half. Wrap to create a cone and staple to secure.

Heat a large pan of water, add a little salt and vegetable oil and bring to the boil. Take a large container of ice-cold water and keep to

CHINESE DUCK WRAP

FOR THE MARINADE:

300ml (½ pint) light soy sauce

3 tablespoons dry sherry

2 tablespoons yellow bean paste

2 tablespoons caster sugar

4 star anise

2 teaspoons five-spice powder

1 walnut-sized piece of fresh ginger, peeled and finely grated

3 cloves garlic, peeled and crushed

600ml (1 pint) dark chicken stock

Vegetable oil

3 duck breasts

FOR THE WRAP:

5 x 30cm (12in) spinach tortillas

500g (1lb 1oz) sour cream

½ cucumber, peeled, deseeded and finely sliced

5 spring onions, washed, dried and cut into fine strips

2 baby gem lettuces, washed, dried and finely shredded

200g (6½oz) plum sauce

Place all the ingredients for the marinade into a large saucepan. Bring to the boil, then turn down to a simmer for approximately 10 minutes to infuse the flavours. Meanwhile, heat a sauté pan with a little oil and seal the duck breasts until golden all sides. Add the duck to the marinade, return to the boil, remove from the heat, and leave to cool. When cold, put the duck and marinade in an airtight container, and place this in the fridge.

To make the wraps, remove the duck breasts from the marinade and pat dry. Slice each duck breast into 8 strips. Place the tortillas on a work surface, spread evenly with the sour cream, followed by the cucumber, spring onions and lettuce. Lay the strips of duck on top and drizzle with plum sauce. Roll up the wraps and seal with cling film. Chill until ready to serve, then cut each wrap into ten at an angle.

one side. Cook the egg noodles in the boiling water for 4–5 minutes, then drain in a colander and drop into the ice-cold water to refresh. Once cold, drain and place into a large bowl, drizzle with a little vegetable oil and toss to prevent the noodles sticking.

Heat a wok, add a little vegetable oil, add the garlic and ginger and sauté the vegetables. Place in a large bowl and mix in the noodles. Leave to cool, then cover and place in the fridge.

To make the dressing, put the soy sauce, sweet chilli sauce, lime juice and sugar in a bowl. Mix well until the sugar is dissolved. Stir

(Above) Banana Leaf Cones filled with Noodle Salad. (Right) Parmesan Baskets filled with Butternut Squash Risotto.

in peanut oil; pour into a container with a lid and place in the fridge.

To serve, dress the noodles, add the coriander and mix well. Place the banana cones in ice-cream stands or baskets. Fill with the noodles and sprinkle with a few sesame seeds. Serve with a fork.

PARMESAN BASKETS FILLED WITH BUTTERNUT SQUASH RISOTTO

FOR THE PARMESAN BASKETS:
500g (1lb 1oz) grated Padano Parmesan
4 wine corks

FOR THE RISOTTO:
1 litre (1^1/2 pints) vegetable stock
Extra virgin olive oil
*1 medium butternut squash, peeled and finely
  diced*
90g (3oz) unsalted butter
3 shallots, peeled and finely chopped
2 cloves garlic, peeled and finely chopped
250g (8^1/2 oz) Arborio rice
1 glass of dry white wine
60g (2oz) Reggiano Parmesan, grated
*^{1}/2 cup flat leaf parsley, washed, dried and
  chopped*
Sea salt and finely ground black pepper

TO MAKE THE BASKETS:
Preheat the oven to 180°C/350°F/gas mark 4. Do not put the oven on a fan cycle or the Parmesan will blow over the oven. Line a baking tray with nonstick baking paper or a silicon baking mat. Place a 5cm (2in) round cutter on the prepared baking tray, place a heaped teaspoon of the grated Parmesan inside the cutter, remove the cutter and repeat this five times. Place in the oven for about 5 minutes until the cheese is bubbling and golden. Remove and while the discs are still hot, mould over the corks to form a basket. You will have to work quickly while the cheese is hot. Repeat until all the Parmesan is used. When cold, place in an airtight container in a cool place. These can be made a day in advance.

TO MAKE THE RISOTTO:
Place the vegetable stock in a saucepan and bring to the boil, then reduce to a gentle simmer. Meanwhile, heat a large sauté pan with a little olive oil. When the oil begins to smoke, add the squash and sauté until golden and soft. Season and place to one side. In a saucepan, melt 30g (1oz) of the butter, add the shallots and cook until transparent, then add the garlic and cook but do not brown, add the rice, and coat each grain, add the wine, reduce by three-quarters, then slowly add the stock. When the rice has absorbed all the stock and is cooked through but still al dente, add the Parmesan, the remaining butter, parsley and squash, reserving some to garnish the tops of the baskets.

To serve, place the Parmesan baskets on a serving tray, fill with the risotto and garnish with the reserved squash.

TOASTED BREAD BOXES FILLED WITH CREAMED WILD MUSHROOMS

FOR THE BOXES:
*1 x 800g (1lb 10oz) white tin loaf, unsliced but
  with all crusts removed*
300ml (^{1}/2 pint) extra virgin olive oil

FOR THE FILLING:
3 shallots, peeled and finely chopped
2 cloves garlic, peeled and finely chopped
2 teaspoons soft thyme
250g (8^1/2 oz) mixed wild mushrooms, brushed
150ml (5fl oz) medium Madeira
450ml (^{3}/4 pint) double cream
*^{1}/2 cup flat-leaf parsley, washed, dried and
  chopped*
Sea salt and finely ground black pepper

TO MAKE THE BOXES:
Preheat the oven to 200°C/400°F/gas mark 6. Line a baking tray with nonstick baking paper or a silicon baking mat. Using a sharp bread knife, cut the loaf into 2.5cm (1in) cubes. Place the cubes in a bowl and pour over the olive oil and toss well until all the cubes are covered.

Season. Place on the baking tray in the oven and bake for 6–10 minutes until golden. Cut out a hole 1.5cm ($^1/_2$in) square in the centre of each cube. Place in an airtight box and store in a cool place.

TO MAKE THE FILLING:

Heat a little olive oil in a large frying pan and sauté the shallots, but do not brown. Add the garlic and thyme and cook for a further 2 minutes, but do not allow to brown. Add the wild mushrooms and sauté for approximately 5 minutes. Add the Madeira, reduce until sticky; add the double cream, reduce by half or until thick. Season. Remove from the heat, leave to cool; stir in the parsley. Cover and place in an airtight container in the fridge.

TO SERVE:

Preheat the oven to 180°C/350°F/gas mark 4. Prepare a baking tray with nonstick paper or a silicon baking mat. Place the bread boxes on the tray, fill with the mixture and heat for approximately 5 minutes.

CRAB CAKES WITH CORN CHOWDER DIP

FOR THE CRAB CAKES:

300ml ($^1/_2$ pint) white fish stock
60g (2oz) unsalted butter
60g (2oz) plain flour
500g (1lb 1oz) white crab meat, all shell removed
90g (3oz) capers, chopped
5 spring onions, washed, dried and finely chopped
3 large free-range eggs, hard boiled and finely chopped
$^1/_2$ cup flat leaf parsley, washed, dried and finely chopped
Sea salt and finely ground black pepper

FOR THE CHOWDER DIP:

450ml ($^3/_4$ pint) light chicken stock

450ml ($^3/_4$ pint) milk
3 corn cobs, cut into three
150ml ($^1/_4$ pint) double cream
60g (2oz) soft unsalted butter
30g (1oz) plain flour
2 tablespoons chives, chopped
A good pinch of cayenne pepper

TO COAT THE CRAB CAKES:

250g ($8^1/_2$oz) plain flour, seasoned
4 free-range eggs, beaten
250g ($8^1/_2$oz) fine breadcrumbs

Line a 42 x 30 x 1.5cm ($16^1/_2$ x 12 x $^1/_2$in) baking tray with nonstick baking paper. Bring the fish stock to the boil in a saucepan. In another saucepan make a roux with the butter and flour and cook for about 5 minutes over a low heat, but do not allow to colour. Leave to cool for about 5 minutes, return to a medium heat and slowly add the fish stock, whisking all the time. When thick, cook for about 5 minutes, stirring all the time; do not allow to stick or burn. Remove from the heat, leave to cool for about 15 minutes, then add the crab, capers, onions, eggs, parsley and pepper. Stir well and season. Spoon onto the prepared tray and smooth with a palette knife to an even thickness. When cool, cover and place in the freezer till required.

TO MAKE THE DIPPING SAUCE:

Place the stock, milk and corn in a saucepan, bring to the boil, cover and simmer for about 30 minutes. Remove the corn and cut the corn kernels from the cob. Return the kernels to the saucepan, add the cream and return to the boil. When boiling, cover and reduce to a simmer. Make a beurre manié by mixing the soft butter and flour together until smooth. Slowly whisk the beurre manié into the chowder, then cook over a low heat for about 10 minutes. Remove from the heat, and leave to cool. When cold, purée the chowder. Cover and refrigerate.

TO COAT THE CRAB CAKES:

Remove the crab mixture from the freezer, cut into small cakes with a 4cm ($1^1/_2$in) round cutter. Place the flour, egg and breadcrumbs into three separate bowls. Take the crab cakes; roll first in the flour, then in the eggs and breadcrumbs and place on a clean baking tray.

TO COOK AND SERVE THE CRAB CAKES:

Pour the corn chowder into a saucepan and warm. Heat a deep-fat fryer to a temperature of 180°C/350°F. Deep-fry a few cakes at a time, then place on a tray lined with absorbent paper in the oven, leaving the door open slightly. Pour the chowder into a dipping bowl and arrange the crab cakes on a serving dish.

RED PEPPER AND GINGER SOUP SIP

This can be served hot or cold in shot glasses.

Extra virgin olive oil
4 shallots, peeled and finely sliced
90g (3oz) fresh ginger, peeled and finely chopped
3 cloves garlic, peeled and finely chopped

(Below) Muffalata. (Right) Sandwiches.

5 red peppers, quartered, deseeded, roasted
and peeled
4 plum tomatoes, peeled and chopped.
1.6 litres (2¹/₂ pints) vegetable stock
300ml (¹/₂ pint) double cream
¹/₂ cup coriander, washed, dried and chopped
Salt and finely ground black pepper

Heat a little olive oil in a saucepan, add the
shallots and cook until transparent. Add the
ginger and garlic, cook for about 2 minutes but
do not allow to brown. Add the peppers,
tomatoes and stock, season and cook slowly
for 1 hour. Add the cream and stir well. Check
the seasoning. Remove from the heat and cool.
When cold, purée and pass through a fine
sieve. Cover and refrigerate.

To serve, warm the soup in a saucepan.
Add the chopped coriander, stir well, pour into
a jug, and then into the shot glasses.

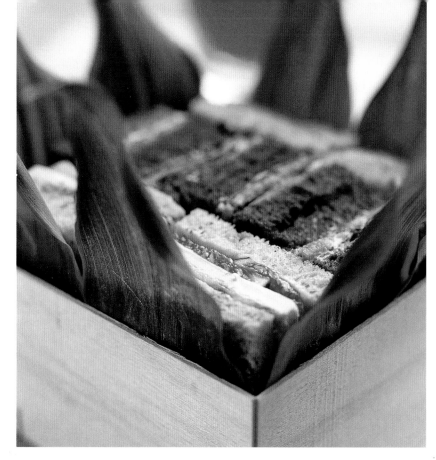

MUFFALATA

4 French sticks 60cm (24in) long
24 slices salami, cut in half
2 aubergines, thinly sliced and chargrilled
4 medium courgettes, thinly sliced and
chargrilled
8 red peppers, roasted, cut into quarters,
deseeded and peeled
1.4kg (2lb 9oz) Taleggio cheese, rind removed
and sliced into 5mm (¹/₈in) thickness
48 basil leaves
300ml (¹/₂ pint) extra virgin olive oil
Sea salt and freshly ground black pepper

Cut the French sticks in half lengthways.
Evenly layer with all the ingredients, seasoning
between layers. (Do not allow any of the
ingredients to fall over the edges.) Drizzle with
olive oil, wrap tightly in cling film, press down
with heavy weights and place in the fridge for
at least 12 hours. To serve, remove the cling
film, slice off the ends and cut into bite-sized
pieces.

SANDWICHES

SALT BEEF AND ROCKET

40 slices dark rye bread, crusts removed
250g (8¹/₂oz) unsalted butter
450ml (³/₄ pint) good quality mayonnaise
4 tablespoons grain mustard
500g (1lb 1oz) cooked salt beef, sliced
200g (6¹/₂oz) wild rocket
Sea salt and freshly ground black pepper

Spread the bread with butter, mayonnaise and
grain mustard. Season and layer with the beef
and rocket. Cut into squares or hearts and
serve.

PRAWN WITH AVOCADO
MAYONNAISE

450ml (³/₄ pint) good quality mayonnaise
2 large Hass avocados
Zest and juice of 2 lemons
40 slices granary bread, crusts removed
250g (8³/₄oz) unsalted butter
80 large Mediterranean prawns, peeled and
sliced lengthways
¹/₂ cup chives, chopped
Sea salt and freshly ground black pepper

Place the mayonnaise in a bowl. Purée the
avocados with the lemon zest and juice. Mix
the purée with the mayonnaise and season.
Cover and place in the fridge until ready for
use. Spread the bread with the butter, followed
by the avocado mayonnaise. Layer the prawns,
season and sprinkle with the chopped chives.
Cut into squares or hearts and serve.

GOAT'S CHEESE AND FIG
WITH ROASTED COURGETTES

20 slices walnut bread, crusts removed
250g (8¹/₂oz) unsalted butter
5 courgettes, sliced lengthways and chargrilled
10 large figs, sliced lengthways

800g (1lb 10oz) goat's cheese, sliced
Sea salt and freshly ground black pepper

Lay the bread on a chopping board and spread with the butter. Layer the courgettes, figs and goat's cheese, season and cut into squares or hearts to serve.

HEART PAVLOVAS

7 free-range egg whites
500g (1lb 1oz) icing sugar

FOR THE FILLING:
300ml (¹/₂ pint) double cream
30g (1oz) icing sugar
1 vanilla pod
25 blackberries
25 raspberries
50 blueberries
50 redcurrants

Line a baking tray with nonstick baking paper. In an electric mixer whisk the egg whites to stiff peaks, add the icing sugar and whisk for 15 minutes. Place the mixture into a piping bag. Secure the edges of the paper to the tray with a little of the mixture. Pipe into 50 small hearts. Leave overnight on a pilot light (or the lowest setting of an electric oven) in the oven to dry. Remove from the oven. When cold, store in an airtight container in a cool place.

To serve, whip the cream, icing sugar and vanilla together in a bowl until thick. Cut the blackberries and raspberries in half. Fill the meringues with the cream, garnish the tops with half a raspberry, half a blackberry, one blueberry and one redcurrant.

(Right) clockwise from top left:
Passionfruit Heart Tartlets,
Ginger Chocolates, Heart Pavolvas
and Little Heart Fruit Tarts.

PASSIONFRUIT HEART TARTLETS

FOR THE CURD:
250g (8¹/₂ oz) unsalted butter, cubed
250g (8¹/₂ oz) caster sugar
20 large passionfruit, strained to make 250ml
(8¹/₂ fl oz) purée
10 large free-range eggs, beaten

FOR THE PASTRY:
375g (12¹/₂ oz) unsalted butter
250g (8¹/₂ oz) icing sugar
5 large free-range egg yolks
625g (1lb 5oz) plain flour
12g (4oz) ground almonds

FOR THE TOPPING:
10 passionfruit
4 leaves gelatine, soaked in water

SPECIAL EQUIPMENT:
50 small heart moulds

TO MAKE THE CURD:
Place the butter and sugar in a heavy-bottomed saucepan and slowly bring to the boil, whisking all the time until smooth. Lower the heat, add the purée and whisk in the eggs. Do not allow the mixture to boil or the eggs will curdle. Continue cooking until thick. Remove from the heat. Pour into a metal bowl to cool. Place a damp piece of greaseproof paper on top to prevent a skin forming. When cold, cover and place in the fridge.

TO MAKE THE PASTRY:
Cream the butter and icing sugar together until light. Beat in the yolks one at a time, then add the flour and ground almonds. Mix to a dough. Turn onto a floured work surface and knead until smooth. Wrap in cling film and leave in the fridge for about 1 hour.

Remove from the fridge. Roll out thinly and line the moulds. Line the pastry with greaseproof paper and place ceramic baking beans on top. Return to the fridge for about 30 minutes.

Preheat the oven to 150°C/300°F/gas mark 2. Bake for 15 minutes or until golden brown. Remove from the oven. Leave to cool, then remove the pastry from the moulds and store in a cool place.

TO SERVE:
Scoop out the passionfruit flesh into a saucepan. Squeeze out any excess water from the gelatine and add the gelatine leaves to the passionfruit. Slowly melt the gelatine into the passionfruit, stirring well. Remove from the heat. Lay the tartlets out on a tray. Place the curd in a piping bag and fill the tarts. Carefully glaze the tops of the tarts with passionfruit and serve.

LITTLE HEART FRUIT TARTS

FOR THE PASTRY:
375g (12¹/₂ oz) unsalted butter
250g (8¹/₂ oz) icing sugar
5 large free-range egg yolks
625g (1lb 5oz) plain flour
125g (4¹/₂ oz) ground almonds

FOR THE FILLING:
300ml (¹/₂ pint) double cream
60g (2oz) icing sugar

FOR THE TOPPING:
200 raspberries
Icing sugar

TO MAKE THE PASTRY:
Cream the butter and icing sugar together until light. Beat in the yolks one at a time, then add flour and ground almonds. Mix to a dough. Turn onto a floured work surface and knead until smooth. Wrap in cling film and place in the fridge for about 1 hour. Remove from the fridge. Roll out thinly and line the moulds. Line the pastry with greaseproof paper and place ceramic baking beans on top. Return to the fridge for about 30 minutes.

Preheat the oven to 150°C/300°F/gas mark 2. Bake for 15 minutes or until golden brown. Remove from the oven. Leave to cool, then remove the pastry from the moulds and store in a cool place.

TO SERVE:
Place the tarts on a tray. Lightly whip the cream with the icing sugar until it just holds its shape. Place into a piping bag and pipe the cream into the cases. Top with the raspberries and dust with icing sugar.

GINGER CHOCOLATE BOX

250g (8¹/₂ oz) sugar
10 large free-range egg yolks
5 leaves gelatine, soaked in cold water
5 teaspoons ginger cordial
1.5 litres (2 pints) double cream, lightly
whipped
60g (2oz) stem ginger, grated
500g (1lb 1oz) bitter chocolate, melted
Edible gold leaf

Line a 30 x 42 x 3cm (12 x 16¹/₂ x 1¹/₂ in) baking tray with cling film. Place the sugar in a heavy-bottomed saucepan and cover with water. Boil the sugar to 121°C/275°F. Whisk the yolks until fluffy and pour over the boiling sugar. Continue to whisk until cold. Squeeze the water from the gelatine, place the gelatine in a saucepan with the ginger cordial and dissolve over a low heat. Remove from the heat and fold into the egg mix. Lastly, fold in the cream and ginger. Pour into the tray and leave to set in the fridge. When set, cut into 3cm (1¹/₂ in) squares and freeze. To serve, dip the squares into melted chocolate. Once set, decorate the tops with a little gold leaf.

buffet of mediterranean flavours

This colourful buffet menu for 20 people has been inspired by the flavours of the Mediterranean. The creations have proved very popular and there are dishes here that appeal to everyone.

(Below) A selection of antipasti.

CHARGRILLED VEGETABLE STACK

*2kg (4¹/₂ lb) courgettes, cut lengthways into
  5cm (2in) wide strips*
*2kg (4¹/₂ lb) aubergines, cut lengthways into
  7.5cm (3in) wide strips*
Olive oil
25 red peppers, halved, roasted and peeled
120g (4oz) Reggiano Parmesan, grated
5 tablespoons pesto sauce
Sea salt and freshly ground black pepper

Preheat the oven to 200°C/400°F/gas mark 6.
Line a 40 x 25 x 6cm (16 x 10 x 2¹/₂in) baking
tray with baking parchment. Heat a chargrill
plate. Brush the courgettes and aubergines
with olive oil and season. Chargrill until bar
marks are visible. Place half the peppers
presentation open side up on the lined tray,
sprinkle with Parmesan and layer with half
the courgettes. Spread with pesto and
sprinkle with more Parmesan. Repeat with
the aubergine, followed by more red pepper,
courgette and aubergine layers, ending
with red pepper on the top. Season between
each layer. Cover with foil and bake in the
preheated oven for approximately 15 minutes.
Remove from the oven, leave to cool and
refrigerate. To serve, place on a board and
cut into small squares, then transfer to a
serving plate.

GRILLED ASPARAGUS WITH PORTOBELLO MUSHROOMS

12 Portobello mushrooms
Olive oil
180 spears of asparagus, blanched, refreshed
and cut into 10cm (4in) lengths
4 cloves garlic, peeled and finely sliced
3 shallots, peeled and finely sliced
Sea salt and freshly ground black pepper

Heat a chargrill plate, brush the mushrooms with olive oil, season and chargrill on both sides for approximately 5 minutes. Place on a baking tray and set aside. Repeat with the asparagus and place on the tray with the mushrooms. Then sprinkle with garlic and shallots and drizzle with olive oil. Cover and refrigerate.

GRILLED BABY AUBERGINES WITH RED ONION JAM

10 baby aubergines
Olive oil
5 tablespoons red onion jam
Sea salt and freshly ground black pepper

Heat a chargrill plate. Halve the aubergines lengthways, score the flat side with a knife, brush with olive oil, season and cook for approximately 5 minutes until soft. Remove and leave to cool. When cold, cover and refrigerate. Serve topped with red onion jam.

BABY PEPPERS FILLED WITH CAPONATA

10 baby red peppers
10 baby green peppers
Olive oil
30g (1oz) red onions, peeled and finely diced
30g (1oz) courgettes, finely diced
30g (1oz) aubergine, finely diced
30g (1oz) fennel, finely diced
30g (1oz) red pepper, finely diced
2 cloves garlic, puréed
1/2 cup flat-leaf parsley
5 plum tomatoes, peeled, deseeded and finely
diced
3 tablespoons good balsamic vinegar
Sea salt and freshly ground black pepper

Preheat the oven to 200°C/400°F/gas mark 6. Remove the tops of the baby peppers, discard the seeds, place in a bowl and dress lightly with olive oil; season. Place on a baking tray and bake in the oven for approximately 8 minutes until soft and blistered. Remove and leave to cool.

Heat a large sauté pan and individually sauté the vegetables except the tomatoes, adding the garlic and seasoning. Remove from the heat and place in a bowl. When cold, add the parsley, tomatoes and balsamic vinegar, mix well and fill peppers. Cover and put in the fridge.

GRILLED FIGS AND BABY MOZZARELLA SALAD WITH BASIL

1kg (2¼ lb) baby Mozzarella balls
300ml (1/2 pint) olive oil
3 shallots, peeled and finely sliced
2 cloves garlic, peeled and finely sliced
10 black figs, cut into quarters
60g (2oz) caster sugar
1 cup green basil leaves
1 cup purple basil leaves
Salt and freshly ground black pepper

Place the baby Mozzarella in a large bowl, pour in the olive oil, add the shallots and garlic and set aside. Heat a large frying pan, dip the figs in sugar and pan-fry until caramelised. Arrange the Mozzarella, figs and basil leaves on a serving dish, season and drizzle with the marinade.

(Above) Goat's Cheese, Lemon and Herb Risotto served in Squash with Parmesan Crisps.

GOAT'S CHEESE, LEMON AND HERB RISOTTO

150ml (6 fl oz) olive oil
6 cloves garlic, unpeeled
2.3 litres (4 pints) vegetable stock
120g (4oz) unsalted butter
5 shallots, peeled and finely diced
3 cloves garlic, puréed
2 tablespoons soft thyme leaves
1kg (2lb 2oz) Arborio rice
1 glass of dry white wine
120g (4oz) unsalted butter
Juice and zest of 3 lemons
120g (4oz) grated Parmesan
1kg (2lb 2oz) of goat's cheese such as
Golden Cross
1 cup flat-leaf parsley
2 squash, hollowed
Sea salt and freshly ground black pepper

In a saucepan heat the olive oil. When it is hot, add the whole garlic cloves and slowly cook for about 30 minutes. It should be soft, not brown. Remove from the heat, leave to one side in the pan. In a large pot bring the stock to the boil. Heat a large pan with the butter; when foaming, add the shallots and the garlic and sauté for about 5 minutes; do not colour. Add the thyme and rice; coat the rice grains with the butter. Add the white wine and slowly add the stock a ladleful at a time, stirring all the time. After 20 minutes the rice should be cooked through but still al dente. Stir in the butter, juice and zest of lemons, Parmesan, goat's cheese and parsley. Check consistency; if too thick add a little boiling water. Season. Pour into the squashes and garnish with the whole garlic cloves and parmesan crisps.

PARMESAN CRISPS

MAKES 30 ROUNDS

Experiment with various shapes and sizes. They also make tasty snacks with cocktails. Store in an airtight container, layered with greaseproof paper. They are fragile so take care. I usually make a few extras to allow for breakages.

300g (11oz) Parmesan cheese

Preheat oven to 190°C/375°F/gas mark 5. Grate the Parmesan with a fine grater. Line a baking tray with a sheet of greaseproof paper or (for better results) a silicon mat. Place a 10cm (4in) ring cutter onto the greaseproof paper or a silicon mat; evenly sprinkle grated Parmesan inside the cutter. Remove mould and bake for 4 minutes. When the crisps are ready they should be slightly bubbling and golden. Remove tray from oven. Using a palette knife place the discs on a wire cooling rack, cool and store.

TUSCAN CHICKEN

2 litres (3$^{1}/_{2}$ pints) white chicken stock
4 teaspoons saffron
20 skinless chicken breasts
3 fennel bulbs, cut into medium-sized pieces
2kg (4$^{1}/_{2}$ lb) medium-sized potatoes, peeled with a knife
6 tablespoons cornflour, dissolved in a little cold water
4 large artichokes, cut into medium-sized pieces
5 red peppers, roasted and cut into strips
10 plum tomatoes, peeled, quartered and deseeded
$^{1}/_{2}$ cup flat-leaf parsley, chopped

Bring the stock to the boil in a large saucepan, then turn down to a simmer. Add 3 teaspoons of the saffron and the chicken breasts and poach for about 10 minutes until chicken is cooked. Remove the chicken from the saucepan, bring the stock back to the boil, add the fennel and cook for about 5 minutes. Remove and set aside. Place the potatoes in the saucepan with salt and the remaining saffron and cook for about 15 minutes. Drain (reserving the stock) and set aside.

Cut the chicken into cubes, bring the stock back to the boil, whisk in the cornflour and cook for about 5 minutes. Add the chicken, fennel, potatoes, artichokes and red peppers. When hot, add the tomatoes and parsley and ladle into a warm dish to serve.

HERB-CRUSTED TUNA WITH SHAVED FENNEL SALAD AND RED PEPPER AÏOLI

Olive oil
300ml (11fl oz) runny honey
3 tablespoons Dijon mustard
4 free-range egg yolks
2.5kg (5$^{1}/_{2}$ lb) tuna loin, skin removed
2 cups parsley, chopped
1 cup marjoram, chopped
1 cup dill, chopped
$^{1}/_{2}$ cup flat leaf parsley
Sea salt and freshly ground black pepper

FOR THE SALAD:
6 fennel bulbs
4 shallots, peeled and finely sliced
1 cup dill

(Left) Grilled Figs and Baby Mozzarella Salad with Basil.

FOR THE DRESSING:

Juice and zest of 3 lemons

2 cloves garlic, peeled and sliced

300ml (11fl oz) olive oil

FOR THE RED PEPPER AÏOLI:

6 red peppers, roasted and peeled

3 cloves garlic, peeled and puréed

Juice of 2 lemons

900ml (1 1/2 pints) mayonnaise

Sea salt and freshly ground black pepper

Preheat the oven to 200°C/400°F/gas mark 6. Pour some olive oil into a roasting tray to a depth of about 2mm (1/8 in). Place in the oven and heat for approximately 10 minutes. In a bowl mix the honey, mustard and egg yolks; season the tuna with salt and pepper, roll in the honey mix, then roll in the mixed herbs. Place the tuna in the roasting tray. Bake for approximately 10–15 minutes, remove and cool.

To make the aïoli, finely dice one of the red peppers and place in a bowl. Place the remaining peppers, garlic and lemon juice in a food processor and blend until smooth; add the mayonnaise. Blend again, ensuring all the ingredients are mixed well. Pour into a bowl and mix with the diced pepper. Season and pour into a serving bowl.

Cut the fennel in half lengthways and thinly shave on a mandolin. Place in a bowl, add the shallots and dill. When ready to serve, add the juice and zest of the lemons, sliced garlic, olive oil and season with salt and pepper and arrange on a serving dish. Slice the tuna into thin steaks, layer over the fennel salad and serve with red pepper aïoli.

INDIVIDUAL PANETTONE

FILLS 12 DARIOLE MOULDS SIZE 5 X 5.5CM (2 X 2 1/2 IN)

300g (10oz) strong flour

1 teaspoon salt

1 tablespoon sugar

2 teaspoons yeast

75ml (3fl oz) milk

2 free-range eggs

1 free-range egg yolk

90g (3oz) butter, cubed

30g (1oz) sultanas

30g (1oz) candied peel

Butter, for greasing

Mix the flour, salt and sugar together. Dissolve the yeast in the milk and combine with the eggs and egg yolk. Stir into the flour and mix until smooth. Pour into the bowl of an electric mixer and with the mixer on a slow speed, add the butter cube by cube, then add the sultanas and mixed peel. Transfer the dough to a clean bowl, cover with cling film and leave in a warm place to prove for about 1 hour or until doubled in size.

Turn the dough out onto a floured surface and knead until smooth. Divide into 12 even-sized pieces. Roll into balls and place into greased dariole moulds. Leave in a warm place to prove for 30–40 minutes or until doubled in size. Brush the tops with a little beaten egg and bake at 180°C/350°F/gas mark 4 for 15–20 minutes or until well risen and golden brown. Remove from the oven and demould while still warm. Once cold, wrap in brown paper collars and tie with a raffia bow.

LEMON POTS

FILLS 6 TEA GLASSES EACH HOLDING 100ML (4FL OZ)

600ml (1 pint) double cream

120g (4oz) caster sugar

Juice of 2 lemons

Redcurrants, to garnish

Bring the cream and sugar to the boil in a saucepan. Add the lemon juice and pass through a fine sieve or chinois. Leave to cool slightly then fill the tea glasses and leave in the fridge to set. Garnish the tops with a strand of 3–5 redcurrants

CRÈME BRÛLÉE

FILLS 6 100ML (4FL OZ) TEA GLASSES.

600ml (1 pint) double cream

1 vanilla pod, split in half

2 free-range eggs

5 free-range egg yolks

60g (2oz) caster sugar

FOR THE CRAQUELIN:

60g (2oz) caster sugar

15g (1/2 oz) flaked almonds

Boil the double cream and vanilla pod together in a pan. Whisk the eggs, egg yolks and caster sugar together until smooth, then pour on the boiling cream and whisk until combined. Continue to whisk over a pan of boiling water until the mixture thickens (this should take about 5–10 minutes). Remove from the heat and pass through a fine sieve or chinois, then fill the glasses and leave in the fridge to set.

To make the craquelin, boil the sugar to a light caramel and pour onto a silicon baking mat or sheet of baking parchment. Sprinkle with the almonds and leave until cool. Blitz in a food processor until fine. Sprinkle evenly onto a greased tray and return to the oven at 180°C/ 350°F/gas mark 4 until fully melted and golden brown. Remove from the oven and leave to cool slightly, then cut into triangles and remove from the tray while still warm. Stick into the tops of the brûlée just before serving.

BITTER CHOCOLATE MOUSSE

FILLS 6 100ML (4FL OZ) TEA GLASSES

30g (1oz) glucose

120g (4oz) bitter chocolate

1 leaf gelatine

200ml (1/3 pint) double cream, whipped

Chocolate pieces, to garnish

Dissolve the glucose in a pan with 30ml (1fl oz) water. Melt the chocolate in a bowl over a pan of hot water. Soak the gelatine in a little cold water and dissolve in the glucose mix. Stir the glucose mix into the melted chocolate and fold in the whipped cream. Pour into the tea glasses and leave in the fridge to set. Serve garnished with abstract chocolate pieces.

WHITE CHOCOLATE TART

MAKES 1 TART 35 X 11CM (14 X 4½IN)

FOR THE PASTRY:
150g (5oz) plain flour, sifted
60g (2oz) icing sugar
60g (2oz) unsalted butter, cubed
1 free-range egg

FOR THE FILLING:
300ml (½ pint) double cream
6 free-range egg yolks
60g (2oz) caster sugar
210g (7oz) white chocolate, melted

FOR THE FROSTED REDCURRANTS:
1 punnet redcurrants
1 free-range egg white
30g (1oz) caster sugar

To make the pastry, mix the flour, icing sugar and butter in an electric mixer until it has the consistency of breadcrumbs and all the butter is combined. Add the egg and mix to a smooth dough. Wrap the pastry in cling film and leave to rest in the fridge for 2 hours or until the dough is firm.

Roll out the pastry and line the tin, making sure there are no holes in the lined case. Rest in the fridge for a further 30 minutes. Preheat the oven to 160°C/325°F/gas mark 3. Line the inside of the case with greaseproof paper and fill with baking beans and bake for about 30 minutes. Remove the beans and bake for a further 10 minutes or until the case is golden brown. Remove from the oven.

To make the filling, bring the cream to the boil. Whisk the egg yolks and sugar together until light and creamy in colour. Pour one-third of the boiling cream onto the egg yolk mix and whisk until smooth. Whisk the remaining cream onto the chocolate and then combine the two mixtures until smooth. Fill the tart and bake at 110°C/225°F/gas mark ¼ for 30–40 minutes or until the tart is set but with no colour.

To frost the redcurrants, simply brush the strands of currants with a little egg white and then coat with the sugar. Leave in a warm place overnight so that they become crisp and then use to garnish the tart.

(Left) Bitter Chocolate Mousse, Crème Brûlée and Lemon Pots.

picnic on the lawn

Attractive Nantucket baskets, filled with interesting foods full of flavour are waiting for guests to carry them away for a picnic in the garden. Blankets, cushions, small tables and chairs are placed on the lawn, inviting guests to relax and enjoy the day. A bar is decorated and placed in a spot easily accessible for the guests to serve themselves. At the end of the afternoon when the bride and groom have left, the guests leave with their baskets as a memento of the happy day. This is a very good way of entertaining a large number of guests.

ADULTS' PICNIC
SERVES 50

Square Rolls filled with Roasted Vegetables and Parmesan

Gravlax and Horseradish Cream Cheese Wrap

Miniature Chicken Pies

Home-made Potato Crisps

Chilli and Tomato Feta Salad

Cup Cake with Preserved Roses

CHILDREN'S PICNIC
SERVES 15

Square Rolls filled with Egg Mayonnaise

Miniature French Stick filled with Chicken Salad

Home-made Potato Crisps

Toffee Apples

Butter Popcorn

Clown Cookies

Crayons and Colouring Books

ADULTS' PICNIC

SQUARE ROLLS FILLED WITH ROASTED VEGETABLES AND PARMESAN

2 large aubergines
4 large courgettes
Extra virgin olive oil
50 square crusty rolls
200g (6½ oz) pesto sauce
13 red peppers, quartered, deseeded, roasted and peeled
250g (8½ oz) Reggiano Parmesan, shaved
Sea salt and freshly ground black pepper
Yellow ribbon

Heat a chargrill plate. Thinly slice the aubergines and courgettes approximately 2mm (¹/₁₀in) thick, brush with olive oil and season. Chargrill until bar marks are visible, place on a tray and leave to cool. Cut the rolls in half lengthways, brush with pesto then layer with the aubergine, courgette, red pepper and Parmesan. Tie a yellow ribbon around the roll, to resemble a present.

GRAVLAX AND HORSERADISH CREAM CHEESE WRAP

1kg (2lb 2oz) cream cheese
120g (4oz) creamed horseradish
½ cup chives, chopped
13 spinach tortillas
2kg (4lb 4oz) gravlax, sliced
7 hard-boiled eggs, cut into 8 segments
250g (8½oz) capers

In a bowl mix the cream cheese, horseradish and chives, then place into a container. Lay out the tortillas on a work surface and spread with the cream cheese. Cover one side with the

gravlax. Place 4 egg segments and a few capers on each tortilla, roll up tightly with cling film and place onto a tray in the fridge. To serve, remove the cling film and cut each wrap into 4 segments on a diagonal cut. Wrap in waxed paper and tie with raffia.

MINIATURE CHICKEN PIES

FOR THE FILLING:
Extra virgin olive oil
25 skinless chicken breasts
1 glass of good port
2.5kg (5lb 4oz) mixed wild mushrooms, brushed and finely chopped
10 shallots, peeled and finely chopped
½ cup flat-leaf parsley, finely chopped
½ cup fresh sage, chopped
3 tablespoons fresh soft thyme leaves

FOR THE PASTRY:
2.5kg (5lb 4oz) plain flour
45g (1½ oz) sea salt
600g (1lb 4oz) lard, cubed
600g (1lb 4oz) unsalted butter cubed
5 large free-range eggs, beaten

300ml (½ pint) milk
10 large free-range egg yolks, beaten
2.6 litres (3½ pints) rich brown chicken stock
25 leaves gelatine, soaked in cold water
Sea salt and freshly ground black pepper

SPECIAL EQUIPMENT:
50 x 7cm (2½ in) ring moulds

TO MAKE THE FILLING:
Heat a large sauté pan with a little olive oil, seal the chicken breasts on all sides until golden. Season and place to one side. Deglaze the sauté pan with the port, and pour over the chicken. Leave to cool. When cold, slice each chicken breast into 4 lengthways. Cover and place in the fridge. Heat a large sauté pan with a little olive oil, sauté the

mushrooms, adding a few shallots at a time.
Season, drain and place in a bowl; add the
herbs and mix well.

Leave to cool. Place the ring moulds onto
trays that will fit in the fridge. Layer the moulds
starting with the mushrooms, chicken, and
repeat until the moulds are full. Cover and
place in the fridge.

TO MAKE THE PASTRY:
Sieve the flour and salt into a large bowl. Make
a well in the middle, add the lard and butter

into the well and rub into flour until it
resembles breadcrumbs. Add the eggs and
750ml (1^1/$_2$ pints) cold water; mix well until it
forms a dough. Turn out onto a floured cool
work surface. Knead until smooth. Wrap in
cling film and place in the fridge for 1 hour.

TO MAKE THE PIES:
Remove the pastry from the fridge. Place on a
floured board, roll out 50 16cm (6^1/$_2$in) circles
of pastry 4mm (^{1}/$_{10}$in) thick. Layer the pastry
between non-stick paper on baking sheets and

place in the fridge. Roll out the remaining
dough and cut out 50 6.5cm (2 ^{1}/$_2$in) circles for
the top. Store as for the large pastry discs.

Preheat the oven to 190°C/375°F/gas
mark 5. Line baking sheets with nonstick
baking parchment. Remove the chicken and
the large pastry circles from the fridge. Place
the pastry circles on a floured work surface.
Place the ring mould in the centre of the

pastry, remove the mould, place the smaller pastry disc on top. Add the milk to the beaten egg yolks and brush the pastry. Pull the sides of the pastry to the top of the chicken mixture. Brush the lip of the pastry with the egg glaze, and seal. Brush the pies all over with the egg glaze. Make a 1cm ($^1/_2$in) hole in the centre of each pie. Place on the prepared trays and bake in the oven until golden brown for 30–40 minutes.

Meanwhile, heat the stock in a large saucepan. When the stock has boiled, remove from the heat and leave for about 10 minutes. Add the soaked gelatine and whisk into the stock. Strain into jugs. Remove the pies from the oven and place on cooling racks. With a funnel, pour the heated stock into the centre of each pie. This will need to be topped up about three times, or until the stock is visible. Leave to cool. When cold, wrap in greaseproof paper and place in an airtight container in the fridge.

HOME-MADE POTATO CRISPS

10 large King Edward potatoes
250g (8$^1/_2$oz) unsalted butter
1 clove garlic
Sea salt and freshly ground black pepper

50 cellophane bags
Ribbon

Preheat the oven to 200°C/400°F/gas mark 6. Line a few baking trays with some greaseproof paper. On a mandolin slice the potatoes to approximately 1mm thick; put the sliced potatoes in cold water to stop discoloration. Place the butter and garlic in a saucepan and slowly melt the butter. Remove from the heat and keep warm.

Take a medium-sized heart-shaped cutter and cut out hearts from the potato slices, pat dry with kitchen paper and place on the prepared baking trays. Brush with the garlic

butter, sprinkle with sea salt and freshly ground black pepper, cover with a piece of parchment paper and bake until crispy and golden. Remove and leave to cool. When cold, store in an airtight container in a cool place. To serve, place the crisps in cellophane bags, and tie with ribbon.

CHILLI AND TOMATO FETA SALAD

10 x 250g (8$^1/_2$oz) punnets small cherry
*   tomatoes*
4 red onions, peeled and finely sliced
5 red chillies, deseeded and finely shredded
1 cup basil, shredded
1 cup mint, shredded
1 cup coriander, shredded
450ml ($^3/_4$pint) lemon olive oil
Juice of 3 lemons
2kg (4lb 4oz) feta, cut into 1cm ($^1/_2$in) cubes
Sea salt and freshly ground black pepper

Place all the ingredients, except the feta, in a large bowl, season, and mix well. Carefully mix in the feta in and spoon into little dishes.

CUP CAKES WITH PRESERVED ROSES

FOR THE GARNISH:
50 open roses, 2.5cm (1in) in diameter
100 mint leaves
2 large free-range egg whites
120g (4oz) caster sugar
Silica gel

FOR THE ROSE WATER SYRUP:
Petals from 3 large scented roses, washed
*   and dried*
100g (3$^1/_2$oz) caster sugar

FOR THE CUP CAKES:
720g (1lb 8oz) unsalted butter

720g (1lb 8oz) caster sugar
12 large free-range eggs, beaten
720g (1lb 8oz) self-raising flour, sifted

FOR THE ICING:
300g (10oz) white fondant icing (from a good
*   pastry supply shop)*

SPECIAL EQUIPMENT:
White cup cake paper cases
Muffin tins

TO PRESERVE THE ROSES & MINT:
Do this two days before the wedding. Paint each rose and mint leaf with a little egg white and dip in the caster sugar. Leave in a warm place overnight to harden. Store in an airtight container with silica gel.

TO MAKE THE ROSE WATER SYRUP:
Place the ingredients into a large saucepan with 100ml (3$^1/_2$fl oz) water over a low heat, bring to a simmer and remove from the heat. Cover and leave to infuse for about 1 hour. When cold, strain into a jug.

TO MAKE THE CUP CAKES:
Preheat the oven to 180°C/350°F/gas mark 5. Place the baking cases into the muffin tins. Cream together the butter and sugar in an electric mixer until light and fluffy. Gradually add the beaten eggs. Do not allow to curdle. Fold in the flour. Spoon the mixture into the baking cases. Bake for about 20–30 minutes until well risen and golden brown. Remove from the oven, place the cakes onto cooling racks and drizzle each cake with the rose water syrup.

TO ICE THE CUP CAKES:
Carefully heat the fondant in a saucepan over a low heat. When it is liquid, spoon a little fondant over each cake, making sure they have a smooth, even coating. Leave uncovered to harden the icing. To serve, place a rose on the centre of each cake, and place in the basket.

CHILDREN'S PICNIC

SQUARE ROLLS FILLED WITH EGG MAYONNAISE

15 large free-range eggs, hard-boiled and
*   shelled*
200g (6¹/₂oz) mayonnaise
2 punnets cress
15 square crusty rolls
200g (6¹/₂oz) unsalted butter
Sea salt and freshly ground black pepper
Yellow ribbon

Grate the eggs into a bowl. Mix in the mayonnaise and cress and season. Halve the rolls, butter each side and fill with egg mayonnaise. Tie with a ribbon.

MINI FRENCH STICK FILLED WITH CHICKEN SALAD

Extra virgin olive oil
8 chicken breasts, skin removed
15 thin French sticks, approximately 16cm
*   (6¹/₂in) long*
200g (6¹/₂oz) unsalted butter
200g (6¹/₂oz) mayonnaise
4 baby gem lettuces, washed and dried
Sea salt and freshly ground black pepper

Preheat the oven to 200°C/400°F/gas mark 6. Heat a sauté pan with a little olive oil. Season the chicken breasts and seal on both sides until golden. Transfer to a roasting tray, place into the oven and cook for 10 minutes. Remove and leave to cool. When cold, thinly slice and set aside.

Halve the French sticks, butter both sides and spread with mayonnaise. Layer the chicken and the lettuce and season.

HOME-MADE POTATO CRISPS

Repeat the recipe for the Adults' Picnic, but omit the garlic.

TOFFEE APPLES

15 Lady apples
15 liquorice root (buy from health stores)
1kg (2lb 2oz) caster sugar

Wash, dry and remove the stalks from the apples. Place a liquorice root into the base of each apple. Set to one side. Place the sugar in a heavy-bottomed saucepan with 120ml (4fl oz) cold water. Over a low heat, melt the sugar, increase the heat and cook to a temperature of 174°C/350°F or to a light caramel colour. Remove from the heat. Cover your hand and arm with a long oven glove, and dip each apple into the caramel, making sure the apple is completely covered and the caramel forms a coating around the base of the liquorice root, to seal the apple completely. Place on a baking tray lined with silicon paper and leave to cool. When cold, store in a cool place.

BUTTER POPCORN

60g (2oz) butter
120g (4oz) popping corn

FOR THE CARAMEL:
120g (4oz) demerara sugar
30g (1oz) golden syrup
30g (1oz) unsalted butter
30ml (1fl oz) malt vinegar

Cellophane bags
Ribbon

Melt the butter in a heavy-bottomed saucepan with a lid. Add the corn and replace the lid.

Shake continuously over a high heat until the popping stops. Remove from the heat and transfer to a tray to cool.

Place all the ingredients for the caramel in a saucepan with 30ml (1fl oz) water and stir over a high heat until all the ingredients have dissolved. Leave to boil for 3 minutes or until golden brown. Add the popcorn and stir until thoroughly coated. Remove from pan and leave to cool. Store in an airtight container in a cool place. To serve, fill the cellophane bags with the popcorn and tie with ribbon.

CLOWN COOKIES

MAKES 20
240g (8oz) unsalted butter
400g (13oz) caster sugar
2 large free-range eggs
600g (1lb 4oz) plain flour
1 teaspoon salt
15ml (¹/₂fl oz) vanilla essence
Zest of 2 large lemons

FOR THE ICING:
3 large free-range egg whites
600g (1lb 4oz) icing sugar
Juice of 1 large lemon
Various colours and sanding sugars

TO MAKE THE CLOWN COOKIES:
Preheat the oven to 170°C/325°F/gas mark 5. Line a baking tray with nonstick baking parchment paper or a silicon mat. Cream the butter and caster sugar in an electric mixer until light and fluffy. Add the eggs gradually and beat until smooth. Carefully fold in the remaining ingredients. Remove, place onto a floured surface and knead until smooth. Cover with cling film and rest in the fridge for 1 hour or until firm.

Place the dough on a floured work surface and roll out to 5mm (¹/₄in) thick. Cut out with a clown cookie cutter and place on the tray. Bake in the preheated oven for 15–20 minutes or until golden brown. Remove from the oven and cool on a wire rack. When cold, store in an airtight container in a cool place.

TO MAKE THE ROYAL ICING:
Place the egg white and icing sugar in an electric mixer and beat until stiff. Add the lemon juice and beat until smooth. Colour as required and decorate as desired.

(Above) Children's picnic baskets filled with home-made snacks and treats.

formal dinner

Our formal dinner for 20 people has been created for you to take time over and enjoy each course, perhaps with a dance in between. Linger over the delicious dessert and macaroons with a cold glass of pink champagne.

FIRST COURSE
Quail and Foie Gras Salad with Truffle Dressing

FISH COURSE
Vichyssoise of Seafood with Caviar Cream

MAIN COURSE
Lamb Niçoise with Thyme and Black Olive Jus

DESSERT
Chocolate Top Hat

Pistachio Macaroons

QUAIL AND FOIE GRAS SALAD WITH TRUFFLE DRESSING

Olive oil

2kg (4lb 4oz) mixed small wild mushrooms, cleaned

4 shallots, peeled and finely diced

1 tablespoon soft thyme leaves

10 quail's eggs, soft-boiled, peeled, placed in a container and covered with water

40 quail breasts, trimmed and bone removed

2kg (4lb 4oz) foie gras, cut into 20 slices, placed in a bowl and just covered with milk

40 baby leeks, blanched and chargrilled

500g (1lb 1oz) mixed salad leaves

120g (4oz) black truffle, finely shaved

Sea salt and freshly ground black pepper

FOR THE DRESSING:

3 tablespoons sweet white wine vinegar (such as Condimento Morbido)

4 tablespoons white truffle oil

2 tablespoons extra virgin olive oil

Sea salt and freshly ground black pepper

Heat a large frying pan with a little oil, sauté a few mushrooms and shallots at a time, season. When all the mushrooms have been sautéed, mix with the thyme leaves and set aside.

Reheat the pan with a little more olive oil; season the quail breasts on both sides, pan-fry until golden brown and still slightly pink inside. Remove and keep warm.

(Below) Quail and Foie Gras Salad with Truffle Dressing.

Remove the foie gras from the milk and pat dry. Line a metal tray with kitchen paper. Reheat the pan to almost smoking hot. Season the foie gras, sear a few slices at a time for approximately 30 seconds on each side. Place on the lined tray and keep warm.

Mix all the dressing ingredients together. Drain and dry the quail's eggs and cut lengthways; thinly slice the quail breasts. Arrange all the salad in the centre of the plate and top with half a quail's egg. Drizzle the dressing over and around the salad.

VICHYSSOISE OF SEAFOOD WITH CAVIAR CREAM

FOR THE SOUP:
2 tablespoons extra virgin olive oil
6 shallots, peeled and finely sliced
4 cloves garlic, peeled and crushed
1.2kg (2lb 8oz) white part of leeks, washed, dried and finely sliced
600g (1lb 4oz) Desirée potatoes, peeled and diced
6 litres (10$^1/_2$ pints) vegetable stock

800g (1lb 10oz) green part of the leeks, washed, dried and finely sliced
450ml ($^3/_4$ pint) double cream

FOR THE SEAFOOD:
4 x 600g (1lb 4oz) lobsters, poached, meat removed and sliced
1kg (2lb 2oz) cooked squid rings
60 Mediterranean prawns, peeled and split lengthways
100 cooked mussels
40 medium scallops, poached and sliced widthways
1 cup dill
Sea salt and freshly ground black pepper

FOR THE GARNISH:
250g (8$^1/_2$oz) Sevruga caviar

Heat the olive oil in a frying pan. When hot add the shallots, garlic and white of the leek and sauté, but do not colour. Add the diced potatoes and vegetable stock, bring to the boil and simmer for 40 minutes. Add the green leeks, season and cook for a further 10 minutes. Remove from heat and leave to cool. Blend until smooth. Pass through a fine sieve into a container. Stir in the double cream, check the seasoning, cover and refrigerate.

To serve, layer the seafood and dill in the centre of each bowl, seasoning each layer. Carefully pour the soup around the seafood and place a spoonful of caviar on top.

LAMB NIÇOISE WITH THYME AND BLACK OLIVE JUS

2 litres (3$^1/_2$ pints) extra virgin olive oil
60 small shallots, unpeeled
60 cloves garlic, unpeeled
60 red cherry vine tomatoes
20 baby aubergines, top and bottom removed
150g (5oz) unsalted butter
2kg (4lb 4oz) spinach, washed and stalks

removed
10 x 300g (10oz) lamb loins, trimmed
Sea salt and freshly ground black pepper

FOR THE SAUCE:
1.2 litres (2 pints) lamb jus
20 black olives, finely diced
5 plum tomatoes, peeled, deseeded and diced

Heat the olive oil in a flameproof casserole on a low heat. Carefully add the shallots and cook for 40 minutes. Once cooked, remove and place onto a roasting tray. Repeat with the garlic but this time for 30 minutes. (The garlic and shallots should be nice and soft.) Do the same with the cherry tomatoes for 2 minutes. Reserve the oil to use later in the recipe.

Take a sharp knife and criss-cross the top and bottom of the aubergine, place in a bowl, drizzle with a little of the oil and season. Heat a large pan with a little oil and sauté the aubergines on all sides until soft, then place on the roasting tray with the other vegetables.

Heat a large saucepan, add half the butter. When foaming add half the spinach and sauté until wilted. Season, place in a colander and drain. Repeat with the remaining spinach and leave to cool. Pick out 60 of the undamaged leaves and lay flat on a tray. With the remaining spinach, make 60 balls about 2.5cm (1in) across and wrap each ball with the reserved spinach leaves; place onto a metal tray. Cover with foil and place in the fridge.

Heat a little oil in a frying pan. Season the lamb. When the oil is hot, seal the lamb until brown on all sides, then place on a baking tray and set aside.

To serve, preheat the oven to 200°C/400°F/gas mark 6. In a saucepan bring the lamb jus to the boil, then simmer over a low heat. Place the lamb in the oven. After approximately 5 minutes, add the vegetables

(Left) Vichyssoise of Seafood with Caviar Cream. (Right) Lamb Niçoise with Thyme and Black Olive Jus.

and cook for a further 10 minutes. Remove the lamb and vegetables from the oven and keep warm. Slice each lamb loin into 4 and place 2 pieces in the centre of each warmed plate. Place 1 aubergine next to the lamb and arrange 3 of each of the vegetables around the lamb. Scatter black olives and diced tomato around the plate and drizzle with the jus.

CHOCOLATE TOP HAT

FOR THE RASPBERRY SORBET:
750ml (³/₄ pint) raspberry purée (made from
    2kg (4lb 4oz) fresh raspberries)
Juice of 2 lemons
400g (14oz) sugar

FOR THE MOUSSE:
800g (1lb 10oz) milk chocolate
700g (1lb 7oz) praline paste (if you cannot find
    the paste, Nutella works just as well)
10 leaves gelatine, soaked in 300ml (¹/₂ pint)
    cold water
1.5 litres (2¹/₂ pints) double cream

FOR THE CHOCOLATE CIGARS:
210g (7oz) extra bitter chocolate

FOR THE TOP HATS:
600g (1lb 10oz) bitter chocolate

FOR THE CARAMEL SPRINGS:
300g (10oz) caster sugar
60g (2oz) glucose

FOR THE GARNISH:
300g (10oz) caster sugar
180 whole hazelnuts
1kg (2lb 2oz) fresh raspberries, sieved to make
    400ml (12fl oz) raspberry coulis
20 mint sprigs

SPECIAL EQUIPMENT:
20 cylinder moulds 5 x 8cm (2 x 3¹/₄ in)
Clean wallpaper scraper
6 sheets of acetate
8cm (3¹/₄ in) and 3cm (1¹/₂ in) round cutters
4 artist's brushes, 6cm (2¹/₂ in) long

TO MAKE THE SORBET:
Place all the sorbet ingredients into a pan with
250ml (8fl oz) water, heat until dissolved,
remove from the heat, cover and leave to cool.
When cold place in an electric ice-cream
maker and churn according to the

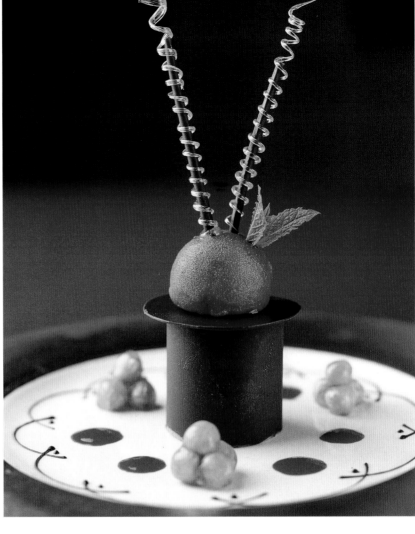

manufacturer's instructions. When ready,
remove and place in a container, cover and
store in the freezer.

TO MAKE THE MOUSSE:
Line baking trays with nonstick parchment
paper and place the moulds on the trays.
Place a saucepan half-filled with water over
the heat. Place a bowl on top containing the
chocolate and praline paste and gently melt.
Remove from the heat. Place the soaked
gelatine and water in a saucepan and heat
gently. When the gelatine has melted, mix
into the melted chocolate. Whip the cream
until it just holds its shape, but do not
over-beat or it will curdle when you fold into
the chocolate. When the chocolate mixture
is slightly warm, fold in the whipped cream.
Pour into moulds and leave to set in the
fridge.

(Above) Chocolate Top Hat.

TO MAKE THE CHOCOLATE CIGARS:
Place a clean baking tray upside-down on the
work surface. Melt the bitter chocolate in a
bain-marie to blood heat, then spread very
thinly with a palette knife onto the back of the
tray and put into fridge to set. When set, hold a
clean wallpaper scraper at a 45-degree angle
and scrape up the chocolate to make cigar
shapes. Place in an airtight container in fridge.

TO MAKE THE TOP HATS:
Cut 20 5.5 cm x 12cm (2¹/₄ x 4¹/₂ in) sheets
from the acetate. Place the remaining sheets of
acetate on a cool work surface. Line baking
trays with nonstick baking parchment.
    Place the chocolate over a bain-marie to
melt. Meanwhile, take the mousses from the
fridge and remove from the moulds. Place on

the trays with a good distance between each mousse. Return to the fridge.

Once the chocolate has melted, remove the bowl from the heat and leave to cool until almost set. Return the bowl to the bain-marie, and stir until the chocolate is smooth. Remove the bowl of chocolate and use a palette knife to spread the chocolate evenly onto the sheets of cut acetate. Wrap each sheet around the mousses. Return to the fridge to set.

Spread the remaining chocolate evenly onto the remaining sheets. Using the large cutter, cut a disc, then place the small cutter in the centre of the disc and cut around. Leave the chocolate to set. When set, remove the small disc of chocolate from the centre. This can be used again as the chocolate has been tempered. Remove the mousse from the fridge. With a hot knife, cut off the excess mousse above the chocolate collar. Make sure the tops are all level. Remove the acetate, place a disc of chocolate on each mousse to finish the top hat. Return to the fridge until required.

TO MAKE THE CARAMEL SPRINGS:

Oil the artist's brushes with non-scented vegetable oil. Place to one side. In a heavy-bottomed saucepan bring the sugar, glucose and 60ml (2fl oz) cold water to the boil and boil until light caramel in colour. Remove from the heat and leave to cool. Once cool enough to handle, leave in the saucepan and pull off small balls about 2.5cm (1in) in diameter. Pull the caramel and wrap around the brushes to form a spring – this will have to be done quickly as the sugar breaks once cold. Store in airtight containers in a cool place.

TO MAKE THE HAZELNUT GARNISH:

Line a baking tray with nonstick baking parchment. Place the sugar in a heavy-bottomed saucepan, just cover with water and melt the sugar over a low heat. When melted, increase the heat and boil until a light caramel colour. Remove from the heat. Dip the hazelnuts in the caramel individually using with a fork, and place in clusters of four on the prepared tray. When cold, store in an airtight container in a cool place.

TO BALL THE SORBET:

Line a baking tray with nonstick paper and place in the freezer for about 30 minutes. Remove the sorbet from the freezer and leave for about 10 minutes. Using an ice-cream scoop, make 20 balls to fit the top of the mousse. Place on the prepared tray and return to the freezer.

TO SERVE:

Melt the remaining chocolate and pour into a piping bag fitted with a very thin nozzle. Pour the raspberry coulis into another piping bag also fitted with a very thin nozzle. Make a pattern on the plates with the chocolate and coulis. Place a top hat on the centre of the plate. Put three hazelnut clusters around the plate. Top each cylinder with a ball of sorbet. Place two chocolate cigars in the sorbet and slide over the caramel springs. Finish with a sprig of mint.

PISTACHIO MACAROONS

225g (7¹/₂oz) icing sugar
125g (4¹/₂oz) ground almonds
30g (1oz) pistachio paste (available from specialist food stores)
4 free-range egg whites
30g (1oz) caster sugar

FOR THE FILLING:
60g (2oz) bitter chocolate
60ml (2fl oz) double cream

TO MAKE THE MACAROONS:

Line baking trays with nonstick baking parchment. Sieve together the icing sugar and almonds and mix in a bowl with the pistachio paste. Whisk the egg whites in an electric mixer until they form stiff peaks. Slowly add the caster sugar and whisk until very stiff. Remove the bowl from the mixer and gently fold in the pistachio mix. Spoon into a piping bag fitted with a 1cm (¹/₂in) nozzle and pipe onto trays. Leave for about 1 hour to form a skin.

Preheat the oven to 150°C/300°F/gas mark 4. Cook the macaroons for 4 minutes, then turn the tray round, reduce the heat to 100°C/225°F/gas mark ¹/₂ and cook for a further 10 minutes. Remove from the oven. Sprinkle cold water on a work surface, slide the baking paper onto the water then return them to the hot tray to create steam to release the macaroons from the paper. Once cold, take them off the parchment paper and store in an airtight container in a cool place.

TO MAKE THE FILLING:

Place the chocolate and cream in a heavy-bottomed saucepan, slowly bring to the boil but do not allow the chocolate to stick to the bottom of the pan. Stir until smooth. Remove from the heat and leave to cool.

TO SERVE:

Place the chocolate mixture into a piping bag. Pipe the mixture into the centre of the macaroons and sandwich together.

(Below) Pistachio Macaroons.

wedding cakes

Wedding cakes are important symbols and rituals of the wedding celebrations. Various countries have their own styles of cakes. France has the magnificent croquembouche – little choux balls filled with crème pâtissière, stuck together with caramel, then covered with spun sugar and decorated with almonds. Italy has fabulous large single-layer cakes filled with cream and fruits. The British have taken American-style cakes to heart, with beautiful tiers of sponge cakes of various flavours, decorated with fruits and flowers. In the West Indies dried fruits soaked in rum for up to six months create a very rich and moist dark cake, which is then iced with traditional royal icing and sugar flowers.

For an informal afternoon wedding, raspberry mousse cake decorated with flowers makes an original statement. Choose flowers and fruits that are in season – you do not want to set your heart on summer berries and flowers and then find they are not available, so let the season be your guide. Whatever your choice, make sure it reflects your personality, style and is the most delicious treat.

Did you know the design of the traditional tiered cake was modelled on the steeple of St Bride's in London's Fleet Street?

HEART FRAISES DES BOIS WHITE CHOCOLATE CAKE

SERVES 150 This lovely heart-shaped wedding cake contains fresh little wild strawberries. Bands of white chocolate are wrapped around the heart-shaped vanilla sponge which is filled with tiny wild strawberries (fraises des bois) and cream.

HEART TINS:

16 x 13cm (6¹/₂ x 5in)
20 x 16cm (8 x 6¹/₂ in)
23 x 19 cm (9 x 7³/₄ in)
60g (2oz) unsalted butter, for greasing tins
60g (2oz) plain flour, for dusting tins

FOR THE SUGAR SYRUP:

150g (5oz) caster sugar
50ml (1¹/₂ fl oz) sweet white wine

FOR THE SPONGES:

630g (1lb 5oz) caster sugar
18 large free-range eggs
1kg (2lb 2oz) plain flour, sieved

FOR THE STRAWBERRY AND VANILLA CREAM FILLING:

4 punnets fraises des bois
2 vanilla pods
750ml (1¹/₄ pints) double cream
00g (00oz) sugar

FOR THE CHOCOLATE CASING:

1kg (2lb 2oz) white chocolate buttons

TO GARNISH:

10 punnets fraises des bois

Line the bottom of heart tins with baking parchment paper. Melt the butter and brush the insides of the tins. Dust with the flour. Place the prepared tins on baking trays.

TO MAKE THE SUGAR SYRUP:

Place 150ml (¹/₄ pint) cold water in a heavy-bottomed saucepan with the sugar and wine, bring to the boil and simmer until the sugar has dissolved. Remove from the heat, leave to cool.

TO MAKE THE SPONGES:

Preheat the oven to 180°C/350°F/gas mark 5. Warm the sugar in a metal bowl in the oven. In an electric mixer whisk the eggs. Add the sugar and continue to whisk on high speed until the mixture is frothy and thick. Fold in the flour, then pour the mixture into the heart tins. Place in the oven and bake until golden, from approx-imately 20 minutes for the smallest to 35 minutes for the largest. Remove from the oven. Leave the sponges in the tins for 2–3 minutes, then gently turn out onto a cooling rack. When cold, cut all three sponges horizontally in half. Brush on generous amounts of the sugar syrup to moisten and flavour the sponge.

TO PREPARE THE STRAWBERRY AND VANILLA CREAM:

Gently wash the fraises des bois, dry with kitchen paper and place in a bowl. Cut the vanilla pods in half lengthways and scrape the seeds into the cream. Whisk the cream and sugar together until firm, but do not over-beat or you will not be able to handle the cream. Using a palette knife, spread an even layer of cream on both sides of the sponges. (Retain a little of the cream for 'gluing' the cakes together – see assembly notes below.) Sprinkle a generous layer of the fraises des bois over the bottom layers and sandwich together. Run the palette knife along the sides of the cakes to smooth the cream. Store in a cool place.

TO PREPARE THE WHITE CHOCOLATE:

Place the chocolate in a clean metal bowl over a saucepan of water. Bring to a simmer; remove from the heat when the chocolate has melted. Place the heart sponges on separate cooling racks. Pour a thin layer of chocolate over the cakes to cover the top and sides. This may need a little help with a warm palette knife.

Cut 3 strips of acetate 6.5cm (2¹/₂in) wide by the outer measurement of the tins. Place the strips on a large baking tray. Check chocolate is still warm and spoon enough over

(Left and above) Heart Fraises des Bois White Chocolate Cake.

the acetate to cover the strips; spread it gently with the palette knife. Swiftly pick up the furthest corners of the strip and carefully wrap it around the cake, joining neatly at the back. The acetate strip will stand 1cm (¹/₂ in) higher than the sponge. Repeat with the remaining cakes. Leave the acetate on the cakes until ready to assemble.

TO ASSEMBLE:

Place a spoon of vanilla cream on the top of the two largest sponges and place one on top of the other in size order. Gently peel off the acetate. Decorate each layer with generous amounts of fraises des bois.

A BASKET OF SUMMER BERRIES SERVES 150

This delicate basket cake is overflowing with glistening summer berries.

TINS:

30cm (12in) square x 8cm (3 1/2 in) deep
20cm (8in) square x 8cm (3 1/2 in) deep
10cm (4in) square x 8cm (3 1/2 in) deep
60g (2oz) unsalted butter, for greasing tins
60g (2oz) plain flour, for dusting tins

FOR THE SPONGES:

20 large free-range eggs, separated
600g (1lb 4oz) caster sugar
4 tablespoons orange and lemon zest
250ml (6 1/2 fl oz) extra virgin olive oil
500ml (16fl oz) Sauternes
560g (1lb 3oz) self-raising flour
1 teaspoon salt
8 large free-range egg whites
2 teaspoons cream of tartar

FOR THE VANILLA CREAM:

1 litre (1 3/4 pints) double cream, lightly
   whipped
2 vanilla pods

FOR THE BUTTERCREAM:

1kg (2lb 2oz) caster sugar
10 large free-range egg whites
1.5kg (3lb 3oz) unsalted butter, cubed
Zest of 10 oranges

FOR THE FILLING:

800g (1lb 10oz) raspberries
800g (1lb 10oz) blackberries
820g (1lb 11oz) blueberries
500g (1lb 1oz) strawberries
150g (5oz) redcurrants

TO GARNISH:

240ml (8fl oz) light corn syrup
800g (1lb 10oz) raspberries
800g (1lb 10oz) blackberries
820g (1lb 11oz) blueberries

500g (1lb 1oz) strawberries
150g (5oz) redcurrants

TO MAKE THE SPONGES:

Line the bottom of the tins with baking parchment paper. Melt the butter and brush the insides of the tins. Dust with plain flour. Place the prepared tins on baking trays.

Preheat the oven to 180°C/350°F/gas mark 5. In an electric mixer beat the egg yolks with half the sugar until they reach the ribbon stage. Fold in the citrus zest, olive oil and Sauternes, then fold in the flour and salt. In a separate clean bowl, whisk all the egg whites with the cream of tartar until stiff. Slowly beat in the remaining sugar to stiff peak stage, then fold into the yolk mixture. Pour into the prepared tins and bake for 20–30 minutes. Open the oven, cover the top of the cakes with a greased nonstick paper and turn off the oven. Leave for 10 minutes, then remove from the oven. When cool, turn out on to cooling racks. When cold, wrap in greaseproof paper, store in airtight tins in a cool place or in the freezer.

(Above) A Basket of Summer Berries.

TO PREPARE THE VANILLA CREAM:

Place the cream in the bowl of an electric mixer. Split the vanilla pods and scrape the seeds into the cream. Whisk the cream until it just holds its shape. Do not over-beat. Place in an airtight container in the fridge.

TO PREPARE THE BUTTERCREAM:

Place the sugar in a heavy-bottomed saucepan and just cover with cold water. Slowly bring to the boil, then boil to 112°C/225°F. Meanwhile, whisk the egg whites in an electric mixer to stiff peaks. Still whisking, slowly pour onto the boiling sugar. When all the sugar is whisked into the mixture, whisk in the butter cube by cube, add the orange zest and whisk until the mixture is cold. Place in a piping bag fitted with a basketweave nozzle.

TO SERVE:

Slice each sponge into three layers. Spread each layer with the vanilla cream, then add a layer of berries; repeat, finishing with a layer of sponge. Place one sponge on top of each other, starting with the largest and finishing with the smallest. Starting from the bottom pipe a basketweave pattern, illustrated opposite, up the sides of the cake. Mix the garnish berries with the corn syrup and decorate the top and sides of the cake.

FOUR-TIER CHOCOLATE CAKE SERVES 200

This comforting, rich chocolate cake is just perfect for a winter wedding.

TINS:

28cm (11in) square x 8cm (3¹/2 in) deep
20cm (8in) square x 8cm (3¹/2 in) deep
12cm (5in) square x 8cm (3¹/2 in) deep
5cm (2in) square x 8cm (3¹/2 in) deep
60g (2oz) unsalted butter, for greasing tins
60g (2oz) plain flour, for dusting tins

FOR THE FRAMBOISE SYRUP:

250g (8¹/2 oz) caster sugar
60ml (2fl oz) framboise liqueur

FOR THE SPONGES:

450g (1lb) unsalted butter
32 large free-range eggs
900g (1lb 13oz) caster sugar
675g (1lb 6oz) plain flour
225g (7¹/2oz) cocoa powder

FOR THE CHOCOLATE
GANACHE FILLING:

1.5kg (3lb 3oz) extra bitter chocolate
1 litre (1³/4 pints) double cream
300ml (¹/2 pint) light corn syrup
12 punnets raspberries

FOR THE CHOCOLATE SPRAY:

600g (1lb 4oz) bitter chocolate
200g (6¹/2 oz) cocoa butter (from a specialist food store)

FOR THE DECORATION:

Glacé fruits

SPECIAL EQUIPMENT:

Chocolate spray gun or a paint diffuser, available from good hardware stores

TO MAKE THE SYRUP:

Place the ingredients into a saucepan with 250ml (8¹/2fl oz) water and bring to the boil. Remove from the heat and leave to cool. When cold, store in an airtight container in the fridge.

TO MAKE THE SPONGES:

Line the bottom of the tins with baking parchment paper. Melt the butter and brush the insides of the tins. Dust with the plain flour. Place the prepared tins on baking trays.

Preheat the oven to 200°C/400°F/gas mark 6. Place the butter in a heavy-bottomed saucepan over a medium heat to melt. In an electric mixer, whisk the eggs and sugar together until doubled in volume.

Meanwhile, sift the flour and cocoa powder together. Carefully fold the flour and cocoa mix into the eggs and sugar, then rapidly stir in the melted butter. Pour into the prepared cake tins and bake for the following times:

28cm (11in) square cake tin: 40–50 minutes
20cm (8in) square cake tin: 30 minutes
12cm (5in) square cake tin: 25 minutes
5cm (2in) square cake tin: 20 minutes

Test whether the cakes are ready by pressing your finger on the tops – they should spring back. Remove from the oven, leave to cool, then turn onto cooling racks. When cold, wrap in nonstick or greaseproof paper and place in airtight containers and store in a cool place or in the freezer.

TO MAKE THE GANACHE:

Place the chocolate, cream and corn syrup in a heavy-bottomed saucepan over a low heat to melt. Stir until smooth. Remove from the heat,

pour into a container and cover. Leave to one side. Do not place in the fridge.

TO ASSEMBLE:

Slice all cakes into three layers and drizzle over the syrup. Spread each layer with some of the ganache and the raspberries. Sandwich together. Cover each cake with the remaining ganache, smoothing it with a palette knife. Place all layers in the freezer for 1 hour.

TO MAKE THE CHOCOLATE SPRAY:

Melt the chocolate and cocoa butter together and leave to cool a little as a better result is achieved if the mix is only slightly warm.

TO FINISH:

Remove from the cakes from the freezer. Stack them on a cake board. Pour the chocolate mixture into the spray gun at setting number 4 and spray each cake. The chocolate will resemble cocoa powder. Put in the fridge to set. Remove from the fridge and place on a cake stand. Decorate with glacé fruits.

(Below) Four Tier Chocolate Cake.

RASPBERRY MOUSSE CAKE SERVES 32

This very different wedding cake doubles as the dessert.

FOR THE MOUSSE:

500g (1lb 1oz) caster sugar

7 free-range egg whites

17 leaves gelatine, soaked in cold water

1 litre (1³/₄ pints) raspberry purée (made from
3kg (6lb 6oz) fresh raspberries)

Juice of 2 large lemons

30ml (1fl oz) Kirsch

2 litres (3¹/₂ pints) double cream

FOR THE DECORATION:

Edible flowers

Fresh raspberries

SPECIAL EQUIPMENT:

32 cylinder moulds, 5 x 8cm (2 x3¹/₂ in)

Cake boards (see the assembly notes below)

Place the caster sugar in a heavy-bottomed saucepan with just enough cold water to cover. Bring to the boil and boil until the temperature reaches 121°C/275°F. Meanwhile, place the egg whites in the clean, dry, stainless-steel bowl of an electric mixer and whisk to stiff peaks. Continue whisking, slowly pouring in the sugar when it has reached the correct temperature, and whisk until cold.

Squeeze the water from the gelatine. Place the gelatine in a saucepan with a little of the raspberry purée and melt over a low heat, stirring all the time. Place the raspberry purée with the dissolved gelatine in a large mixing bowl. Stir well and fold into the egg whites with the lemon juice and Kirsch.

Finally, fold in the cream. Fill the moulds to the top and put in the fridge to set.

TO ASSEMBLE:

It's best to assemble this cake on the table where it will be cut and served from. De-mould

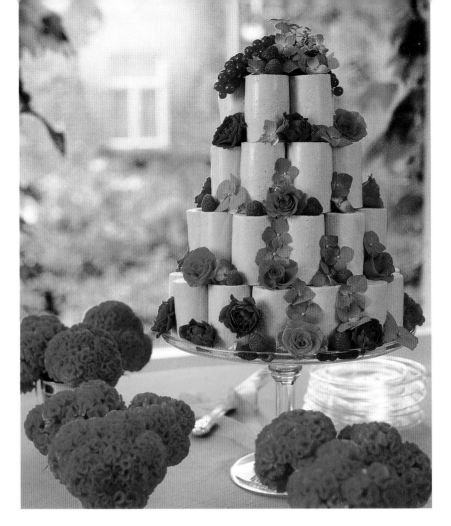

all the mousses. Place on a tray in a cool place. Starting with a 30cm (12in) cake stand, place a ring of mousses on the edge of the cake stand. The next layer is made by placing a 22cm (9in) cake board on top of the mousses. Repeat with 15cm (6in) and 8cm (3in) boards. Finish the top layer with the mousses. Decorate with flowers and raspberries.

LARGE CROQUEMBOUCHE

SERVES 150

A traditional French wedding cake is one of my favourites, and it looks and tastes wonderful. Serve as a dessert with some fresh berries or ice-cream.

FOR THE CHOUX PASTRY:

30g (1oz) salt

30g (1oz) caster sugar

400g (13oz) unsalted butter

800g (1lb 10oz) plain flour, sifted onto
greaseproof paper

20 large free-range eggs, beaten

FOR THE NOUGATINE:

300g (10oz) fondant icing

15g (¹/₂oz) flaked almonds

FOR THE PASTRY CREAM:

600ml (1 pint) milk

600ml (1 pint) double cream

1 vanilla pod

12 large free-range egg yolks

250g (8¹/₂oz) caster sugar

140g (4¹/₂oz) plain flour

FOR THE CARAMEL:

750g (1lb 8oz) caster sugar

FOR THE DECORATION:

Sugared almonds and flowerheads

HEART CAKE

This recipe is for a delicate pink romantic heart decorated with lace icing and fresh red roses.

FOR THE SPONGE:

6 large free-range eggs, separated
135g (4½oz) caster sugar
125g (4½oz) ground almonds
125g (4½oz) ground hazelnuts
75g (2½oz) plain flour, sieved

FOR THE ICING:

500g (1lb 1oz) packet regal icing
3 drops red food colouring
120g (4oz) icing sugar
1 free-range egg white

TO DECORATE:

Pink ribbon and Red roses

Grease and line a 15 x 12 x 8cm (6 x 5 x 3½ in) heart-shaped cake tin with nonstick baking paper. Preheat the oven to 180°C/350°F/gas mark 5.

In an electric mixer whisk the egg yolks and 75g (2½ oz) of the sugar until doubled in volume and light and creamy, then carefully fold in the ground nuts and flour. In a separate mixer, whisk the egg whites to peaks then slowly add the remaining sugar and whisk until stiff, then carefully fold into the nut mixture. Pour into the prepared tin. Bake for 20–30 minutes or until springy to the touch. Remove

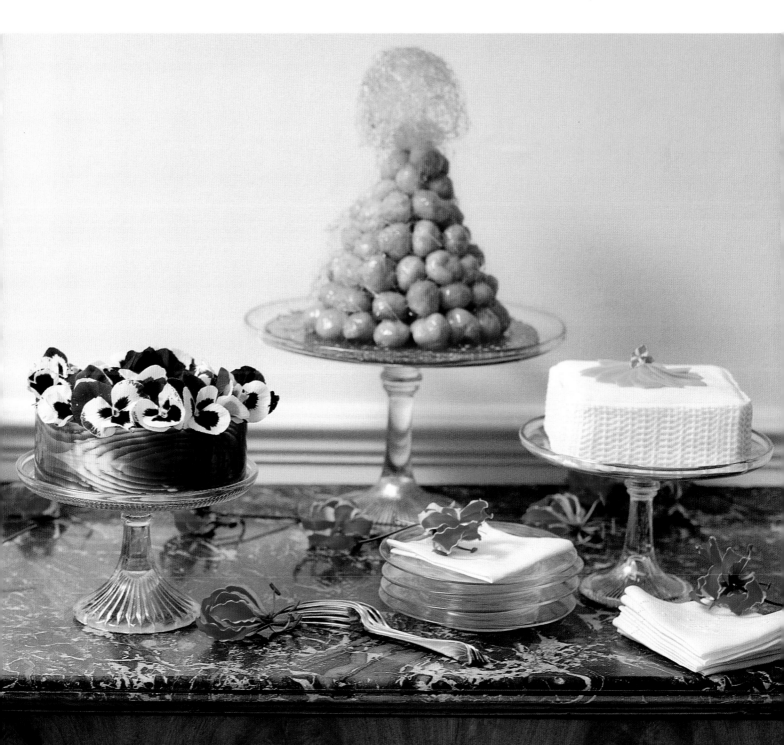

from oven and cool. After about 5 minutes, turn onto a cooling rack. When cold, wrap in nonstick paper and store in an airtight container in a cool place or freeze.

TO MAKE THE ICING:

Remove the regal icing from the packet. Sprinkle a cool work surface with a little icing sugar. Knead the icing into a flat ball with a slight hollow in the centre. Drip the food colouring into the centre and knead until the colour is evenly distributed throughout the icing. There must be no streaks. Roll out to 5mm (¼in) thickness. Cover the cake and trim off excess. Tie the ribbon around the base. Beat the icing sugar into the egg white until stiff, then pipe the desired pattern on top.

TO SERVE:

Place the cake on a stand and decorate with red roses.

MINI CROQUEMBOUCHE

A miniature version of the large cake featured on page 162.

FOR THE CHOUX PASTRY:

200g (6¹/₂oz) unsalted butter
1 teaspoon salt
1 teaspoon caster sugar
400g (13oz) plain flour
10 large free-range eggs, plus 1 egg to glaze

FOR THE NOUGATINE:

250g (8¹/₂oz) fondant icing
30g (1oz) flaked almonds

FOR THE PASTRY CREAM:

600ml (1 pint) milk
600ml (1 pint) double cream
3 vanilla pods
12 free-range egg yolks
250g (8¹/₂oz) caster sugar
180g (6oz) plain flour

FOR THE CARAMEL:

750g (1lb 8oz) caster sugar

TO MAKE THE CHOUX PASTRY:

Preheat the oven to 190°C/375°F/gas mark 5. Line baking trays with nonstick baking paper or silicon mats.

Place 500ml (16fl oz) water, the butter, salt and sugar in a large heavy-bottomed saucepan. Over a gentle heat, stir until the mixture is boiling. Add the flour and cook until the paste forms a dough in the centre of the saucepan and has a shiny texture. Remove from the heat and put into an electric food mixer fitted with a paddle. Gradually beat in the 10 eggs, one at a time.

When all the eggs are incorporated, place the mixture into a piping bag fitted with a 2cm (³/₄in) nozzle. Pipe balls no bigger than 2cm (³/₄in) in diameter onto the trays. Place the trays in the oven and bake for 15 minutes until the pastry is well risen and golden brown. Reduce the heat to 160°C/325°F/gas mark 4 and cook for a further 15–20 minutes until the

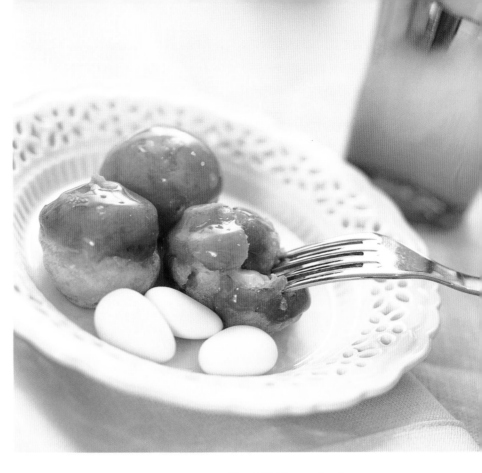

(Above) Mini Croquembouche.

choux balls are dry to the touch when broken in half. Remove from the oven and leave to cool. When cold, store in airtight containers in a cool place or freeze.

TO MAKE THE NOUGATINE DISC:

Preheat the oven to 180°C/350°F/gas mark 5. Line a baking tray with nonstick baking paper, and prepare a second tray with nonstick baking paper with a greased 25cm (10in) flan ring in the centre.

Place the fondant icing in a small saucepan over a medium heat and stir until liquid. Leave on the heat and bring to a caramel; it is important not to stir the caramel at this stage as it will crystallise. Pour onto the lined tray and scatter over the flaked almonds. Leave until cold. When cold, break the caramel into small pieces and place in a food processor and blend to a fine powder. Sprinkle a thick, even layer of the nougatine in the ring. Place in the oven and cook until the sugar has dissolved heat. Stir in the purée, mix well, pour into an electric ice-cream-maker and churn according to the maker's instructions. Remove, spread smoothly into the metal trays and freeze.

TO MAKE THE RIBBON BISCUITS:
These biscuits can be made three days before they are required. Beat the egg white, icing sugar and flour together until smooth. Beat in the melted butter, cover and leave to cool. When cold, place in the fridge and rest for 1 hour.

Preheat the oven to 180°C/350°F/gas mark 4. Prepare a baking tray with nonstick silicon paper or a silicon mat. Place the stencil on the nonstick baking mat and spread the biscuit mixture evenly; repeat (you may need to wipe the stencil a few times). Place in the preheated oven and bake for 5–7 minutes or until golden brown.

While the biscuits are baking, take two wooden spoons and place the ends on the sides of a cooling rack. When the biscuits are cooked, remove them from the oven, peel them off the nonstick baking mat and mould them over the wooden spoons to make a ribbon. When cold, pipe the couple's initials and date on the ribbons in chocolate. Leave to set. When cold, layer with nonstick paper in an airtight container in a cool place.

TO ASSEMBLE:
If required, add icing sugar to the blackcurrant coulis. Wash and dry the fruit for the garnish. Cut out the blackcurrant ice-cream with a 9cm (3¹/₂ in) cutter, the raspberry ice-cream with a 6cm (2¹/₂ in) cutter and the strawberry ice-cream with a 4cm (1¹/₂ in) cutter. Build up into a pyramid and freeze.

TO SERVE:
Pour the blackcurrant coulis into a plastic squeezy bottle and drizzle around the ice-cream cakes in a pattern. Arrange the berries around the sauce. Place ribbon biscuits on top and serve.

GATEAUX DE MARIAGE
My editor, Helen Woodhall, was a guest at a wedding in France. When the croquembouche appeared on a large serving board, it was surrounded by little cakes. This has inspired us to create these little wedding cakes to be served buffet-style.

CARROT CAKE
A moist, spicy and nutty carrot cake with pretty, caramelised carrot flowers.

FOR THE CARROT CAKE:
225g (7¹/₂ oz) plain flour
2 teaspoons bicarbonate of soda
1 teaspoon cinnamon powder
1 teaspoon grated nutmeg
¹/₂ teaspoon salt
400g (13oz) soft dark brown sugar
250ml (6¹/₂ fl oz) unscented vegetable oil
4 large free-range eggs
400g (13oz) carrots, peeled and grated
275g (9oz) walnuts, chopped

FOR THE FROSTING:
150g (5oz) unsalted butter
400g (13oz) caster sugar
400g (13oz) cream cheese
Zest of 3 large oranges

FOR THE GARNISH:
200g (6¹/₂ oz) caster sugar
1 large carrot, peeled and thinly sliced on a mandolin

TO MAKE THE CAKE:
Preheat the oven to 180°C/350°F/gas mark 5. Grease and line a 12cm (5in) square, 8cm (3¹/₂ in) deep cake tin with nonstick baking paper. Sieve the flour, soda, spices and salt together into a bowl. Set aside. In an electric mixer, beat the sugar, oil and eggs together until smooth. Stir in the remaining ingredients, mix well and pour into the

prepared tin. Bake for 40–50 minutes or until firm to the touch. Remove from the oven and cool. When cold, place in an airtight container in a cool place or freeze.

TO PREPARE THE FROSTING:
In an electric mixer beat the butter and sugar together until light and fluffy. Beat in the cream cheese and orange zest. Cover and refrigerate.

TO MAKE THE GARNISH:
Place the sugar and 200ml (6fl oz) cold water in a saucepan and bring to the boil. Turn down to a simmer, add the sliced carrot; continue to reduce until the mixture becomes thick and syrupy. Remove from the heat and place the carrot strips on nonstick baking parchment. Leave to cool. When cold, twist into flowers. Leave to one side.

TO ASSEMBLE:
Place the cream cheese frosting into a piping bag fitted with a basketweave nozzle. Place the carrot cake on a cake stand. Starting at the bottom, pipe a basketweave pattern all over the cake and arrange the thin slices of candied carrot on the top to form a flower.

CHOCOLATE WOOD CAKE
A Lulu Guinness handbag inspired this lovely cake. If pansies are not in season, large open roses have just as much of an impact.

FOR THE CAKE:
8 large free-range eggs
225g (7¹/₂ oz) caster sugar
120g (4oz) unsalted butter
150g (5oz) plain flour
60g (2oz) cocoa powder

FOR THE BLACKBERRY SYRUP:
90g (3oz) caster sugar
1 tablespoon crème de mûre

FOR THE GANACHE:

300ml (1/2 pint) double cream

60ml (2fl oz) light corn syrup

375g (12 1/2 oz) bitter chocolate, chopped

450g (1lb) blackberries

FOR THE WOOD BARK AND
DECORATION:

Sheet of acetate 6 x 52cm (2 1/2 x 21in)

75g (2 1/2 oz) extra bitter chocolate

100g (3 1/2 oz) white chocolate

Wood-graining tool

*Pansies, blown garden roses or any edible
  flowers*

TO MAKE THE SPONGE:

Preheat the oven to 200°C/400°F/gas mark 6.
Grease and line a 12cm (5in) round, 8cm
(3 1/2 in) deep cake tin with nonstick baking
paper.

   Place the eggs and sugar together in an
electric mixer and whisk until doubled in
volume. Meanwhile, place the butter in a
heavy saucepan over a medium heat to
melt. Sift the flour and cocoa powder into a
bowl. When the egg mixture is ready, carefully
fold in the flour/cocoa mix, and rapidly stir in
the melted butter. Pour into the prepared
cake tin. Bake for 20–30 minutes or until
springy to the touch. Remove from the oven.
Leave to cool for about 5 minutes, then turn
out onto a cooling rack. When cold, store in
an airtight container in a cool place or place
in the freezer.

TO MAKE THE SYRUP:

Place the ingredients in a saucepan with 90ml
(3 1/2 fl oz) cold water and bring to the boil.
Leave to cool. When cold, store in an airtight
container in the fridge.

TO MAKE THE GANACHE:

Bring the cream and syrup to the boil in a
heavy-bottomed saucepan over a high
heat. Pour onto the chocolate and stir until
smooth.

TO ASSEMBLE:

Slice the sponge into three widthways. Soak
each layer in the syrup and spread with a little
ganache. Put half the blackberries onto the
bottom layer and cover with more ganache;
repeat with the second layer and finish with the
final piece of sponge on top. Smooth the
remaining ganache over the top and sides of
the cake. Place the cake on a stand.

TO MAKE THE BARK
AND FINISH THE CAKE:

Cut one strip of acetate the circumference of
the cake. Melt the bitter and white chocolates
over water in two separate pans. Spread the
acetate with the bitter chocolate with a wood-
graining tool and leave to set. Spread the white
chocolate evenly over bitter chocolate and
wrap the strip around the cake. When set, peel
off the acetate and cover the top of the cake
with flowers.

**From left to right: Heart Cake, Mini Square
Meringue Cake, Chocolate Wood Cake, Mini
Croquembouche and Carrot Cake.**

TO MAKE THE CHOUX PASTRY:

Preheat the oven to 190°C/375°F/gas mark 5. Line baking trays with nonstick baking paper or silicon mats. Place 1 litre (1$^3/_4$ pints) cold water, the salt, sugar and butter in a large heavy-bottomed saucepan over a gentle heat. Stir until the mixture is boiling. Add the flour and cook until the paste forms a dough in the centre of the pan and has a shiny texture. Remove from the heat and put into an electric food mixer fitted with a paddle. Gradually beat in the eggs one at a time.

When all the eggs are incorporated, place the mixture in a piping bag fitted with a 1.5cm ($^3/_4$in) nozzle. Pipe balls no bigger than 3cm (1$^1/_2$ in) onto the baking trays. Place the trays in the oven and bake for 15 minutes until the pastry is well risen and golden brown. Reduce the heat to 160°C/325°F/gas mark 4 and cook for a further 15–20 minutes until the profiteroles are dry to the touch when broken in half. Remove from the oven and leave to cool. When cold, store in airtight containers in a cool place or freeze.

TO MAKE THE NOUGATINE DISC:

Preheat the oven to 180°C/350°F/gas mark 5. Prepare one tray lined with nonstick baking paper and a second tray lined with nonstick baking paper with a greased 30cm (12in) flan ring in the centre.

Place the fondant in a small pan over a medium heat and stir until liquid. Leave on the heat and bring to a caramel – it is important not to stir the caramel at this stage as it will crystallise. Pour onto the plain lined tray and scatter over the flaked almonds. Leave until cold. When cold, break the caramel into small pieces and place in a food processor and blend until a fine powder. Sprinkle a thick even layer of the nougatine into the ring on the second tray. Place in the oven and cook until the sugar has dissolved (about 10 minutes). Remove from the oven and leave for about 10 minutes. Remove the ring. When cold, store in an airtight container in a cool place.

TO MAKE THE PASTRY CREAM:

Bring the milk, cream and vanilla pod to the boil in a heavy-bottomed saucepan. While the milk and cream are coming to the boil, whisk the egg yolks, sugar and flour together in an electric mixer until pale and fluffy. Pour the boiling liquid onto the yolks and whisk until smooth. Return to the heat and whisk for a further 5 minutes or until the pastry cream boils. Remove from the pan, place a disc of damp greaseproof paper on top to prevent a skin forming. Leave to cool. When cold, cover with cling film and refrigerate.

TO FILL THE CHOUX BALLS:

Make a hole in the flat side of the profiteroles. Place the pastry cream in a piping bag and fill each choux bun. Leave in a cool place.

TO MAKE THE CARAMEL:

Place the sugar in a heavy saucepan and just cover with water. When the sugar has dissolved, increase the heat and cook the sugar to a dark caramel. Remove from the heat.

TO ASSEMBLE:

Place the nougatine disc on a cake stand. Dip the rounded sides of the choux balls into the caramel and stick onto the base. Continue doing this until a pyramid is formed. Dip the ends of the sugared almonds into the caramel and arrange on the choux balls. Decorate with flowerheads. This cake will last for up to 3 hours on a table.

(Left) Raspberry Mousse Cake.
(Below) Large Croquembouche.

ICE-CREAM CAKES

MAKES 10

This makes a wonderful alternative to a wedding cake. Each guest has their own special cake.

FOR THE BLACKCURRANT
ICE-CREAM:

1 litre (1³/₄ pints) double cream

400g (13oz) caster sugar

1 litre (1³/₄ pints) blackcurrant purée (made from 3kg (6lb 6oz) fresh blackcurrants)

FOR THE RASPBERRY
ICE-CREAM:

500ml (1 pint) double cream

200g (6¹/₂oz) caster sugar

500ml (1 pint) raspberry purée (made from 2kg (4lb 4oz) fresh raspberries)

FOR THE STRAWBERRY
ICE-CREAM:

250ml (¹/₂ pint) double cream

120g (4oz) caster sugar

250ml (¹/₂ pint) strawberry purée (made from 1kg (2lb 2oz) fresh strawberries)

FOR THE RIBBON BISCUITS:

1 large free-range egg white

90g (3oz) icing sugar

75g (2¹/₂oz) plain flour

75g (2¹/₂oz) unsalted butter, melted

30g (1oz) bitter chocolate, melted

Stencil cut from card, 10cm (4in) long and 2.5cm (1in) wide with van dyke ends

FOR THE GARNISH:

200ml (7fl oz) blackcurrant coulis (made from 800g (1lb 10oz) fresh blackcurrants)

(Above) Ice-Cream Cake.

Icing sugar, if required

Raspberries, blueberries, redcurrants and blackberries

TO MAKE THE ICE-CREAM CAKES:
The same method is used for making all the ice-creams.

For the blackcurrant ice-cream line a baking tray 30 x 42 x 3cm (12 x 16¹/₂ x 1¹/₂in) with cling film.

For the raspberry ice-cream use a tray 30 x 30 x 3cm (12 x 12 x 1¹/₂ in).

For the strawberry ice-cream use a tray 30 x 15 x 3cm (12 x 6 x 1¹/₂ in).

Place the cream and sugar in a heavy-bottomed saucepan and dissolve over a low

index of recipes

1x 30cm (12in) diameter

FOR THE ROYAL ICING

3 egg whites

500g (1lb 4oz) icing sugar

1 teaspoon glycerine

EQUIPMENT

Cake turntable

Palette knife

Metal ruler, approximately 40cm (16in)

Pastry scraper

TO MAKE THE FRUIT CAKE

The night before cooking, mix together the currants, sultanas, raisins, cherries and mixed peel. Then add the zest and juice of the lemons and the rum or brandy. Combine well and then leave covered, in a cool place.

Grease and line the cake tins, making sure that the sides are lined with at least two layers of paper. This is to ensure the outside of the cake does not colour too much during cooking.

Preheat the oven to 160°C/320°F/gas mark 3.

Cream together the butter and sugar, until light. Gradually add the beaten egg, mixing well between each addition.

Sieve together the flour, salt, nutmeg and mixed spice, and fold into the mixture.

Finally fold in the soaked fruit and the flaked almonds. Divide the mixture between the cake tins and bake for approximately 4 hours, 2 hours and 1 hour respectively. Insert a skewer into the centre of each cake, and when it comes out clean, the cake is cooked.

Allow to cool in the tins, on a cooling rack, and then turn them out. When completely cold, wrap in fresh parchment paper and cling film.

The cakes are best made three months in advance, and stored in a cool dry place.

Once or twice before decorating your cakes unwrap them and feed with a little extra rum or brandy. This will ensure a moist cake.

Do not use sherry or any other fortified wine as this will cause fermentation while being stored.

TO MAKE THE ALMOND PASTE

Brush the top of the cake with boiled apricot jam, and roll out a piece of almond paste to cover the top. Turn the cake over onto the paste, trim away any excess, and smooth with a palette knife. Turn the cake over again and place into the centre of the cake board.

Roll out another piece of paste in a long strip, and trim to fit the depth of the cake. Brush the sides of the cake with more jam, and place on the strip of paste. Press lightly, but try to avoid making any indentations, as this will show when icing the cake.

Allow the cake to dry for 24 hours before icing. Otherwise the oils from the almonds will show through and spoil the effect of the finished cake.

TO MAKE THE ICING

To ice and decorate a three-tier wedding cake you will need approximately 4 batches of the above recipe.

Place the egg whites in a mixing bowl. Gradually stir in the icing sugar, mixing to a smooth paste. Add the glycerine and beat the icing until it reaches a similar consistency to a stiff meringue. Store in a sealed container or a bowl covered with a damp cloth until required.

The glycerine is added so that the icing will not set too hard. This ingredient can be left out when making the royal icing for any decoration on the cake.

To ensure the best results all the equipment must be free from any grease, so rinse well with very hot water before commencing.

TO FINISH THE CAKE

Place the cake on the turntable. Using a palette knife spread some of the royal icing evenly onto the top. Remove the cake from the turntable and put on a flat surface. Place the metal ruler, at a 45-degree angle, on the side of the cake furthest away. Draw the ruler slowly and evenly towards you, leaving a layer of icing on the cake. Remove any icing from the sides in a downward motion, with a knife or pastry scraper. Allow the top to dry completely before icing the sides.

To ice the sides, again place the cake onto the turntable. With a palette knife in a vertical position, spread the icing onto the cake. Using a scraper, place the edge against the side of the cake. Rotate the cake in one movement, if possible, keeping the scraper stationary. Remove any excess icing on the top; this will ensure that the edges of the cake are smooth.

Allow to dry before continuing with the layers. As described, the technique is to ice the top and sides alternately, allowing each coat to dry before applying the next one. It is recommended that the cake should have 4 coats on the top and 3 coats on the sides.

(Left) Lemon Parcel Cake.
(Below) Traditional Wedding Cake.

index

(about 10 minutes). Remove from the oven and leave for about 10 minutes, then remove the ring. When cold, store in an airtight container in a cool place.

TO MAKE THE PASTRY CREAM:

Bring the milk, cream and vanilla pods to the boil in a heavy-bottomed saucepan. Meanwhile, whisk together the egg yolks, sugar and flour in an electric mixer until smooth. Pour the boiling liquid onto the yolks and whisk until smooth. Return to the heat and whisk for a further 5 minutes or until the pastry cream boils. Remove from the pan and place a disc of damp greaseproof paper on top to prevent a skin forming. Leave to cool. When cold, cover with cling film and refrigerate.

TO FILL THE CHOUX BALLS:

Make a hole in the flat side of the choux balls. Place the pastry cream in a piping bag and fill each choux ball with the cream. Leave in a cool place.

TO MAKE THE CARAMEL:

Place the sugar in a heavy-bottomed saucepan and just cover with water. When the sugar has dissolved, increase the heat and cook the sugar to a dark caramel. Remove from the heat.

TO ASSEMBLE:

Place the nougatine disc on a cake stand. Take the choux balls and dip the rounded side into the caramel and use to stick to the base. Continue doing this until a pyramid is formed. Top with spun sugar.

MINI SQUARE MERINGUE CAKE

This is one of my favourites as I love meringue in any shape or form.

FOR THE SYRUP:
120g (4oz) caster sugar
Zest and juice of 1 large lime

FOR THE SPONGE:
8 free-range eggs
300g (10oz) caster sugar
375g (12 1/2 oz) plain flour, sieved

FOR THE FILLING:
500ml (3/4 pint) double cream
30g (1oz) icing sugar
1 vanilla pod, halved and deseeded
1 punnet strawberries
1 punnet raspberries
1 punnet blackberries

FOR THE MERINGUE:
8 large free-range egg whites
400g (13oz) caster sugar

TO MAKE THE SYRUP:
Place the ingredients in a saucepan with 120ml (1/4 pint) water and bring to the boil. Remove and leave to cool. When cold, strain and place in an airtight container in the fridge.

TO MAKE THE SPONGE:
Preheat the oven to 200°C/400°F/gas mark 6. Grease and line a 12cm (5in) square cake tin.

In an electric mixer whisk the eggs and sugar together until light and creamy and doubled in volume. Carefully fold in the flour and pour into the prepared cake tin. Bake for 20–30 minutes or until springy to the touch. Remove and leave for about 5 minutes, then turn out onto a cooling rack. When cold, wrap in greaseproof paper, place in an airtight container and leave in a cool place or in the freezer.

TO MAKE THE FILLING:
Whisk the cream, icing sugar and vanilla together until thickened. Place in a covered bowl in the fridge.

TO MAKE THE MERINGUE:
Whisk the egg whites with 30g (1oz) sugar until stiff. Slowly add the remaining sugar and whisk until thick and glossy.

TO ASSEMBLE:

Slice the sponge into three layers. Drizzle the syrup over each layer. Spread one-third of the cream over the first layer and fill with half the fruit. Repeat and top with final layer of sponge. Cover the top and sides with the remaining cream. Fill a piping bag fitted with a 1cm (1/2 in) nozzle with the meringue. Starting at the base of the cake, pipe 2cm (3/4 in) high spikes to cover the complete cake and glaze with a blow torch. Place on a cake stand.

LEMON PARCEL CAKE

This is the perfect cake for a small wedding party. Here Vince O'Toole has made the prettiest yellow and white sugar ribbon. It takes years of experience to be able to make one, but you could buy striped ribbon from a specialist ribbon store.

FOR THE SYRUP:
300g (10oz) sugar
Zest of 4 lemons

FOR THE SPONGE:
250g (8 1/2 oz) unsalted butter
250g (8 1/2 oz) caster sugar
5 large free-range eggs
250g (8 1/2 oz) plain flour
15g (1/2 oz) baking powder
Zest of 5 lemons

FOR THE LEMON CURD:
250g (8 1/2 oz) unsalted butter, cubed
250g (8 1/2 oz) caster sugar
Juice of 5 lemons
8 large free-range eggs

FOR THE ICING:
750g (1lb 10oz) packet regal icing
Icing sugar, for dusting
3 drops yellow food colouring

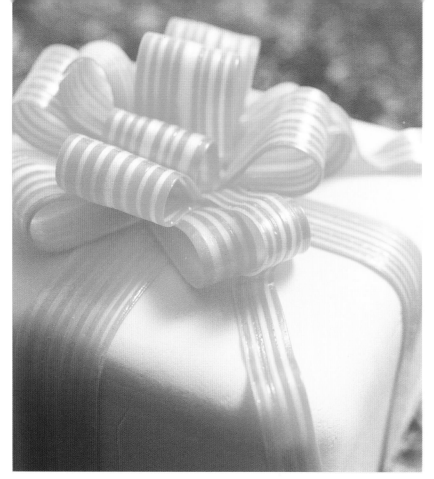

TRADITIONAL WEDDING CAKE SERVES 150

A recipe by Jane Grafton, our ex-pastry chef.

FOR THE WEDDING CAKE:

3kg (6lb 4oz) currants

3kg (6lb 4oz) sultanas

2kg (4lb 2oz) raisins

750g (1lb 9oz) glacé cherries, quartered

750g (1lb 9oz) mixed peel

1kg 500g (3lb 2oz) butter

1kg 500g (3lb 2oz) soft dark brown sugar

25 eggs, beaten

1kg 500g (3lb 2oz) plain flour

large pinch of salt

large pinch of nutmeg

120g (4oz) mixed spice

Zest and juice of 4 lemons

200g (6oz) rum or brandy

500g (1lb 1oz) flaked almonds

Extra rum or brandy to soak the cooked
   cakes

EQUIPMENT:

Cake tins:

1 x 30cm (12in) diameter tin

1 x 25cm (10in) diameter tin

1 x 15cm (6in) diameter tin

Parchment paper

FOR THE ALMOND PASTE

Allow 1.5kg (3lb 2oz) almond paste for the
   30cm (12in) cake

1.5kg (2lb 10oz) for the 25cm (10in) cake

750g (1lb 9oz) for the 15cm (6in) cake

Boiled apricot jam for helping the almond paste
   adhere to the cake

Icing sugar for dusting

EQUIPMENT

Rolling pin

Pastry brush

Palette knife

Cake boards:

1x 40cm (16in) diameter

1x 35cm (14in) diameter

TO MAKE THE SYRUP:

Place the ingredients into a saucepan with 300ml ($^1/_2$ pint) water and bring to the boil. Remove and leave to cool. When cold, strain and place in an airtight container in the fridge.

TO MAKE THE SPONGE:

Preheat the oven to 180°C/350°F/gas mark 5. Line a 20cm (8in) square, 8cm (3$^1/_2$in) deep tin with nonstick baking parchment. In an electric mixer beat the butter and sugar together until light and fluffy. Gradually beat in the eggs, then fold in the flour, baking powder and zest. Bake for 30–40 minutes or until golden and springy to touch. Remove from the oven. After about 5 minutes turn onto a cooling rack. When cold, wrap in greaseproof paper and store in an airtight container in a cool place or in the freezer.

TO MAKE THE LEMON CURD:

Whisk together the butter and sugar in a small saucepan over a low heat until smooth and glossy. Whisk in the lemon juice and then the eggs, return to the heat and whisk until thickened. Pass through a fine conical sieve into a bowl. Cover with wet greaseproof or nonstick paper to prevent a skin forming and leave to cool. When cold, cover with cling film and place in the fridge.

TO FILL THE CAKE:

Cut the cake into three lengthways, drizzle with the syrup and spread each layer with the lemon curd. Cover and place in the fridge.

TO MAKE THE ICING AND FINISH THE CAKE:

Remove the icing from the packet and place on a work surface dusted with icing sugar. Knead to a smooth ball with a slight hollow in the centre. Drop the food colouring into the centre and knead until all the colour is mixed and there are no streaks. Roll out to 5mm ($^1/_4$in) thick, cover the cake with the icing and trim off the excess. Finish with a yellow and white ribbon.

Author's Acknowledgements

In writing and creating *Weddings*, I relied on the support and help of many people. I would like to thank the following:

My staff, without whose professionalism and dedication our weddings would not be perfect. Richard Cubbin, Dave Withers and Paul North for their creativity, and for testing recipes and preparing food for photography.

Ming Veevers Carter, Lizzie and Justine for the most wonderful flowers, bouquets, ideas and kindness. Detta Phillips for her lovely bouquets and rich roses.

Helen Woodhall, my editor, who has made this project effortless and creative.

Pippin Britz, for her help, advice, creativity and energy in bringing my visions and ideas to life.

Tim Winter and Jo Fairclough for making the days of photography great fun.

Bryan and Nanette Forbes for their encouragement and support in writing this book, and for use of their beautiful lake and gardens for our summer wedding by a lake.

Joan White for reading and correcting my text.

Special thanks for the gracious generosity of the following companies and friends:

Graham, Terry and Sophie of Jones Hire for the loan of their china, glassware, cutlery, linen, chairs and tables. Annie and William Melon of Top Table who also loaned their beautiful china, cutlery and glassware. Maryse Boxer for the pretty glasses and china. The Wedding Shop for our brides' and bridesmaids' dresses and accessories. Kara Kara for the stunningly wrapped presents and frosted sake glasses. Theo Fennell for advice and magnificent rings. Guinevere Antiques for glasses, cutlery and linen. Sarah White for her encouragement and tablecloths. Gib Edge for arranging the pretty Saxon Church and trap.

The Rev. Frank Mercurio for his advice on weddings in the Church of England. Father Michael for information on marriage in the Roman Catholic Church. The secretary of the St. Johns Wood Synagogue for information on Jewish Weddings.

Derek Thompson and Tom Flaherty for valuable advice on hair and makeup for brides. Marc Staines for information about photography and videos

Last but not least my friends and customers, whose wedding photos grace the end papers.

PHOTOGRAPHIC ACKNOWLEDGEMENTS
The publisher would like to thank the following for their permission for reproducing the images on the following pages: pages 54–55 Getty Images/Telegraph; page 59 Chuck Fishman/Image Bank; page 62 Sally Griffyn; page 64 James Stafford; page 65 Super Stock; page 71 Glamis Castle; page 75 Super Stock; page 76 Emily Stoner; page 98 The Bridal Design Room Ltd.; page 109 Journal Für Die Frau/Camera Press.